INTERMEDIATE
MODERN STUDIES

Guch Dhillon, Alison Elliott
and Vicki A. Jolly

Editor: Frank Cooney

HODDER
GIBSON
AN HACHETTE UK COMPANY

The Publishers would like to thank the following for permission to reproduce copyright material:

Photo credits Page 1 (top) © Murdo MacLeod/murdophoto.com, (bottom) © PA Archive/Press Association Images; page 4 (left) © Rex Features, (right) © Scottish Parliamentary Corporate Body; page 5 © PA Wire/Press Association Images; page 13 © Scottish Parliamentary Corporate Body; page 14 © PA Wire/Press Association Images; page 15 © Scottish Parliamentary Corporate Body; page 16 © Scottish Parliamentary Corporate Body; page 33 © Scottish Parliamentary Corporate Body; page 35 (left) © Simon Walker/Rex Features, (right) © Jonathan Player/Rex Features; page 43 © PA Wire/Press Association Images; page 45 © PA Archive/Press Association Images; page 51 © Rex Features; page 55 (top) © PA Archive/Press Association Images, (bottom) © Jeremy Selwyn/ Evening Standard/Rex Features; page 56 © Rex Features; page 61 © European Parliament – Audiovisual Unit; page 64 © Hodder Education; page 66 (top) © PA Wire/Press Association Images, (bottom) © The Sun 30.09.2009/nisyndication.com; page 77 © Murdoch Ferguson/Photofusion; page 82 © Alan Richardson Pix-AR.co.uk/Courtesy Scottish Federation of Housing Associations Ltd; page 85 © Jeff J Mitchell/Getty Images; page 90 © Karen Kasmauski/Corbis; page 95 © Science Photo Library; page 96 © Image Scotland/Alamy; page 102 © Christopher Furlong/Getty Images; page 104 © D.G.Farquhar/Alamy; page 111 © PA Archive/Press Association Images; page 113 © TopFoto; page 114 © PA Archive/Press Association Images; page 115 © AP/Press Association Images; page 117 © PA Archive/Press Association Images; page 119 © © Stuart Conway/Scottish Viewpoint; page 123 © GustoImages/ Science Photo Library; page 127 © John Powell/Rex Features; page 131 © Jonathan Hordle/Rex Features; page 137 (top) © Strathclyde Police Picture Library, (bottom) © Central Scotland Police; page 145 © Per-Anders Pettersson/Getty Images; page 147 (left) © Sipa Press/Rex Features, (right) © 1999 Topham Picturepoint/TopFoto; page 148 © Louise Gubb/Corbis; page 149 © Per-Anders Pettersson/Getty Images; page 151 (left) © Alexander Joe/AFP/Getty Images, (right) © Don Boroughs/Still Pictures; page 154 © Action Press/Rex Features; page 156 © Peter Anderson/Alamy; page 158 © Nic Bothma/epa/Corbis; page 159 © AP/Press Association Images; page 161 (top) © AP/Press Association Images, (bottom) © Rajesh Jantilal/AFP/Getty Images; page 163 © Gianluigi Guercia/AFP/Getty Images; page 166 © Rick Gershon/Getty Images; page 170 © Dennis Cox/Alamy; page 173 © China Photos/Getty Images; page 181 © Michael Loewa/Visum/Still Pictures; page 190 © Robert Francis/Robert Harding/Rex Features; page 192 © Mark Henley/Panos; page 193 © STR/AFP/Getty Images; page 197 © Dwight Cendrowski/Alamy; page 198 © AP/Press Association Images; page 204 (left) © Alfred Buellesbach/Visum/Still Pictures, (right) © W. G. Allgoewer/Still Pictures; page 207 © Steve Starr/Corbis; page 208 (left) © Clive Brunskill/Getty Images, (right) © EMPICS Sport/Press Association Images; page 213 © The Granger Collection, NYC/TopFoto; page 216 © The US Senate Picture Studio; page 217 (both) © Rex Features; page 220 © Chip Somodevilla/Getty Images; page 222 © AP/Press Association Images; page 223 © Sipa Press/Rex Features

Every effort has been made to trace all copyright holders, but if any have been inadvertently overlooked the Publishers will be pleased to make the necessary arrangements at the first opportunity.

Although every effort has been made to ensure that website addresses are correct at time of going to press, Hodder Gibson cannot be held responsible for the content of any website mentioned in this book. It is sometimes possible to find a relocated web page by typing in the address of the home page for a website in the URL window of your browser.

Hachette's policy is to use papers that are natural, renewable and recyclable products and made from wood grown in sustainable forests. The logging and manufacturing processes are expected to conform to the environmental regulations of the country of origin.

Orders: please contact Bookpoint Ltd, 130 Milton Park, Abingdon, Oxon OX14 4SB. Telephone: (44) 01235 827720. Fax: (44) 01235 400454. Lines are open 9.00 – 5.00, Monday to Saturday, with a 24-hour message answering service. Visit our website at www. hoddereducation.co.uk. Hodder Gibson can be contacted direct on: Tel: 0141 848 1609; Fax: 0141 889 6315; email: hoddergibson@ hodder.co.uk

Cover photos © Paul Springett02/Alamy (Houses of Parliament), © Steve Lindridge/Alamy (Scottish Parliament) and © Glow Images/photolibrary.com (White House).
Running head photo © Photodisc/Getty Images.
Illustrations by Jeff Edwards and Pantek Arts Ltd
Typeset in Latin 725 BT 11/14.5pt by Pantek Arts Ltd, Maidstone, Kent
Printed in Dubai

A catalogue record for this title is available from the British Library

ISBN-13: 978 0340 990 483

Contents

Background to the Scottish Parliament

Prior to the Act of Union 1707, Scotland had its own parliament. When the Act of Union took effect on 1st May 1707, the Kingdom of England and the Kingdom of Scotland became a single United Kingdom of Great Britain. The Scottish and English parliaments were dissolved and replaced with a new parliament of Great Britain, which would be based at Westminster in London. The two countries had shared the same King since 1603 when Elizabeth I died and was succeeded by James VI of Scotland, who also became James I of England. Although England and Scotland were then ruled by a single monarch, they had separate governments.

Scottish Identity

The terms and conditions of the Act of Union meant that Scotland could keep its own educational and legal systems. Scotland also had its own church (the Church of Scotland) whilst England had the Church of England. It also had a Secretary of State who acted as a link between Scotland and the UK government and ensured that Scottish interests were represented.

Between 1707 and 1999, Scotland was governed by the UK parliament at Westminster in London. Scotland was still different from England in many ways. For example, Scotland had a different legal system in terms of courts and verdicts. Scotland's courts can deliver a 'not proven' verdict, but England's courts cannot. There are still different education systems whereby English pupils sit GCSEs and A levels whilst Scottish pupils sit Standard Grade, Intermediate, Higher and Advanced Higher exams, although this will change again with the advent of *A Curriculum for Excellence*. Scotland also had its own national football team and still does today.

Creating the Scottish Parliament

For many years in Scotland there had been disagreements and debates about how Scotland should be governed. From 1979 to 1997 the Conservative Government in Westminster was governing Scotland, although it only had a very small number of MPs in Scotland. They had passed unpopular policies under the Prime Minister Margaret Thatcher, for example, introducing the poll tax in Scotland and privatising industries such as British Rail and British Steel.

Labour won the general election in 1997 and no Conservative MPs were elected in Scotland. Labour had promised to hold a referendum on devolution for Scotland and Wales if they were elected to power. Newspapers such as *The Sun* backed Labour and even claimed that they had helped Labour win the general election: 'It's the Sun Wot Swung It' was a famous headline at the time (see the section on the role of media, pages 63–70). Labour's campaign theme tune of 'Things Can Only Get Better' seemed to capture the mood of the British people at that time.

Labour had run a 'YES YES' campaign, encouraging people to vote 'yes' to both the option of setting up a Scottish Parliament and

Figure 1.1 Labour's 'YES YES' campaign

to the Scottish Parliament being able to set its own tax rates.

The Scottish people were asked to give a 'yes' or 'no' response to two questions in the referendum:

Question 1: I agree that there should be a Scottish Parliament.

Question 2: I agree that a Scottish Parliament should have tax-varying powers.

Almost 75 per cent of people voted 'yes' to Question 1, whilst 63.5 per cent voted 'yes' to Question 2.

Table 1.1 Question 1 votes cast

	Number of votes	Percentage of votes
Yes (agree)	1,775,045	74.3 %
No (disagree)	614,400	25.7 %

Table 1.2 Question 2 votes cast

	Number of votes	Percentage of votes
Yes (agree)	1,512,889	63.5 %
No (disagree)	870,263	36.5 %

The voter turnout for the referendum was 60.4 per cent, which might have been viewed as disappointing for those who wanted a clear national statement of support for devolution. Over one-third of those entitled to vote did not do so.

The fact that the majority of people voted 'yes' to Question 2 meant that the Scottish Parliament gained the power to raise or lower taxes. To date, these powers have never been used.

The first elections for the Scottish Parliament were held on 6th May 1999, and the first meeting of the Scottish Parliament took place

Figure 1.2 Official opening of the Scottish Parliament in 1999

on 12th May 1999. On 1st July 1999, the Scottish Parliament was officially opened by the Queen and received its full legislative powers.

Devolved and Reserved Matters

The Scotland Act 1998, which established the Scottish Parliament, gave powers to the Scottish Parliament to make laws in certain areas which would apply to Scotland only. These were to be called **devolved matters**. Areas which were deemed to be of national (UK-wide) importance remained **reserved matters**, controlled by Westminster. Reserved matters were set out in Schedule 5 of the Scotland Act. Scotland, England, Northern Ireland and Wales cannot make their own laws in these areas.

Devolved Matters
- Health
- Education
- Training
- Local Government
- Social Work
- Housing
- Planning
- Tourism
- Economic Development
- Some aspects of Transport
- Justice

Reserved Matters
- Defence
- Social Security
- Foreign Affairs
- Time
- Currency
- Immigration
- Gambling
- Energy (nuclear, coal, oil, gas, electricity)
- Broadcasting
- Weights and Measures
- Economic Policy
- Elections
- Equal Opportunities
- Data Protection

ACTIVITIES

1 Give two reasons why many people in Scotland supported the setting up of the Scottish Parliament.

2 Define the term 'referendum'.

3 'Most people in Scotland wanted a Scottish parliament. Few people turned out to vote in the 1997 referendum.' (View of Derek Mooney)
Using the information on page 2, give one reason to support and one reason to oppose the view of Derek Mooney.

4 What is the Scotland Act 1998?

5 Explain the difference between devolved and reserved matters.

6 Look at the list of devolved and reserved matters below. Draw a table with one column headed 'Devolved Matters' and the other headed 'Reserved Matters'. Place each of the matters in this list under the correct headings.
- NHS
- local councils
- building new schools
- RAF
- National Lottery
- wind farms
- links with foreign countries
- football
- planning permission to build a nuclear power station in Scotland
- building new prisons
- free prescriptions for everyone in Scotland
- ID cards
- increasing benefits

Conflict between Westminster and the Scottish Government

As well as the reserved and devolved matters, there are some 'grey areas' which can lead to conflict between the Scottish Government and Westminster. For example, two nuclear power stations in Scotland need to be replaced. The issue of planning permission lies with the Scottish Parliament, but the issue of nuclear power lies with Westminster. The SNP Government is opposed to nuclear power and therefore opposes building new nuclear power plants. They can effectively veto the building of these power stations through their planning permission powers. Meanwhile, Westminster is in favour of replacing these power stations and favours the expansion of nuclear power stations to ensure the security of energy supplies in the future and to help the UK meet its CO_2 reduction targets.

↑ **Figure 1.3** Dounreay nuclear power station

More Powers for the Scottish Parliament?

The main agenda for the SNP is full independence for Scotland and, as such, they have consulted the people of Scotland via the National Conversation (www.scotland.gov.uk/Topics/a-national-conversation) and promised a referendum in 2011 if re-elected into power. In the short term, the SNP are also in favour of more powers for the Scottish Parliament.

In February 2008, Gordon Brown (the UK Prime Minister) backed a review of the powers of the Scottish Parliament, including taxation policy. The Commission on Scottish Devolution (sometimes called the Calman Commission after its chairman Sir Kenneth Calman) was set up with the backing of Labour, the Liberal Democrats and the Conservatives to look at ways of improving Scottish devolution.

↑ **Figure 1.4** The Calman Commission

The Commission's First Report was published on 2nd December 2008. One of the major findings was that devolving full fiscal autonomy (economic independence) to Scotland would be inconsistent with the running of the United Kingdom. The report also highlighted that, while devolution had been a great success since it came about in 1999, matters such as defence and national security could only be dealt with at a UK level.

The Commission's second report was published in June 2009 and made 24 other specific recommendations, including giving Scotland the power to set its national speed limit and to change the drink-driving limits. It also argued that the Scottish Parliament should be responsible for the administration of Scottish elections and the regulation of air guns and that it should be given greater control of its budget to make it more accountable.

Alex Salmond and the SNP Government have carried out their own initiatives and campaigned for changes in reserved areas that they feel very strongly about, such as broadcasting and nuclear weapons. For example, Alex Salmond has set up a Broadcasting Commission to look into the case for broadcasting to be devolved to Scotland amid his party's concerns over the level of television production carried out in Scotland.

Despite defence being an issue reserved to Westminster, the SNP has tried to make their voice heard on the issue of nuclear weapons. One way in which they have done this is through the nuclear Non-Proliferation Treaty (NPT). This is a treaty set up to limit the spread of nuclear weapons. There are currently 189 countries who are part of the treaty, five of which have nuclear weapons: the United States, the United Kingdom, France, Russia, and China. Scotland doesn't have a separate say on these matters as this matter comes under the UK's reserved control of defence, but Alex Salmond has tried to ensure that the SNP have their views recognised by writing to 122 NPT state parties, asking them to support a request for Scotland to be given 'observer status' at future meetings of the NPT members. The Scottish Government held their own summit on the replacement of trident nuclear weapons in 2007.

↑ **Figure 1.5** A trident submarine

ACTIVITIES

1 Why might the Scottish Government and the Westminster Government come into conflict with each other? Give examples to explain your answer.
2 What kind of governance does the SNP want for Scotland?
3 Explain the role of the Calman Commission and give a brief outline of its proposals.
4 Describe how the SNP Government has tried to make their voices heard over reserved matters.

Founding Principles of the Scottish Parliament

Following the referendum on setting up the Scottish Parliament, a Consultative Steering Group (CSG) was established to guide the practical operation of the new Parliament. It published its report 'Shaping Scotland's Parliament' in January 1999. This report identified four key principles, which have been adopted by the Parliament:

- sharing of power
- accountability
- access and participation
- equal opportunities

The Scottish Parliament has many procedures

Sharing of Power

The Scottish Parliament should embody and reflect the sharing of power between the people of Scotland, the legislators and the Scottish Executive.

Accountability

The Scottish Executive should be accountable to the Scottish Parliament, and the Parliament and Executive should be accountable to the Scottish people.

Access and Participation

The Scottish Parliament should be accessible, open and responsive. Procedures should allow participation in the development, consideration and scrutiny of policy and legislation.

Equal Opportunities

The Scottish Parliament should promote equal opportunities for all in its appointments and operations.

in place to ensure that the founding principles are met. They are mainly met through the legislative process, the committee system and the electoral system.

Sharing of Power

The electoral system used to elect MSPs to the Scottish Parliament is the Additional Member System (AMS) and this meets the principle of sharing power. This system produces a more representative result than other electoral systems and has allowed small parties such as the Greens to have MSPs elected. Scotland currently has a minority SNP Government and previously there was a Labour–Liberal Democrat coalition. This is a result of the type of voting system used.

Access and Participation

The public petitions process is a key part of the Scottish Parliament's commitment to participation, openness and accessibility. It allows individuals, community groups and organisations to participate in scrutinising policy by raising issues of concern with the Parliament. Once petitions are submitted, they are considered by the Public Petitions Committee. Any person or group may submit a petition to the Parliament. The Parliament now also has e-petitions whereby petitions can be submitted or signed online. See: http://epetitions.scottish.parliament.uk.

For example, in 2009, Ron Beaty submitted an e-petition about bus safety. He called on the Scottish Parliament to urge the Scottish Government to establish proper safety signage and lights on school buses, to be used only when school children were on the bus, and also to make overtaking a stationary school bus a criminal offence.

The Scottish Parliament allows openness by allowing members of the public to sit in on committee meetings, debates and questions.

Accountability

Procedures such as the involvement of committees in the legislative process ensure the principle of accountability. Ministers and First Minister's questions also hold the Scottish Government to account. Committees can scrutinise legislation, suggest amendments and call for evidence. For example, the Education Committee rejected the Scottish Government Graduate Endowment Bill at Stage 1, after the convener used her casting vote.

Thousands of young students have taken part in visits to the Scottish Parliament or have involved MSPs in their school projects through the Education Service.

Equal Opportunities

In terms of equal opportunities, the Scottish Parliament is said to be more 'family friendly' than the UK Parliament, offering crèche facilities and an official office hours approach, unlike the regular late-night sittings in Westminster. The Scottish Parliament has one of the highest female representations in Europe.

Although a reserved power, the Scottish Parliament has set up an Equal Opportunities Committee which investigates and debates current issues relating to equal opportunities.

All of these examples illustrate the ways in which the Scottish Parliament meets its four founding principles.

The Voting System of the Scottish Parliament

The name of the voting system used to elect the 129 MSPs to the Scottish Parliament is known as the Additional Members System (AMS). It is a mixed system of proportional representation, which means there is a closer link between the number of seats (MSPs) a party gets and the number of votes it receives.

Under AMS, everybody has two votes. 73 MSPs are elected using First Past the Post and 56 MSPs are elected using the List System. Both types of MSP have equal status in the Parliament. Each voter has two votes on one ballot paper. Each side of the ballot paper is a different colour to make it clear to the voter which type of MSP that side refers to: regional or constituency.

ACTIVITIES

1 Create a simple memory map which illustrates the four founding principles of the Scottish Parliament and what they mean.
2 Copy and complete the table below to illustrate how the Scottish Parliament meets its four founding principles.

Founding principle	How it is met
Sharing power	
Accountability	
Access and participation	
Equal Opportunities	

Regional Vote

In the regional vote, Scotland is divided up into eight regions e.g. the Highlands and Islands region. Each region elects seven MSPs. In the regional vote, the electorate vote for a political party, not a candidate.

> 8 regions x 7 MSPs each = 56 regional MSPs

Party A
- Derek Hope
- Nicola McGuire
- Christie MacPherson
- John MacIntosh
- Raj Singh
- Natalia Zukowska
- Archie Donnelly

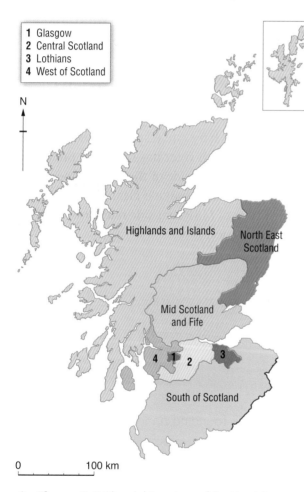

1 Glasgow
2 Central Scotland
3 Lothians
4 West of Scotland

N

Highlands and Islands

North East Scotland

Mid Scotland and Fife

4 1 2 3

South of Scotland

0   100 km

Figure 1.6 The eight regions of Scotland for AMS elections

Each political party will have a list of their candidates in rank order. For example, look at the Party List of candidates for 'Party A.'

If Party A were to win five MSPs in a regional vote, then they would choose the first five people on their list above to take up those seats. The number of MSPs each party receives is calculated using a standard formula. The party then selects their MSPs based on the order their candidates were ranked on their list.

Constituency Vote

In the constituency vote, the voter marks an X next to the candidate of his/her choice. In this vote, the candidate with the most votes wins the seat. Look at the result below for Moray in 2007. Which candidate won the seat?

Table 1.3 2007 Election results for the constituency of Moray

Name	Party	Votes
Richard Lochhead	Scottish National Party (SNP)	15,045
Mary Scanlon	Scottish Conservative and Unionist Party	7,121
Lee Butcher	Scottish Labour Party	4,580
Dominique Rommel	Scottish Liberal Democrats	3,528
	Majority	7,924
	Total Electorate	60,959
	Total Votes Cast	30,274
	Turnout Percentage	49.66 %

Source: Scottish Parliament Election Results 2007

Table 1.4 2003 Scottish election results

Political Party	Constituency MSPs	Regional List MSPs	Total MSPs	% Votes*	% Seats
Labour	46	4	50	31.9	38.8
SNP	9	18	27	22.3	20.9
Liberal Democrat	13	4	17	13.6	13.2
Conservative	3	15	18	16.0	14.0
Green	0	7	7	6.9	5.4
Scottish Socialist Party	0	6	6	6.4	4.7
Save Stobhill Hospital Party	1	0	1	0.6	0.8
Scottish Senior Citizens Unity Party	0	1	1	0.8	0.8
Independents	1	1	2	1.5	1.6
Total	73	56	129	100	100
Turnout	**49.4 %**				

* Average of the percentage of constituency votes and regional list votes for each party.

Table 1.5 2007 Scottish election results

	Constituency MSPs	Regional List MSPs	Total MSPs	% Votes*	% Seats
SNP	21	26	47	33	36.4
Labour	37	9	46	31	35.7
Conservative	4	13	17	16	13.2
Liberal Democrats	11	5	16	14	12.4
Greens	0	2	2	2	1.6
Independents	0	1	1	0.5	1
Total	73	56	129	100	100
Turnout		**51.7 %**			

* Average of the percentage of constituency votes and regional list votes for each party.

Table 1.6 Summary of total seats (MSPs) by political party 1999–2007

Party	1999	2003	2007
SNP	35	27	47
Labour	56	50	46
Conservative	18	18	17
Liberal Democrats	17	17	16
Greens	1	7	2
SSP	1	6	0
Others	1	4	1

Impact of the Additional Member System

Type of Government

To date, no political party has achieved an overall majority i.e. more than 50 per cent of the seats (MSPs). AMS is likely to result in coalition or minority governments. From 1999–2007, Labour and the Liberal Democrats formed a coalition government. In 2007, the SNP formed a minority government with 47 MSPs. They have an 'informal coalition' with the Greens where the Green Party have said that they will support them in passing legislation. In return, the Greens were given a convener on a committee. As such, the SNP may find it difficult to get legislation passed, for example, they were defeated on the Edinburgh Trams Bill and didn't pass their 2008 budget on the first attempt.

Some argue that coalition governments encourage cooperation on policy which is beneficial for voters. For example, during their coalition, the Liberal Democrats negotiated the policy of Free Personal Care for the elderly, but had to compromise on their pledge to end tuition fees. The Liberal Democrats also forced Labour to concede to a move to the Single Transferable Vote system (see pages 26–27) for Scottish local government elections. As a minority government, the SNP will have to govern on an issue by issue basis.

However, some would say that nobody voted for a coalition and so it was wrong to have one created. From 1999–2007 the Liberal Democrats were only the fourth largest political party, but they were able to from part of the government by going into partnership with Labour.

Smaller Parties

AMS is fairer to smaller parties as it gives a proportionally representative outcome. The total percentage of MSPs a political party gains will be quite proportional to the percentage of votes a party receives. Therefore, arguably, this more closely reflects the views of the Scottish voters. As such, it is fairer to smaller political parties as opposed to voting systems like First Past the Post. In the 2003 elections there was a significant increase in the number of MSPs from smaller parties such as the Greens (who won seven seats) and the Scottish Socialist Party (who won six seats) in addition to two independent MSPs and one SSCUP MSP.

The Green Party has been particularly successful with AMS as they have decided to put candidates forward for the regional votes only because they know they have little chance of winning a constituency vote.

However, in 2007 smaller political parties did not do as well as there was a swing towards the SNP. The Scottish Socialists were completely wiped out, as were the SSCUP. The Greens were reduced from seven to two MSPs, though Margo MacDonald (Independent) retained her seat.

Greater Representation?

Voters are represented by both a constituency and regional MSP. Some argue that this gives greater representation, but some argue that it creates confusion about which MSP a voter should go to with any issue they might have and there has been an ongoing debate about the status of regional MSPs. Although officially there is equal status, regional MSPs are not always regarded as such. Voters are unsure of the role of List MSPs and they may not be known to the public in the same way.

The political party that dominates the constituency results tends to do badly in the regional results. In 2007 Labour, with 37 MSPs, had the most constituency MSPs, but only had nine regional MSPs. In contrast, the SNP had 21 constituency MSPs but significantly had 26 regional MSPs, which made the SNP the largest political party.

Choice

AMS gives voters greater choice. Voters could vote for two different political parties in theory e.g. a Labour candidate in the constituency vote and the Green Party on the regional vote. However, some say the voting system is too complicated. In 2007 some people were unaware of the changes made to the ballot paper. Almost 150,000 ballot papers were spoiled in the 2007 elections. Local government elections were also held on the same day which used a different voting system. Local government elections and Scottish parliament elections will now be held on different days.

The voting systems of the Scottish parliament is such that a majority government made up of one political party is unlikely. The most likely forms of government that we will see are minority and coalition governments. The 2007 elections saw the first minority government of the SNP in power.

Coalition Governments

Advantages

Coalitions governments are more democratic as they tend to have a greater share of the votes compared to having one political party alone in government.

Coalition governments encourage political parties to work together, compromise and share power. Free personal care for the elderly and the abolition of student tuition fees were Liberal Democrat policies which may not have been passed if only Labour had been in power.

There will be a wider range of talent and experience within the government and Cabinet. This may mean that decisions are more heavily debated and thought through.

Disadvantages

Coalitions government can actually be less democratic because the smaller political parties who come in third or fourth place can still get into government. Between 1999 and 2007, the Liberal Democrats were in government with Labour despite coming fourth in the election in terms of numbers of MSPs. Nobody voted for a coalition like this.

Some people argue that people did not vote for parties to compromise on their manifesto policies. Free personal care for the elderly and an end to student tuition fees were Liberal Democrat policies which Labour agreed to discuss if the Liberal Democrats would enter into coalition with them.

Coalitions governments can be unstable as the political parties may not always agree and could come into conflict with each other, meaning that it can take longer to pass policy, which is not in the best interests of the electorate.

Minority Governments

Advantages

The results reflect more accurately how people have voted as the largest political party has formed the government. The political party with the most votes (MSPs) governs the country.

Legislation must be passed on an issue by issue basis as the political party won't have enough MSPs to pass legislation. Every single vote is a challenge for a minority government, meaning that decisions should be more carefully considered and also more reflective of the electorate's wishes. For example, opposition MSPs voted against the SNP's proposal to abolish the plans for a trams network in Edinburgh.

Disadvantages

A minority government may not be able to fully carry out their manifesto policies if they don't receive the support of other political parties. Alex Salmond struggled to get the SNP Budget Bill passed in 2008 and had to make concessions to other parties before it was passed.

Other political parties may use tactical voting against the government and stop policies being passed. This can mean that the decision making process may be slowed down and decisions are not made in the best interests of the people.

ACTIVITIES

1 Using the headings below, write a summary of the voting system used in the Scottish Parliament:
  - name of the voting system
  - number of votes
  - ballot paper
  - number of MSPs (seats)
  - different types of MSP

2 Which candidate won the constituency of Moray in 2003? Give a reason for your answer.

3 Study Table 1.6 and write down differences between the 2003 result and the 2007 result. Mention two differences in your answer.

4 Using the 2003 and 2007 Scottish Parliament election results, what conclusions can be drawn about the results of the Scottish Parliament elections in 2003 and 2007?
You should give one conclusion about each of the following:

- the success of the main political parties in both elections
- the success of smaller political parties in both elections
- the fairness of the Additional Member System in both elections

5 Complete the table below to illustrate the impact of AMS.

Area of impact	Advantage	Disadvantage
Type of government		
Smaller political parties		
Choice		

6 Do you think a minority government or a coalition government is best for Scotland? Give reasons for your answer.

The Work of an MSP

Each person in Scotland is represented by one constituency MSP and seven regional MSPs. Anyone can stand as a candidate to be an MSP as long as they are 18 or over on the day they are nominated as a candidate.

MSPs are elected by the Scottish people to represent them and make decisions on devolved matters for Scotland, such as education and health. MSPs have a responsibility to work on behalf of their constituents. They do this in two main ways:

- the work they do in their constituency or region
- the work they do in the Parliament

Constituency and Regional Work

MSPs generally work within the constituency on a Monday and a Friday. They hold 'surgeries' where constituents can speak to MSPs about any concerns or problems relating to devolved matters. For example, a constituent may contact their MSP regarding his/her thoughts on a proposed school closure. The MSPs will discuss their concerns with them and decided on any appropriate action. Some MSPs have online surgeries and use their websites to keep constituents up to date with their constituency and parliamentary work and even produce newsletters.

MSPs will also attend local events and speak to local groups to keep abreast of what is happening in the local area. Have a look at the Independent MSP Margo MacDonald's website to find out about her parliamentary and constituency work: www.margomacdonald.org/

Parliamentary Work

The parliamentary work of MSPs usually takes place between Tuesday and Thursday. Parliamentary committees usually meet on Tuesday and Wednesday mornings.

For example, Ken MacIntosh, constituency MSP for Eastwood, is a member of the education committee and takes part in the work of that committee on Tuesday and Wednesday mornings.

Figure 1.7 Ken MacIntosh, constituency MSP for Eastwood

The sitting days of the Scottish Parliament are Tuesdays, Wednesdays and Thursdays. Much of the Scottish Parliaments business is done through committees and most MSPs are members of committees. There are 16 committees and each one is made up of between seven and 11 MSPs. One of these committee members is chosen as the convener and another as the deputy convener.

Committees

In committees, MSPs scrutinise the government's proposals for new legislation in the form of Bills. The MSPs who sit on the committees consider the bills at various stages (see page 19 for details of the passing of Bills).

For example, at Stage 1 of the Graduate Endowment Bill there was a tie in the committee vote. This meant that the MSP acting as convener of that committee had the casting vote. The convener voted to reject the Bill. However, the Bill was eventually passed in the Parliament when all MSPs voted.

Debates and Motions

MSPs can take part in debates in Parliament. Members can speak in debates and they can also put forward motions which may be debated. Motions are used by MSPs to initiate debate or propose a course of action.

For example, in September 2008, MSP Margaret Curran (who is the Labour Party Health Spokesperson) proposed a motion (Motion S3M-2524) which was successful in being accepted for a debate. The motion was about a fatal outbreak of a hospital superbug that had been linked to 18 deaths in Vale of Leven Hospital in Dunbartonshire.

Decision Time

MSPs can vote at Decision Time which is usually at 5 pm on sitting days for the Parliament. As the current SNP Government is a minority government, MSPs from non-government political parties have greater influence over the

CASE STUDY

Graduate Endowment Bill

Students no longer have to pay the Graduate Endowment Fee when they finish university, after MSPs voted to abolish the charge in 2008. MSPs voted by 67 to 61 in favour of scrapping the one-off charge of £2,289. Approximately 50,000 students will benefit from the abolition.

↑ Figure 1.8 The Scottish Parliament debating chamber

Labour and the Conservatives voted against abolition, after they failed to force the Scottish Government to set up a review into university funding. The Bill was supported by the SNP, the Liberal Democrats, the Greens, Margo MacDonald and one Labour MSP, Elaine Smith. All the other Labour MSPs and the Conservatives argued that the £17 million cost to the Government of abolishing this fee could be better spent.

The committee, through the casting vote of the convener, did not agree that abolishing the Graduate Endowment Fee was the most effective way of removing barriers to access to higher education. During Stage 1 scrutiny, a number of significant criticisms of the Bill were highlighted but there was a lack of alternative approaches. Once the Bill passed from the committee to the Stage 1 parliamentary debate on 20th December 2007, the general principle was passed. The Bill became an Act of Parliament on 4th April 2008.

voting process compared with the previous Labour–Liberal Democrat coalition government.

Each sitting day, MSPs decide on all of the motions and amendments that have been moved through the Parliament that day. The Presiding Officer asks questions about the motions and amendments by reading out the name of the motion or amendment and asking 'are we all agreed?', to which the chamber first votes orally. If there is disagreement, the Presiding Officer announces 'there will be a division' and members proceed to an electronic vote using the keypad on their desks. The outcome of most votes is known within seconds.

For example in October 2008, a motion was moved through Parliament in the name of

MSP Jamie McGrigor. It was passed, and so the Parliament agreed that the Scottish Register of Tartans Bill was passed and became law.

Figure 1.9 Richard Lochhead, Moray MSP and Cabinet Secretary

CASE STUDY

Richard Lochhead: Moray MSP and Cabinet Secretary for Rural Affairs and the Environment

Sunday 7th June

Daytime: Spent time with family and attended the Elgin Rotary Marathon event. This is a local bi-annual event which has raised over £400,000 for various charities.

Evening: Attended the European elections count in the local town hall.

Monday 8th June

Daytime: Met with the Rural Development Council to discuss impact of recession on rural economy and how to move forward. (The Rural Development Council tries to help develop and regenerate rural areas for the better.)

Evening: Attended a reception in Bute House after the European elections. I was the guest Minister and I spoke to new MEPs and retiring MEPs about the future role of the European Union.

Tuesday 9th June

Daytime: Visited Lothian Towhead Farm to look at conservation project. Met with Government agricultural official regarding a ministerial statement I am making in parliament tomorrow on the future role of Government support to agriculture and food.

Attended a Cabinet meeting at Bute House with Alex Salmond and the five other Cabinet Secretaries.

Wednesday 10th June

Daytime: Visited a farm in Fife to attend an event organised by the Royal Highland Education Trust (RHET). RHET aims to create an opportunity for each child in Scotland to experience the countryside.

Delivered ministerial statement in parliament on the future role of Government support to agriculture and food at 14:05 for 15 minutes. The statement detailed a package of new measures to support agriculture and the rural economy. Took questions from MSPs for 30 minutes on my statement.

Met with officials who are launching the UK Climate Projections 2009 Report. This project will outline how climate change will affect the UK including Scotland over the next few decades.

Evening: Meetings with officials regarding the UK Climate Change report.

Thursday 11th June

Daytime: Office work in Holyrood. This involves dealing with constituency work, ministerial work and clearing papers.

Met environment ministers and waste policy officials to discuss today's debate on waste policy plans.

Attended First Ministers Questions.

Evening: Attended a debate on a waste policy plan. Roseanna Cunningham, Environment Minister, opened the debate and I closed it.

Attended a Gala dinner, made a speech and presented prizes in Drymen for the world Fly Fishing Championships, 27 countries were represented.

Friday 12th June 2009

Daytime: Carried out ministerial work and constituency work at home.

Opened new premises of The Quarriers (A Scottish charity) in my local constituency.

Held my surgery at 3 pm in Elgin Youth Café to meet constituents to discuss issues in the local area.

Evening: Spent time with family.

Saturday 13th June 2009

Daytime: Attended a school summer fete at my son's local primary school.

Spent time with my family at Keith and Dufftown Railway.

In addition to my week's diary I also carry out the activities below on a regular basis:

- Read newspapers and press cuttings given to me by my communications team.
- Speak with my constituency office in Elgin regarding local concerns and call local constituents.
- Reply to emails. I receive 60–70 emails a day. I have people who

work for me in a ministerial office who can answer some of these emails on my behalf, some I answer personally.

- Meet SNP colleagues to discuss forthcoming business.
- Attend local primary and secondary schools to talk about my work as an MSP and as a member of the government.

Questions

MSPs can ask questions at General Question Time and First Ministers Question Time. Both take place on a Thursday; General Question Time takes place first, followed by First Ministers questions at 12 noon for 30 minutes.

The First Minister will know the first question that each MSP will be asking him in advance. However, MSPs can be given the opportunity to ask supplementary questions, which the First Minister will not have beforehand, and may try to 'catch the First Minister out'.

The Presiding Officer

Alex Fergusson is the current Presiding Officer and was previously a Conservative MSP for Galloway and Upper Nithsdale.

The Presiding Officer of the Scottish Parliament has many responsibilities, including chairing proceedings in the parliamentary Chamber. He has other duties, which include the selection of questions to the First Minister, as well as the

selection of supplementary questions and amendments.

The Presiding Officer is supported by two Deputy Presiding Officers, currently Alasdair Morgan MSP and Trish Godman MSP. The Presiding Officer must remain politically impartial (neutral) in everything that he does.

Who is in the Government?

The Scottish Government is responsible for devolved matters in Scotland, which include issues of day-to-day concern regarding health, education, justice, rural affairs and transport.

The Scottish Government is financed by the Westminster Government via something called the Barnett Formula. In the 2008–2009 session it managed an annual budget of more than £30 billion. MSPs vote on the government proposals for spending the budget. At least 65 of the total 129 MSPs must vote in favour of the proposed budget for the government's plans to go through.

The government was known as the Scottish Executive when it was established in 1999, following the first elections to the Scottish Parliament. The current SNP administration was formed after elections in May 2007 and they renamed the 'Scottish Executive' the 'Scottish Government'.

The First Minister and his Scottish Cabinet make up the Scottish Government. The First Minister leads the government and appoints the other Scottish Ministers (Cabinet Secretaries) who make up the Cabinet.

↑ **Figure 1.10** A gathering of some key SNP Cabinet Ministers in 2009

From left to right: Kenny McAskill, Justice Secretary, John Swinney, Finance Secretary, Nicola Sturgeon, Health Secretary and Deputy First Minister, Alex Salmond, First Minister, Fiona Hyslop, Culture Secretary, Richard Lochhead, Cabinet Secretary for Rural Affairs

Each Cabinet Secretary is responsible for a department and has junior ministers and civil servants to support him/her in their work. The First Minister and Cabinet Secretaries also have to answer written and oral questions about the work of their department. The Scottish Cabinet normally meets weekly (while Parliament is sitting) at Bute House in Charlotte Square, Edinburgh.

The Role of the First Minister

The First Minister is the leader of the Scottish Government. The 129 MSPs vote for who the First Minister will be but it is usually the leader of the largest political party. The current First Minister is Alex Salmond of the SNP Party. His Party has formed a minority government in the Scottish Parliament.

One of the First Minister's powers is that he appoints MSPs to become Scottish Ministers as Cabinet Secretaries, becoming a part of the government. He can also reshuffle them if he wishes. With his Cabinet, the First Minister will discuss issues relevant to Scotland, ultimately making the decisions which become government policy.

ACTIVITIES

1 Describe the kind of work that an MSP may carry out in their local constituency.
2 Using the list below, describe the ways in which an MSP can represent people in the Scottish Parliament. Remember to include examples.
   ● Committees
   ● Debates and Motions
   ● Decision Time
   ● Questions
3 Describe the role of the Presiding Officer.
4 Copy and complete the diagram below, filling in the correct names and titles using the wordbank below.
   The Scottish Government

   The Scottish electorate elects MSPs. MSPs vote for the ▭ who selects the Scottish Government. The Scottish Government is made up of ▭ and is accountable to the ▭ who are accountable to the ▭ .

   > **Word bank:**
   >
   > Scottish electorate   First Minister   Scottish Parliament   Cabinet Secretaries

5 Imagine that someone is coming to visit the Scottish Parliament on holiday. Create an information Fact File on the role of the First Minister.

The First Minister's main role is to represent Scotland in devolved matters and lead the country forward. Each year the First Minister lays out their legislative programme for the year.

The First Minister is also accountable to the Scottish Parliament and must answer questions during First Minister's Questions for 30 minutes every Thursday. As Alex Salmond has a minority government, it is harder to push through legislation compared to the previous government. For example, his local income tax plans have met with much controversy, so much so that the SNP have had to scrap their plans for this tax due to little support in the parliament for it.

Passing Laws in the Scottish Parliament

The Scottish Parliament considers and makes laws on devolved matters. Proposals for new laws are introduced in the parliament as Bills. When the Scottish Parliament was set up, one of the key principles behind the shaping of it was the sharing of power. This was to ensure that no one party had too much power and to allow smaller parties a chance of influencing legislation. It was also decided that individual MSPs could propose new laws in addition to committees and the government.

There are four types of Bills:

- Executive Bill
- Members' Bill
- Committee Bill
- Private Bill

Executive Bill

These are introduced by the Executive (Cabinet Secretaries and Ministers) and account for the majority of legislation. The Scottish Parliamentary Pensions Act was introduced by the SNP Government in 2008 and passed in February 2009.

The Abolition of Bridge Tolls (Scotland) Bill was introduced by John Swinney and passed in January 2008. This Bill removed the charge (tolls) for cars passing over the Forth Road Bridge, Erskine Bridge and Tay Bridge.

Member's Bill

Each MSP is entitled to introduce two Bills in each parliamentary session. Approximately 10 per cent of Bills passed each session are Member's Bills. The Wild Mammals Bill of 2002 was a Member's Bill. Also, the Scottish Register of Tartans Bill, which was introduced by Jamie McGrigor MSP in 2008 and proposed the creation of a publicly held and maintained register of tartans and the setting up a system for registering new tartan designs.

Committee Bills

Committee Bills are initiated by a parliamentary committee. Committee Bills only make up a small proportion of Bills passed in the Parliament. The Commissioner for Children and Young People (Scotland) Act was a Bill introduced by the Education, Culture and Sport Committee. It was passed on 26th March 2003.

When new Bills are introduced, the legislative process usually consists of three stages.

If parliament votes in favour, the Bill is passed. Once a Bill has passed there is a four-week period when the Bill can be challenged, but this is only likely to happen if it is deemed not to be a devolved matter. After the four week period, the Presiding Officer sends the Bill for **Royal Assent**. This is when the monarch signs the Bill. This procedure takes place because Scotland is still part of the UK and all UK legislation must receive Royal Assent.

Private Bills

The Stirling to Alloa railway link was established in 2004 due to a Private Bill. A Private Bill is introduced by a promoter, who may be a person, a company or a group of people, and usually relates to development projects.

For more information on current Bills in the Scottish Parliament visit www.scottish.parliament.uk and click on 'Current Bills'.

Stage 1
The appropriate parliamentary committee(s) take evidence on the Bill and produce a report on its general principles.

A meeting of the parliament then considers the report and debates whether to agree to the Bill's general principles. Parliament will debate whether the Bill should proceed during Decision Time.

If the parliament agrees, the Bill moves on to Stage 2.

 If the parliament does not agree, the Bill will fall.

Stage 2
The Bill is considered in detail, and scrutinised line by line by a Committee or, occasionally, by a Committee of the Whole Parliament.

Changes to the Bill, known as **amendments**, can be made at this stage.

If the parliament agrees, the Bill moves on to Stage 3.

 If parliament does not agree, the Bill will fall.

Stage 3
The Bill is considered by the whole parliament.

Amendments to the Bill, can also be made at this stage. Only amendments made at this stage are debated.

The Parliament then votes on the Bill.

If the parliament agrees, the Bill is passed, signed by the monarch and becomes an Act of Parliament.

  If parliament does not agree, the Bill will fall.

 Figure 1.11 The legislative process in the Scottish Parliament

ACTIVITIES

1 Create a simple memory map with examples to illustrate the four different types of Bill in the Scottish Parliament.

2 Passing a law in the Scottish Parliament involves different stages. Complete the table below to summarise what happens at each stage.

Stage	What happens?
Stage 1	
Stage 2	
Stage 3	
Royal Assent	

Committees in the Scottish Parliament

Committees in the Scottish Parliament are where much of the real work of an MSP takes place. Committees are made up of small groups of MSPs.

There are two types of committees: Mandatory and Subject. Mandatory committees are those which must exist under the rules of the parliament i.e. the Parliament's Standing Orders. Subject Committees are based on the responsibilities of the Scottish Government.

Mandatory Committees

Equal Opportunities

European and External Relations

Finance

Public Audit

Public Petitions

Standards, Procedures and Public Appointments

Subordinate Legislation

Subject Committees

Economy, Energy and Tourism

Education, Lifelong Learning and Culture

Health and Sport

Justice

Local Government and Communities

Rural Affairs and Environment

Transport, Infrastructure and Climate Change

The Work of Committees

Committees have many roles, but the major role of committees is to examine legislation and scrutinise the government. The full role includes:

● scrutinising legislation
● conducting inquiries
● gathering evidence
● holding the Scottish Government to account

Gathering Evidence

Committees spend a lot of time gathering evidence and investigating people's views on a matter. Committees can take evidence in different forms: written (via email/letter) or they can invite witnesses to give their evidence in person. Committees can also use video-conferencing to take evidence from witnesses in remote locations and they also go on fact-finding visits.

For example, during the passing of the Disabled Persons' Parking Places (Scotland) Bill, the Local Government and Communities Committee took oral evidence from an Asda representative (Guy Mason) and also from John Donaldson, Sergeant in Strathclyde Police's traffic management department.

Conducting Inquiries

Committees can also conduct enquiries in Scotland to cover lots of different issues which affect the people of Scotland. There have been over 250 enquiries by committees since the Scottish Parliament was created. Inquiries have the potential to bring about changes in laws or even influence policy created or altered by the Scottish Government.

For example, in March 2009 there was an inquiry into the public petitions process by the Public Petitions Committee. The committee wanted to investigate issues highlighted in its 2006 research on the petitions system and to reflect, ten years on, how the petitions system is serving petitioners.

Committee Meetings

The make-up of committees is reflected by the political party balance of the parliament. This means that the number of MSPs in a committee will reflect the percentage of MSPs that a political party has in the parliament.

Each committee has a convener to chair the meetings and a deputy convener who will chair meetings in the convener's absence. The convener is also responsible for calling witnesses to speak.

Each committee also has approximately two clerks who brief and advise the convener and committee members, organise meetings, visits and events and provide support with administrative tasks.

Official reporters write a report in the meeting of the committee, which is usually published a couple of days after the meeting.

Legislation and Scrutiny

Committees can also introduce their own Bills. The most well known example was when the Education, Culture and Sport Committee conducted an inquiry into whether there was a need for a Children's Commissioner for Scotland, and what the roles and responsibilities of a Scottish Children's Commissioner should be. The consultation period lasted about a year and it then reported to parliament on its proposal to introduce a Bill to have a commissioner. The Commissioner for Children and Young People (Scotland) Bill was introduced to parliament on 15th January 2003 and passed on 25th March 2003.

Committees play a very important role in the Scottish Parliament and are central to the way parliament works. The committee system is designed to encourage the key principles of participation, access, power sharing and accountability.

The Scottish Parliament is 'unicameral' (has a single debating chamber) and also a committee-based legislature. A conscious decision was taken not to follow the Westminster model for committees as the system at Westminster has been criticised for being weak, encouraging executive (Cabinet Minister) dominance and not allowing for effective legislative scrutiny.

Committee System

A committee system was preferred because it was felt that this was in line with the key principles outlined in Shaping Scotland's Parliament. In particular, the committee system was designed to:

- encourage significant public involvement in the Scottish Parliament's activities. For example, individuals as well as members of organisations and groups can appear before committees or write to them to give evidence

- enable parliament to hold the Scottish Government to account effectively. Part of a committee's work is to scrutinise the work of the Scottish Government. The Ministers in the Government do not sit on committees but can be asked to appear before the committee to answer questions

- encourage the sharing of power. Committees can investigate any item which falls within their remit, hold inquiries and make recommendations to parliament and the Executive. Committees also have the power to initiate legislation themselves (see the information about the Children's Commissioner for Scotland on page 21)

Source: www.scottish.parliament.uk/vli/education/resources/learningResources/interCommittee.htm

Equal Opportunities in the Scottish Parliament

When the Scottish Parliament was created, it endeavoured to be representative of the Scottish electorate. To be truly representative, the percentage of gender and ethnic groups in the parliament should reflect the percentage in the population.

The number of women in the Scottish Parliament declined by seven to 43 out of 129 (33.3 per cent) following the parliamentary election on 3rd May 2007.

Scotland is ranked eighth within the EU for female representation at 33 per cent. Sweden has the highest proportion with 45.3 per cent female members of parliament. The UK Parliament has 19.5 per cent (126 out of 646 MPs) MPs.

The UK Parliament is more favourable in terms of minority representation with 15 MPs who are ethnic minority. Minorities make up seven per cent of the population in the UK and three per cent of the Scottish population. In 2007, the first ethnic minority candidate was elected to the Scottish Parliament as SNP MSP. Sadly, Bashir Ahmad died in February 2009.

Achievements of the Scottish Parliament

In its first year, the Scottish Parliament passed eight Bills into Acts and a further eleven Bills were going through the parliamentary process. This would never have been achieved at Westminster – on average, the House of Commons would pass one or two Acts a year that are directly related to Scotland. In this respect, it could be argued that the Scottish Parliament has been very successful.

Table 1.7 Female representation in the Scottish Parliament

Election Year	Population of Scotland	Number of Male MSPs	As % of MSPs	Number of Female MSPs	As % of MSPs
1999	51% Female/ 49% Male	82	64	47	36
2003	51% Female/ 49% Male	78	61	51	39.5
2007	51% Female/ 49% Male	86	66.9	43	33.3

Table 1.8 Ethnic minority representation in the Scottish Parliament

Election Year	Ethnic population of Scotland	Number of ethnic minority MSPs	MSPs as % of ethnic minority
1999	2%	0	0
2003	2.2%	0	0
2007	2%	1	0.7

ACTIVITIES

1 Name the two types of committee in the Scottish Parliament and give an example for each.
2 What is a 'temporary committee'?
3 What are the four main roles of committees in the Scottish Parliament? Try to give examples in your answer.
4 How do you think the committee system meets the four founding principles of the Scottish Parliament?
5 'The Scottish Parliament has done well in terms of representing females and ethnic minorities.' (View of Jackie McLaughlin)
Using the tables on female and ethnic minority representation in the Scottish Parliament, to what extent can Jackie McLaughlin be accused of being selective in his use of facts?

The Scottish Parliament has now passed over 100 Acts. These include a ban on smoking in public places to try and help Scotland's appalling health record, free personal care for the elderly (introduced by the Labour/Liberal Democrat coalition 1999–2007), the phasing-out of prescription charges, abolition of the Graduate Endowment Tax and also of bridge tolls in Scotland (introduced by the SNP minority government). In May 2007, the Scottish National Party broke Labour's eight-year dominance of the Scottish Parliament when it won the Holyrood election by one seat.

Some would argue that the Scottish Parliament has also brought decision making in Scotland closer to the Scottish people and engaged with people more than Westminster could have done.

However, the Scottish Parliament has also come under negative publicity in terms of MSP expenses (in October 2005, David McLetchie quit as Scottish Conservative leader, after pressure over his Holyrood taxi expenses) and there was also controversy surrounding the spiralling cost of the parliament building, which finally cost over £400 million. Whilst hospital waiting times are lower in Scotland than England, some argue that not enough progress has been made in this area.

2008 was the first time a Scottish Government budget was rejected, despite ministers making last-minute concessions. The SNP's £33 billion budget plans failed on the casting vote of the Presiding Officer after the vote was tied at 64 votes to 64. After talks with the other political parties, the SNP budget was passed second time round.

ACTIVITIES

1 In your opinion, has the Scottish Parliament been a success? Give reasons for your answer.

Local Government in Scotland

Local Government is the biggest employer in Scotland with approximately 250,000 employees. There are currently 32 local authorities in Scotland and their responsibilities are set out in the Local Government in Scotland Act 2003.

The Scottish Parliament 'devolves' certain powers to local government just as the UK Parliament has 'devolved' powers to the Scottish Parliament.

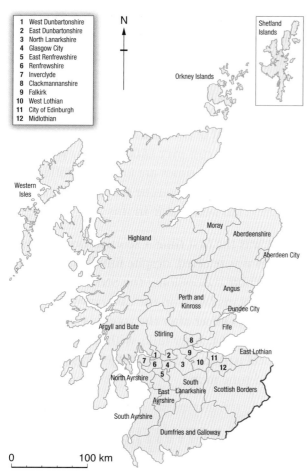

1	West Dunbartonshire
2	East Dunbartonshire
3	North Lanarkshire
4	Glasgow City
5	East Renfrewshire
6	Renfrewshire
7	Inverclyde
8	Clackmannanshire
9	Falkirk
10	West Lothian
11	City of Edinburgh
12	Midlothian

Figure 1.12 Local Authorities in Scotland

Areas of Responsibility

Local councils proved a range of services. Some are mandatory whilst others are discretionary. Mandatory services must be provided by the council by law, whilst discretionary services are the choice of the council.

Local councils must prove that they are providing the highest quality service whilst ensuring it is cost-effective. This is known as providing 'best value' in local government services.

All council services are headed by permanent officials in local councils. They are in charge of the day to day running of council services. They provide advice to councillors to help them make informed decisions. They put into practice policies agreed by council committees.

Mandatory Services	Discretionary Services
Education e.g. schools, teacher's salaries	Leisure facilities e.g. swimming pools, community centres
Police and fire services	Flood control e.g. Moray Council has engaged in a flood alleviation programme as many residents are affected by flooding
Social work, fostering, adoption	Twin-Towning e.g. Forres in Moray is twin-towned with Mount Dora, Florida
Planning e.g. new schools, business premises	Adult education services, residential care for the elderly

Financing

Central Government

Local councils receive the majority of their money (80 per cent) from the Scottish Government, through Aggregate External Finance (AEF). AEF consists of three parts:

- Revenue Support Grants
- Non-Domestic Rates
- Income and Specific Grants

The Scottish Government receives their funding from the UK Government via the Barnett Formula and then the Scottish Government decide how much to allocate to local councils.

Cabinet Secretary for Finance and Sustainable Growth (John Swinney) decides the amount of funding that each council will receive, taking into account things like population, social deprivation, etc.

Council Tax

Councils obtain additional income through council tax. This is a property tax on each house, which the council itself sets. Council tax accounts for approximately 13 per cent of overall funding.

The amount that households pay depends on their band (A to H) which is based on the value of the property as seen in 1991. There are special provisions for single person households, disabled persons and students as well as some other groups. For example, for a band D property in Glasgow (valued between £48,000 and £58,000 in 1991) you would pay £1,213 in council tax for a calendar year.

People with low incomes may be eligible for help through the Council Tax Benefit Scheme.

Non-Domestic (Business) Rates

Occupiers of non-domestic property (usually businesses) in Scotland pay non-domestic rates. These are taxes on local businesses in the area.

Service Charges

This comes mainly from charges to use council facilities such as swimming pools and gyms.

PPP

Public Private Partnerships (PPPs) involve local governments liaising with private companies to finance projects. These partnerships have allowed many local councils to fund projects which they could not have afforded otherwise. PPP uses private consortiums to build hospitals and schools and the local government pays back the firm over a period of time, usually 25 years. For example, the Edinburgh Royal Infirmary and many schools in Glasgow have been built under PPP projects.

East Dunbartonshire council is another example of a local council which has used PPP projects. In 2009, East Dunbartonshire council

completed a five-year £125 million project to build six new secondary schools. The InspirED Education consortium was awarded the contract to build six brand new schools in East Dunbartonshire situated on the north side of Glasgow.

Opinions on the existence and success of PPP projects are divided. Some people believe that PPP projects provide state of the art facilities, which improve patient care in hospitals and education in schools. They also argue that PPP finance offers best value for taxpayers money. However, opponents suggest that schools and hospitals will cost more to build under PPP in the long run than if they were publicly financed using traditional methods.

Role of Local Government

The main role of local government is summarised in the spider diagram below:

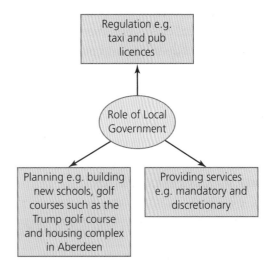

↑ **Figure 1.13** Role of local government

The Work of a Local Councillor

Each local council is split into smaller areas called 'wards'. Depending on the council, each ward will be represented by three or four councillors. For example, there are 79 councillors elected to Glasgow City Council.

There are 21 wards in the city, each having either three or four councillors representing it. Councillors are responsible for making decisions about how the council area e.g. Glasgow City is operated and about the services it provides.

Councillors hold surgeries (like MPs and MSPs) where people in the ward can go to air any concerns or seek solutions to a problem. For example, in the Park Hall ward in West Dunbartonshire, many local residents were against the proposed merger of two secondary schools and presented a petition to their local councillor who raised the matter with the council's education committee.

Like most MSPs, councillors are members of committees. These committees are related to local council services, e.g. the planning committee. Most councillors are members of more than one committee. Councillors will also get involved in the 'local life' of the council area by attending local events and meetings such gala days, school openings and public meetings.

Councillors are now paid a salary for the work they do. Previously they were given a small allowance and were able to claim expenses. As of May 2nd 2007, councillors now receive full training, approximately £15,000 salary and expenses packages once elected.

The Leader of the Council

The leader is the political head of the council, while the Lord Provost is the civic head. The leader is elected by the members of the majority party in the council. The council leader is similar to the role of the First Minister: he or she leads the administration, which is then accountable to the full council, and they are ultimately responsible for the services the administration provides. The Provost is like the Speaker of the Scottish Parliament: he or she presides at meetings of the full council and has a casting vote in the event of a tie. As civic head, the Provost has a number of ceremonial duties (welcoming distinguished guests, and representing the city in an unbiased way).

Elections

Prior to 2007, councillors were elected under a system of First Past the Post (FPP). Since 2007, councillors have been elected using the Single Transferable Voting System (STV). STV is a form of proportional representation and was introduced as part of the 2003–2007 coalition agreement between the Labour/Liberal Democrat Scottish Executive.

Labour were reluctant about the introduction of STV because they fair better under FPP as they have strong geographical support. STV was a large factor in changing the political landscape of local councils in Scotland.

Table 1.9 2007 local council election results

Political Party	Number of Councillors	Net gain/loss compared with 2003 elections
Scottish National Party	363	+182
Scottish Labour	348	−161
Scottish Liberal Democrats	166	−9
Scottish Conservatives	143	+21
Scottish Green	8	+8
Scottish Socialists	1	−1
Solidarity	1	+1
Independent and Other	192	−42
	Total: 1,222	

Under STV, voters rank the candidates on the ballot paper in order of preference. They put a '1' next to their favourite candidate, a '2' next to their second favourite, and so on. Voters can number as many or as few candidates as they like. Candidates need to reach a set quota of votes to be elected. To find out more about how STV works, you can visit www.votescotland.com and take a virtual tour.

Election of Council A, Z Ward

Instead of using a cross, number the candidates in the order of your choice.

Put the number 1 next to the name of the candidate who is your first choice, 2 next to your second choice, 3 next to your third choice, 4 next to your fourth choice and so on.

You can mark as many or as few choices as you like.

Party C	CANDIDATE A	4
Party D	CANDIDATE D	
Independent	CANDIDATE H	1
Party A	CANDIDATE J	2
Party F	CANDIDATE Q	
Party E	CANDIDATE S	
Party B	CANDIDATE W	3
Party A	CANDIDATE Z	

Figure 1.14 An STV ballot paper looked like this in 2007

Table 1.10 Control of local councils by political party 2003 and 2007

Party	2003	2007
Labour	14	2
SNP	1	0
Liberal Democrats	1	0
Conservatives	0	0
Other	5	3
No Overall Control	11	27

Tables 1.9 and 1.10 illustrate the impact of STV on local council results in Scotland. For example, the SNP had one of the largest increases in the percentage of councillors in 2007, whereas Labour had one of the lowest. The increase in the number of SNP councillors had a direct impact on the number of councils controlled by Labour.

The 2007 results also show that the majority of councils in Scotland are not controlled by one political party and that Labour also lost control of 12 out of the 14 councils that it had controlled in 2003. The impact on decision making is such that there will need to be more consensus in politics – councillors from different parties now need to work together to agree on policies to be passed. It is harder for any one political party to push ahead its agenda as there are so many councils with no overall control.

Relations between Central and Local Government

Decisions made by the Scottish Parliament and the House of Commons can affect the work of local councils.

Relationships between central government and local government can be problematic. Between 1979 and 1997 (before there was a Scottish Parliament), the UK elected a Conservative Government but the majority of local authorities in Scotland were dominated by Labour councillors. So there were two different political parties in control of two different layers of government.

Between 1997 and 2007, there was a UK Labour Government, a Labour/Liberal Democrat coalition in Scotland and most Scottish councils were under Labour control. This meant that there was less strain as one political party dominated most levels of government.

The 2007 Scottish Parliament elections produced a different result. Since then, there has been a minority SNP government in

Scotland, a Labour UK Government in Westminster and no political party dominates local councils – it makes for interesting times.

On occasions, there can be conflict over policy implementation between central and local government. Policy that is made by central government often needs to be implemented by local government and sometimes conflict can arise. This is usually over financial issues or differing ideologies.

Free personal and nursing care for the elderly was, and still is, an issue for local authorities. Free Personal Care was a flagship policy of the Liberal Democrats and implemented in 2001 as part of their deal as a coalition with Labour in the 1999 Scottish Parliament elections.

Although Free Personal Care for the elderly is a national policy, it is implemented locally by local councils, and they must find the funding. There is a growing elderly population in the UK and, as more elderly people receive free personal and nursing care, the financial burden on the local authority becomes greater. When one financial burden increases this has an adverse affect on the provision of other services as the councils' books need to balance at the end of the year.

Latest figures reveal that council spending on the nation's flagship policy has rocketed, up 21 per cent on personal care services for people in their own homes (from £185 million in 2006 to £224 million in 2007). The increasing cost and increasing elderly population begs the question of whether or not Scotland can really afford to fully fund the policy which was implemented seven years ago.

Another conflict involved Cabrach School in Huntly, which was set to close in early 2008 under a decision made by Moray Council. The Council's decision was overturned by the Scottish Government. There are currently only two pupils in the school and education heads in Moray Council had questioned whether the high cost – £50,000 a year per child, compared to the Scottish average of £3,300 – were fair to other schools and children. If the decision had not been overturned then the children would have been expected to travel to Dufftown, several miles away, when the new school term began.

Most disagreements between local and central government relate one way or another to funding. For many years there has been disagreement with regard to local authority funding. However, in 2007 the historical concordat (agreement) was made between the Scottish Government and Confederation of Scottish Local Authorities (COSLA). COSLA is an organisation which represents the best interests of local authorities. The concordat led to a freeze in Council Tax levels for the people in Scotland. To compensate for the loss of income this freeze caused, the Scottish Government gave the councils additional funding in the form of grants. Councils are still expected to produce efficiency savings of two per cent each year, although they are allowed to retain the finance from these savings and utilise them in working towards their priorities.

In order for the councils to receive this additional funding, they are required to deliver a number of government priorities through a Single Outcome Agreement. This is an agreement which sets out what councils must achieve. The councils have to meet government objectives and outcomes. There are also 45 national indicators by which performance in these objectives is assessed.

ACTIVITIES

1 How many local authorities are there in Scotland and which one do you live in?

2 a) What is the difference between discretionary and mandatory services?

b) Give some examples of discretionary and mandatory services that you or your family use.

c) For each service, describe how it helps meet the needs of people in the local community.

3 Describe two sources of funding for local councils in Scotland.

4 Create an information leaflet on the work of a councillor. You should include information about:

- wards
- committees
- decisions
- local work
- surgeries
- other work

5 Place the statements in the list below into this table under the appropriate headings.

Local councillors should be paid	Local councillors should not be paid

- Councillors deserve a reward for the amount of time and effort they put into their duties.
- Part time councillors are more in touch with the real world because they are active residents and workers in the local community.
- It would cost a lot of money.
- The importance of the role of the councillor should be recognised.
- Councillors would be able to ensure best value by devoting more time to their duties. They would no longer need to hold down a job.
- Some people would only become councillors for the payments.
- Councillors would probably do a better job of representing their local area.
- Many councillors already do a good job without payments.
- It would attract people of a high standard and change the present mix of councillors.

6 What is the name of the voting system used in local council elections?

7 'The SNP were big losers in the 2007 local council elections. The Scottish Liberal Democrats lost the least number of councillors.' (View of Ann McDermott)
Using the 2007 local council election results, give two reasons why Ann McDermott could be accused of exaggeration.

8 Why might central and local government come into conflict with each other? Give examples to illustrate your answer.

Pressure Groups

A pressure group is made up of people who come together because they feel strongly about an issue. Most pressure groups will try to influence or put pressure on 'decision makers', the people or organisations who have the power to make decisions and initiate changes, e.g. national and local government. This pressure may aim to change existing laws, to stop a Bill being passed, to introduce new laws in the group's favour or to stop the government from acting in a certain way. Although pressure groups seek to influence change, they do not wish to govern the country.

There are thousands of pressure groups in the UK. These range from small, local groups to large national and global groups. Pressure groups usually deal with single issues. More voters, especially younger voters, show more interest in pressure groups which campaign on single issues compared to political parties which have policies on many issues. The number of people who join political parties has fallen but the numbers who have joined pressure groups has risen. It is single issue campaigns, direct action and pressure group politics which are leading to higher levels of political activism. In recent years, more and more people have been taking part in pressure group activity as a way to get things changed.

Why are Pressure Groups Powerful?

Pressure groups are powerful because they usually have many members which mean they have 'power in numbers'. People and organisations are more likely to sit up and take notice if lots of people are making a point about an issue as opposed to only one person.

Pressure groups are also powerful because they have a lot of knowledge and information about their particular cause or issue. In fact the government will often consult pressure groups if it is thinking about introducing or changing a piece of legislation. For example, the government may contact the British Medical Association (BMA) if it was changing or introducing a law in relation to health or the NHS.

Pressure groups which have a large membership base draw attention to problems in society e.g. Greenpeace is able to spread its message using the media because high membership brings with it greater finance.

Types of Pressure Groups

Pressure groups tend to promote a cause or an interest. For example, the SSCPA (Scotland's animal welfare charity) is a cause group, concerned with the cause of improving the care and protection of animals. The SCND (Scottish Campaign for Nuclear Disarmament) is another example of a cause group, it campaigns for the abolition of nuclear weapons in the UK. However, not all pressure groups are cause-based – trade unions promote the 'interests' of their members e.g. pay, working conditions, etc.

Pressure groups can also usually be divided into two categories: 'insider' and 'outsider'.

Methods Used by Pressure Groups

Pressure groups often use a range of methods to get their point across. However, the methods used by a pressure group often depends on the kind of pressure group that they are (insider or outsider). Outsider groups, for example, will often use methods that attract the attention of the media to influence public opinion because they do not have the 'insider status' and are unable to negotiate directly with the government or indeed be invited by the government to provide expert advice.

Insider pressure groups:

- play an important role in governing the country
- have expert knowledge of a particular issue – they have a clear understanding of political decisions
- will be consulted and listened to by the government before it considers policy change e.g. the government would consult the BMA before proposing changes about the NHS etc. because the government is keen to keep such groups 'on side'
- can be very powerful as they are part of the consultation process if a law is to change. They have access to policy makers e.g. the British Medical Association (BMA) gave evidence to the health committee on the ban on smoking in public places
- can have a lot of influence as the public are often more likely to listen to them than the government
- use 'low key' methods to promote their aims e.g. negotiation via talks with government representatives or sending letters

Outsider groups:

- are on the 'outside' or 'margin' of the decision making process and, as such, generally have less influence on the government
- are not consulted and the government often disagrees with their aims and principles
- adopt methods they hope will gain media attention such as protests and demonstrations. Outsider pressure groups like the Scottish Campaign for Nuclear Disarmament (SCND) often break the law by causing disruption

Method	Description	Example
Marches	Groups will march in streets, usually in cities for their cause. There may also be people with loudspeakers making speeches or calling out details of the cause. During demonstrations, groups will often gather outside an organisation carrying placards and banners to attract publicity and media attention.	'Not in my Name' where people protested against the war in Iraq.

Demonstrations can be effective in influencing the government because they show the level of commitment and determination that members of the public have to pursue a cause. When large numbers of people join a march, they show the strength of support a pressure group has. This may persuade representatives to take action or they risk losing votes in the next election. For example, many hundreds of thousands of people protested against the war in Iraq. The Labour Government did not retreat from their position. As a result, in the 2005 General Election, Labour lost many seats and their parliamentary majority was whittled down to just 66 MPs. Indeed, George Galloway (a member of the Respect Party) was a fierce critic of the war and a member of the 'Not in My Name' campaign. He stood against Oona King (Labour Party) in the Bethnal Green and Bow constituency and defeated the Labour candidate.

Method	Description	Example
Lobbying	Lobbying comes from the term 'lobbies' (meaning hallways where MPs and members of the House of Lords would meet before and after debates in the House of Lords and House of Commons). In the past, pressure groups would meet MPs there, but modern day lobbying is a little different. Pressure group organisations will often hire companies which are professional 'lobbyists' to represent their views to parliament. They may try to organise interviews, protests and prepare documents relating to a law which is to be passed/changed.	March 2009 saw a mass lobby of parliament over the government's controversial Welfare Reform Bill involving trade unions e.g. UNISON, non-governmental organisations, and campaign groups e.g. Child Poverty Action Group. They were lobbying the government over the plans of the new Bill to: privatise employment services and the social fund, introduce work for your benefit schemes, abolish income support, cut benefits for single parents and those with long term illness and require all parents of young children to seek work.

Impact of Pressure Groups

Insider groups tend to be more effective in lobbying the government. They have the ear of the government and are in a position to influence policy because Ministers and civil servants rely on them for advice and guidance. However, some people argue that this is unfair as pressure groups are not elected and therefore should not be in a powerful position. Meetings behind closed doors between members of insider pressure groups like the British Medical Association (BMA) and the Health Minister might lead to accusations of secrecy.

Some other pressure groups like Fathers 4 Justice have argued that violent direct action is the only way they can force the government to listen to them. Fathers 4 Justice resorted to these measures because they had exhausted peaceful methods which proved to be ineffective. They are often criticised because members use illegal methods to draw attention to their cause. They hope that this will gain media attention and influence the government.

For example, Fathers 4 Justice acted violently when they ran into the Debating Chamber in

Method	Description	Example
Non-violent direct action	This is action which breaks the law without causing harm/violence towards people, although it may cause some damage to property. A blockade is a form of non-violent direct action.	SCND which campaigns against the nuclear weapons held at Faslane Naval Base near Glasgow often holds blockades at the premises. Sometimes the group will use lock-on tubes which lock protesters arms together and lie down so that they cannot be easily separated.
Violent direct action	Some pressure groups are prepared to break the law by using violent methods against others e.g. physical assault, bomb hoaxing, arson, and damaging property. This is clearly against the law.	Some animal rights activists have carried out direct action of this sort e.g. many are against Huntingdon Life Sciences which is a contract animal-testing company.

the House of Commons and threw purple powder at Tony Blair and other Cabinet Ministers. Fathers 4 Justice were criticised for breaching security and acting in a terrorist-like manner. As a result of negative criticism, they have now disbanded. Lawful members of that pressure group then set up their own pressure group to distance themselves from these irresponsible acts.

Non-violent direct action is also sometimes criticised for using methods that cause disruption and inconvenience to others, such as protesting and demonstrating on busy streets or places of importance. For example, on 21st March 2009, members of the pressure group Plane Stupid were arrested and charged with breach of the peace after dropping a banner reading 'Airport expansion is stupid' from the fourth storey of a car park opposite the Aberdeen airport terminal. Nine group members were also charged after protesters carried out direct action and barricaded themselves inside a 'wire fortress' on the

tarmac at the airport. Seven people were detained on an airport taxiway about five hours after the protest began.

These disturbances cost the economy money by delaying people who might otherwise be at work. In addition, resources are diverted into protecting ordinary people or moving protestors on. Many feel that this is a waste of time for the police as they ought to be tackling 'real crime' such as assault and youth behaviour as opposed to babysitting demonstrators and ensuring fair play.

Petitions are effective in influencing the government because they show the strength of public support. Locally-elected representatives are more likely to take notice of local petitions about council services such as the closure of schools. If the councillor ignores a petition with many local signatures, then they may find themselves voted out of office. People can just choose to vote for another candidate. Furthermore, the Public Petitions Committee

Method	Description	Example
Petitions	Petitions are a collection of signatures from people who feel strongly about an issue. The higher the number of signatures, the greater the level of support. Petitions are then delivered to representatives or the public petitions committee.	The 1000th petition to the Scottish Parliament was from All Saints Secondary pupils in Glasgow, asking the government to consider the public health impact of cheaply available alcohol.

← **Figure 1.15** All Saints Secondary School pupils deliver their petition to the Scottish Parliament

in the Scottish Parliament plays a crucial role in that petitioners can send their petitions online or in person to members of the committee. They would consider the petition and may act on it if they feel that it is a viable proposal. As a result, the issue can be raised in the debating chamber and could possibly turn into legislation should enough MSPs support it.

Another method which pressure groups may use to get their views across is roadshows. In the summer of 2008, Friends of the Earth Scotland ran a national roadshow at various locations in Scotland to raise support for its 'Big Ask Scotland' campaign. The campaign was to ensure the government passed a wide-reaching Scottish Climate Bill, making its way through the Scottish Parliament in 2009. At the roadshows Friends of the Earth spoke to the public about the climate campaign, and asked people to get involved by signing postcards addressed to their MSPs. The Big Ask Scotland campaign was launched at the Radiohead gig on Glasgow Green on 27th June 2008. The event was given a lot of media coverage and featured in the newspapers and on television. The pressure group wanted to try and make sure that they got their point across to as many people as possible and they managed to get 1,000 postcards signed.

ACTIVITIES

1 Describe in your own words what is meant by the term 'pressure group'.
2 Why can pressure groups be powerful?
3 What is the difference between 'insider' and 'outsider' pressure groups?
4 Design a poster which shows the different methods used by pressure groups.
5 Explain in detail why some pressure group methods are criticised.
6 Give one reason to explain why representatives like MSPs should listen to local pressure groups.
7 Why are some pressure groups prepared to break the law in their campaigns?
8 a) Do you feel strongly about a particular issue?
   b) Decide on an issue and write down what you think the government should do about it.
   c) Imagine that you were to form a pressure group for your cause. What would be the name of the pressure group?
   d) What kinds of methods would your pressure group use to get its message across and why?

Introduction

The UK is a **representative democracy**. This means that people vote for representatives to speak and make decisions on their behalf. The UK has a population of over 60 million people and, therefore, direct democracy (where everyone has a say in how the country is run) is not practical. Elections offer the opportunity for the British people to communicate their views on the decisions taken by the government and either re-elect those in power or choose other people. This means that politicians need to answer to the people of their country.

The UK Parliament is divided into three different parts: the House of Commons, the House of Lords and the Monarch. In the UK Parliament, the people of the UK are represented by MPs (Members of Parliament). MPs will represent people in a local constituency. There are currently 646 MPs in the UK. 59 of these MPs are in Scottish constituencies. Do you know who your local MP is?

To give the people of Scotland, Wales and Northern Ireland more say over what happens in their countries, the UK Parliament has devolved some of its powers to other bodies. In Scotland, for example, there is the Scottish Parliament which has elected MSPs who make some decisions for Scotland (see Chapter 1). Wales and Northern Ireland have their own Assemblies and there is also a London Assembly for the Greater London Authority.

The UK Parliament is responsible for creating and changing laws and also for scrutinising the work of the UK government. The UK Parliament makes laws on **reserved matters** which apply to the whole of the UK, such as

Figure 2.1 Westminster: the House of Commons (left) and the House of Lords (right)

defence and foreign affairs, whereas the Scottish Parliament makes laws on **devolved matters** for Scotland.

A constitution is a set of laws on how a country is governed. The British Constitution is unwritten, unlike the constitution in America. The British Constitution can be found in a range of documents. Changes to Britain's unwritten constitution are made in a similar way to how a law is made – by a majority vote in both Houses of Parliament to be followed by the Royal Assent.

The Houses of Parliament are sometimes called Westminster because they are located in the Palace of Westminster in London. There are more than 1,000 rooms and more than two miles of corridors. The building of the Houses of Parliament also includes the famous clock 'Big Ben' which you can see on the front cover of this book.

What is Parliament and Government?

The political party that wins the most seats (MPs) in a general election forms the new government, led by their political party leader – who becomes Prime Minister. However, not all

MPs will be 'in government'. The Prime Minister will appoint a Cabinet, which is a group of about 20 MPs who become ministers of a particular department. Members of the Cabinet tend to be drawn from the House of Commons and the House of Lords. The members of the Cabinet and the Prime Minister are technically 'in government'. Your MP may be a member of the political party forming the current UK government but it doesn't necessarily mean that they are working 'in government'.

Most members of the Cabinet are heads of government departments e.g. the Education Secretary is responsible for the Department of Education. Every Tuesday whilst parliament is sitting (it takes a break for the summer), the Cabinet meets in 10 Downing Street to discuss the big issues of the day.

Elections

General elections must be held at least every five years to elect MPs to the House of Commons, but they can be called before then. The most recent general elections took place in 1997, 2001 and 2005. The next general election will be held no later than May 2010.

Table 2.1 2005 UK general election results

Political Party	Number of seats won (MPs)	Number of votes won	Percentage of total votes (%)	Percentage of total seats (%)
Labour	356	9,552,436	35.2	55
Conservative	198	8,784,915	32.3	30.6
Liberal Democrat	62	5,985,454	22	9.6
Scottish National Party	6	412,261	1.5	0.9
Other	24	1,205,630	9	3.9
Total	**646**	**25,940,702**	**100**	**100**

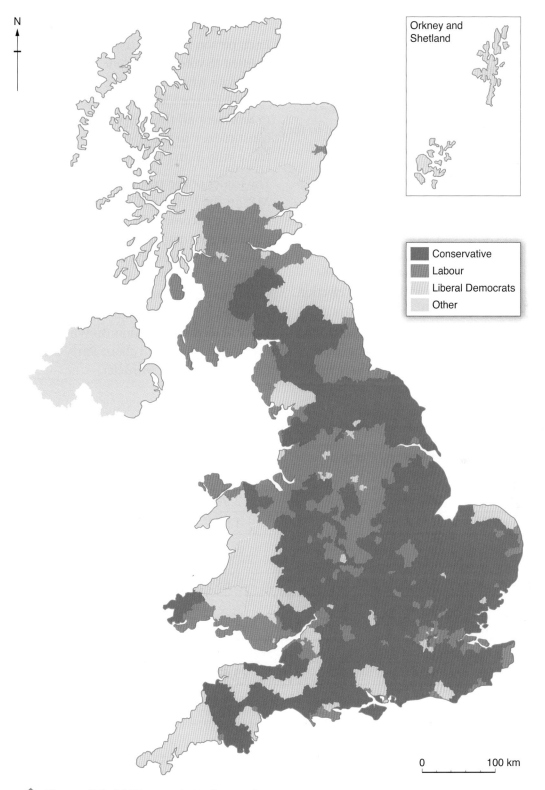

N

Orkney and
Shetland

Conservative
Labour
Liberal Democrats
Other

0   100 km

Figure 2.2 2005 general election results

If a political party wishes to form the government with an overall majority of MPs then it must win 324 or more seats.

In the 2005 general election, Labour won 356 seats in total. The political party which comes second in a general election is known as the **official opposition**. The official opposition to the Labour Government is the Conservative Party.

The voting system used at general elections is known as First Past the Post (FPP) or the simple majority system. It is the second most widely-used voting system used in the world.

During a general election, each of the 646 constituencies in Britain will have an election. Most political parties will put forward candidates to be elected and there may also be some independent candidates who have no affiliation to a political party. The three main political parties in Britain are Labour, Conservative and Liberal Democrat.

Each person living in the constituency who is entitled to vote is given one vote to cast. The candidate who receives the most votes becomes the MP for the local constituency and is elected to represent all the people living in their constituency in the House of Commons, even those who didn't vote for them.

The leader of the political party with the most MPs in the House of Commons is asked by the Queen to become Prime Minister and to form a government that will run the country. The Labour Party received the most seats in the last election in 2005. Tony Blair was the leader at that time and so he became the Prime Minister. After Tony Blair resigned, the Labour Party agreed that Gordon Brown should take over as leader of the Labour Party and he became the Prime Minister.

Table 2.2 Bootle constituency results in 2005 general election

Candidate	Political Party	Number of votes	Percentage of votes
Joe Benton	Labour	19,345	75.5 %
Chris Newby	Liberal Democrat	2,988	11.7 %
Wafik Moustafa	Conservative	1,580	6.2 %
Paul Nuttall	UK Independence Party	1,054	4.1 %
Peter Glover	Socialist Alternative	655	2.6 %
Labour Majority		**16,357**	**63.8 %**
Voter Turnout		**25,622**	**47.7 %**

Safe Seats

A 'safe seat' is a constituency where a particular candidate or political party has won by a large majority. It is safe because it would take thousands of people to change their mind at the next election and vote for someone else for that political party to win the seat. In the 2005 general election, Bootle in north-west England was the safest constituency seat.

Marginal Seats

A marginal seat is a constituency held with a particularly small majority. These seats require a smaller 'swing' to change hands. For this reason, they are usually a focus area during election campaigns. In the 2005 UK general election, Crawley was the most marginal constituency.

Table 2.3 Crawley constituency results in 2005 general election

Candidate	Political Party	Number of votes	Percentage of votes
Laura Moffatt	Labour	16,411	39.1 %
Henry Smith	Conservative	16,374	39.0 %
Rupert Sheard	Liberal Democrat	6,503	15.5 %
Richard Trower	British National Party	1,277	3.0 %
Ronald Walters	UK Independence Party	935	2.2 %
Robin Burnham	Democratic Socialist Alliance: People Before Profit	263	0.6 %
Arshad Khan	Justice Party	210	0.5 %
Labour Majority		**37**	**0.1 %**
Voter Turnout		**41,973**	**58.4 %**

For more General Election results see http://news.bbc.co.uk/1/shared/vote2005/ flash_map/html/map05.stm

Arguments in favour of First Past the Post

- **Strong government:** A single ruling party makes for a strong government. The system of First Past the Post has delivered a strong government with an overall majority for many years. This means that the winning party can usually carry out its manifesto policies without depending on the support of other political parties or having to form a **coalition government**. After all, no one votes for a coalition. First Past the Post in the UK has delivered a **two-party** system, meaning that the general election is usually a contest between the two main political parties: Labour and Conservative.

- **Simplicity:** First Past the Post is easy for members of the public to understand. Voters mark an 'X' next to the candidate of their choice and the person with the most votes wins. The party with the most seats (MPs) usually becomes the government. The result is also known quickly. It doesn't take very long to count all the votes and work out the winner, meaning results can be declared in a matter of hours after polls close.

- **Representative:** Under First Past the Post, voters have a single, local representative who they can contact regarding constituency issues. The system builds a strong relationship between a representative and the constituency.

ACTIVITIES

1 What is meant be a representative democracy?
2 What are the three main parts of the UK Parliament?
3 Who are the people of the UK represented by and how many are there?
4 Explain the difference between being a member of parliament and being 'in government'.
5 'The 2005 general election produced fair results for every political party.' (View of Naomi Dalgleish)
  Using Table 2.1, give one reason to support and one reason to oppose the view of Naomi Dalgleish.
6 a) Explain the difference between a 'safe seat' and a 'marginal seat'. Use the examples of the constituencies Bootle and Crawley to help explain your answer.
  b) Why might voters in Crawley feel that Laura Moffat does not represent their views?
7 Describe, in detail, the arguments for and against First Past the Post.

Arguments against First Past the Post

- **The winner takes all:** Under First Past the Post there are no prizes for second, third or fourth place and so on. Even if the winner only has a few more votes than second place, that person wins the constituency. Sometimes, the votes for other candidates added together make up a bigger total than the number of votes that the winning candidate receives. In fact, the only three MPs elected in the 2005 general election secured more than even 40 per cent of their constituent's votes.

- **Geographical support:** As Labour and the Conservatives have strong geographical support, they often come first in certain constituencies. For example, Labour has traditionally had strong support in Glasgow during general elections and was the dominant party across Scotland for many years. The Conservatives have strong support in the south of England. First Past the Post is therefore not so favourable for parties whose support is spread throughout the country e.g. the Liberal Democrats. They often come second or

third in constituency votes, gathering votes around the UK but not always winning a seat.

- **Unproportional:** Often the percentage of seats a party gains does not reflect the percentage of votes. General elections have consistently shown that the percentage of votes a party receives across the UK is not proportional to the percentage of seats (MPs) it receives. For example, in the 2005 general election, the Labour party gained 35.2 per cent of the votes but gained 55 per cent of the seats in the House of Commons. The Liberal Democrats received 22 per cent of the vote but only 9.6 per cent of the seats.

- **Wasted votes:** Many voters feel that their vote is wasted as their vote in the constituency counts for nothing if their chosen candidate doesn't win. In 2005, 70 per cent of votes were wasted in this way – that's over 19 million ballots. This means that some people do not bother voting as they don't see the point. This is especially the case in safe seats where a particular candidate or party wins election after election with a comfortable majority.

The Role of the House of Commons

All Bills must go through both Houses of Parliament before they become Acts (laws). The House of Commons is the more powerful of the two Houses and is the most important place for discussing policies and making laws. There are only 427 places on the green leather benches in the House of Commons, so when it's full a lot of politicians have to stand!

Members of the Commons (MPs) debate big political issues and proposals for new laws.

Debates

Debates give MPs a chance to discuss important matters and government policy and then reach an informed decision on a matter. These are initiated when a matter of concern or a topic is introduced as a proposal (motion) by MPs. Debates also allow MPs the chance to voice the concerns of their constituents and take their views into consideration. Votes are often held at the end of a debate and are known as a 'division'. MPs vote 'Aye' (for) or 'No' (against) to each proposal by passing through different doors in the House of Commons. This is different to the Scottish Parliament whereby MSPs vote using an electronic keypad.

Debates in the House of Commons are often very animated and sometimes likened to a 'Punch and Judy Show'. MPs will get involved and participate in each other's speeches to support or criticise their views. If MPs wish to speak, they must get the Speaker's attention (called 'catching the Speaker's eye') and usually stand, or half-rise from their seat to do so. This is unlike the Scottish Parliament, where MSPs press an electronic button at their desk which lets the Presiding Officer know that they wish to speak.

MPs address their speeches to the Speaker or their deputy. Normally MPs will speak only once in a debate, although they may 'intervene' with a brief comment on another member's speech. MPs who introduce the subject of debate (called 'tabling a motion') have the right to reply to speeches. You can view the most recent House of Commons debates at: www.theyworkforyou.com/debates/

However, there are rules to ensure that the etiquette of the House is adhered to, these are known as the 'Standing Orders'. The Speaker, currently the Conservative MP John Bercow, is responsible for ensuring order in the Commons and for chairing debates. The Speaker is elected by other MPs. The Speaker is the chief officer and highest authority of the House of Commons and must remain politically impartial at all times. The Speaker sits on the large raised chair at the top of the House of Commons.

Scrutiny

One of the most important roles and powers of the House of Commons is to examine the work of the government. This is mainly done through select committees, Question Time, divisions and opposition.

Parliamentary questions are very important in the House of Commons. They allow Members of Parliament to hold the government to account. MPs can ask the government questions to be answered in person by a Minister (oral questions) or in writing (written questions).

Question Time
This offers MPs the opportunity to question ministers about the work of their departments. Each department has at least one Minister in the House of Commons who can answer other MP's questions. Question Time lasts for one hour from Monday to Thursday and takes place at the start of the business of the day, after prayers. Each government department answers questions according to a rota called the Order of Oral Questions.

Ministers know the questions that MPs are going to ask before Question Time begins as they must submit their questions three days in advance. The questions are then printed in the Commons Questions Book. This allows the minister to prepare an answer in advance. Sometimes MPs are given the opportunity to ask supplementary questions once a Minister has answered the original question. The Minister will not know this in advance and MPs use these supplementary questions to try and catch the Minister out. However, supplementary questions must be on the same subject as the original question.

Prime Minister's Question Time

This takes place at 12 noon every Wednesday for 30 minutes and allows MPs to question the Prime Minister about the work of the government. The Prime Minister will answer questions on the work of the government which will usually involve a wide variety of subjects.

Similar to Ministers' questions, the Prime Minister will know in advance the first question to be asked. This allows the Prime Minister to prepare a scripted answer. However, there is an opportunity for opposition parties to ask supplementary questions. This is where the opposition will try to catch out the government and surprise them as the Prime Minister will not know the next question. The supplementary question has to be about the original topic, which leaves it very open for the MP. However, the Prime Minister's office will be advised by civil servants on all possible supplementary questions which may come up, meaning that the Prime Minister is usually well prepared. The Leader of the Opposition is allowed three or four supplementary questions to follow up their first question and the leader of the next largest opposition party is allowed two. This can leave little time for other parties and backbench MPs to ask questions.

Prime Minister's Questions are the event which most people are likely to see on the evening news at home. It is not particularly effective in changing government policy but it grabs the media attention and has the potential to influence the public's opinion.

Written Questions

Written questions are submitted to the government, usually when MPs want a detailed response or are pushing for some kind of action to be taken. In the parliamentary session 2007–2008 MPs submitted over

Figure 2.3 Gordon Brown at Prime Minister's Question Time

57,000 written questions. Answers are sent directly to the MP who asked the question and, as with oral answers, the text of written answers is given in **Hansard** (a formal record of parliamentary activity). Public debates and results of votes (divisions) in the chamber and in committees of both Houses are also published in Hansard (www.publications. parliament.uk/pa/pahansard.htm).

Select Committees

Select Committees in the House of Commons examine the work of government departments. Select committees examine the work of the government in three main areas: spending, policies and administration. The make up of these committees reflects the party balance in parliament. This means that currently, the Labour Party have a majority of MPs sitting on select Committees.

Select committees are usually small groups of around 11 MPs. A committee of 11 MPs currently has six Labour and three Conservative MPs and two MPs from smaller parties. In scrutinising government departments, Select Committees use a range of methods – they can gather oral and written evidence and call witnesses who are experts in an area and they can also decide on their own topics for inquiry. Government Ministers normally give evidence at some stage, but pressure groups, professors and experts are also given a say. Select Committees will often have a question and answer session with a witness after the witness has submitted written evidence. They can visit people and places in the UK and overseas to see how things work in practice and how other countries handle similar problems. Since 1997 Select Committees have also been able to consider draft Bills. The publication of a Select Committee report is often a major news event and may trigger a government response very quickly.

There are currently 19 departmental select committees. Some examples include; Defence Committee, Education and Skills Committee, Foreign Affairs Committee and Work and Pensions Committee. Each committee has a chairman who is chosen by the committee members at their first meeting. The main role of the chairman is to lead the committee's work and chair the meetings of the committee. The chairman also has a casting vote if there is a tied vote.

Select Committees meet once a week when parliament is in session. Members sit at a horseshoe shaped table, with the chairman in the middle. A meeting starts with a short private period where the committee discusses questions to be given to witnesses, possible future areas of enquiry, any draft reports etc. The committee then goes into public session to take oral evidence from witnesses. They may later go into private session again to hear more evidence or deal with administration.

The importance of select committees was reinforced by the announcement in April 2002 that the Prime Minister would submit himself to the twice-yearly scrutiny of the Liaison Committee. This committee is made up of the chairman of all the various committees. Tony Blair's first session before the committee was in July 2002 when members were able to quiz the Prime Minister on such topics as school spending and the war in Iraq. The session was seen by many as ground-breaking in terms of Prime Ministerial accountability.

Voting (Divisions)

The government needs support from the House of Commons in order to pass laws and take other actions e.g. go to war with another country. When the House of Commons votes, it is called a **division**. MPs vote by walking through either an 'Aye' or a 'No' lobby door. The 'Aye' lobby is to the right of the Speaker's seat and the 'No' lobby is to the left. The names of the MPs are recorded as they walk past the Clerks at the doorway and they are then counted by the Tellers.

Unlike many other parliaments, the House of Commons has not adopted an electronic method of voting. The idea of electronic voting was considered in 1998 by the Modernisation Committee but was rejected because there was no real support for an alternative to the current system.

Her Majesty's Opposition

Her Majesty's Opposition is the political party with the second highest number of MPs in parliament. One of the main roles of the opposition is to challenge the government in debates, at Question Time and in division lobbies. The opposition will seek to make the government explain its policies and check that it does its work properly. The main aim of the opposition is to gain power and become the government at the next election. It prepares for power by developing its own policies should it be elected to govern the country.

The opposition will have a leader and also a **Shadow Cabinet**. The role of the Shadow Cabinet is similar to the actual Cabinet. There will be Shadow Ministers whose job it is to challenge their opposite in government, e.g. the Shadow Chancellor of the Exchequer will challenge the Chancellor of the Exchequer. The influence of Shadow Ministers can be limited, especially if the government has a majority in the House of Commons and can pass legislation through the support of their own MPs alone. However, on occasions, MPs of a political party will revolt and vote against their party. Whips are employed by political parties to try and deal with this situation.

Figure 2.4 The results of a vote (division) being declared in the House of Commons

The Party Whip System

MPs are expected to follow the 'party line' when it comes to divisions because they have been elected to represent that particular political party in parliament. This means that MPs are required to vote in the way that their political party leader wants them to. To ensure that MPs vote as they are expected to, there are Chief Whips and Whips to make sure that this happens.

The political party's Chief Whip will be a member of the Cabinet or Shadow Cabinet. The other Whips will be MPs. Whips issue notices called 'The Whip' to MPs when there is an important division (vote) in the House of Commons. There are three types of Whip that an MP can receive and these are ranked in order of importance by the number of times they are underlined.

Three Line Whip

Important divisions are underlined three times – a 'three line Whip' – and normally apply to major events like the second readings of significant Bills. A three line Whip sends the message that the MP must attend no matter what. However, on occasions MPs will disobey the political party line, which results in 'the Whip' being taken away from an MP. This means that the MP is suspended from their party (but keeps their seat) and must sit as an independent until the Whip is restored. Many MPs revolted against the Labour Party over the vote to go to war in Iraq and also on the 42-Day Terror Detention Bill. MPs usually go against the political party line when they feel that they cannot personally or morally agree to the party's wishes.

Two Line Whip

This usually lets an MP know that they should attend the division unless they have made special arrangements not to attend. This must be approved by a party Whip.

One Line Whip

This lets MPs know that a vote will take place but their attendance, whilst appreciated, is not essential.

Lazy Labour MPs are to get new targets to increase their presence in the Commons under plans being drawn up by the Chief Whip, Nick Brown. Brown is to ask the Prime Minister to crack down on a hardcore of five per cent of members he has identified as responsible for 25 per cent of unauthorised absenteeism and a 'very similar' five per cent who are responsible for 50 per cent of all rebellions.

In a speech to the parliamentary press gallery today, Brown said this group were 'letting the others down'. He said: 'What impresses me is just how hard some Labour parliamentarians work: they wouldn't have to work quite so hard if the others worked harder.'

Brown is to present the Prime Minister with plans for a quota of activity every Labour MP must take part in during the last parliamentary year before a likely general election. Previously, Brown's attempts to curb rebellious behaviour included the threat to prevent any Labour MP who voted against the government from sitting on all-party parliamentary select committees.

Brown said: 'It is not so unreasonable for the electorate and taxpayers to expect members of parliament to be in regular attendance of the House of Commons. It is not unreasonable for people who voted for Labour at the election to expect Labour MPs to vote Labour in the house.

'In order not to let people down, you will be expected in one year to attend so many statutory committees and so many standing committees and so on. It is something the parliamentary party itself has called for in the past and they are lucky – they are going to get it.'

Brown cited research by Nottingham University which scotched the notion that rebellious MPs were more popular within their constituency – being a rebel had no effect on whether or not they were re-elected to parliament, the research found. 'Rebellion does not make you more electable,' Brown said.

Source: Extract from Guardian Newspaper online March 2009

The House of Lords

The House of Lords is the second chamber or 'upper house' of the UK Parliament. It is currently unelected and its members are unpaid (except for Law Lords). Membership of the House of Lords was once a birth right for hereditary peers, but following a range of reforms, the House of Lords now consists mainly of appointed members. In March 2009 the House of Lords had 742 members. There are a number of different routes to becoming a member of the House of Lords.

Elected Hereditary Peers
The House of Lords Act 1999 ended the hereditary peers' right to sit and vote in the House and also the right to pass membership down through their family. This Act cut the number of heredity peers from 700 to 92 which, except for two royal appointments, were elected from within the House. These peers will remain in position until the next stage of The House of Lords Reform.

Non-political Peers and the Peoples' Peers
The Appointments Commission was set up in May 2000. The role of the commission was to make recommendations to the Queen for non-political peers. These were sometimes called 'the people's peers' as the media had suggested that the new peers would be representative of UK society. Their peerage

ACTIVITIES

1 Imagine that you are going to teach your peers about the role of the House of Commons. Create a detailed information poster or PowerPoint presentation on the role of the House of Commons. Include information on:

- debates
- Aye and No lobbies
- scrutinising the government
- Question Time
- Prime Minister's Questions
- Select Committees
- voting
- opposition

2 What is meant by the 'Party Whip' system?

3 Complete this flow diagram below to show the difference between the three types of whip.

One line Whip   Two line Whip   Three line Whip

would run for their whole lifetime. The commission also checks nominations for peerages, including those from political parties. Life peers make up the majority (about 630) of the total membership of the House of Lords.

Law Lords

Law Lords become members of the House through *ad hoc* (as and when necessary) announcements. Law Lords are 'professional' judges who will listen to appeals from the lower courts and carry out official inquiries. They can do this up until they are 70 years old. However, the judicial role of the House of Lords ended in October 2009 when a separate, independent UK Supreme Court was set up.

Archbishops and Bishops

The maximum number of Bishops allowed in the House of Lords is 26. The Bishops who are appointed are done so according to how senior their positions are in the Church of England e.g. the Bishop of London, the Bishop of Durham, and the Bishop of Winchester. This is because the Church of England is the 'established' Church of the State. The Archbishops of Canterbury and York are given seats and life peerages too.

Dissolution Honours

Sometimes peerages may be given to some MPs who are leaving the House of Commons after many years of service.

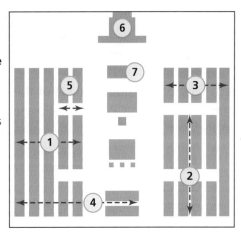

Groups and seating in the chamber

1: Government benches
2: Opposition benches
3: Liberal Democrat benches
4: Crossbenches
5: Bishops' benches
6: The Throne
7: The Woolsack

 Figure 2.5 Seating arrangements in the House of Lords

The Work of the House of Lords

The House of Lords has three main roles, as shown in Figure 2.6.

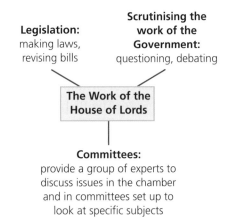

Legislation: making laws, revising bills

Scrutinising the work of the Government: questioning, debating

The Work of the House of Lords

Committees: provide a group of experts to discuss issues in the chamber and in committees set up to look at specific subjects

 **Figure 2.6** The roles of the House of Lords

An additional role for is judicial work. Until October 2009, the House of Lords was the highest court in the land (the supreme court of appeal) made up of full time judges known as Law Lords. However, the UK now has a separate Supreme Court.

The House of Lords complements the work of the House of Commons in many ways, see Figure 2.7.

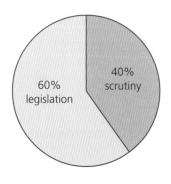

60% legislation

40% scrutiny

 Figure 2.7 How time is spent in the House of Lords

Each sitting day, the members of the Lords start by questioning government ministers in the chamber to find out what they are doing, or propose to do, on any subject. After these Oral Questions, the Lords may then examine and improve draft legislation. This legislation may have begun in the House of Commons or the House of Lords. Members may also debate important topics to highlight what the House thinks on an issue, signalling their views to the country and the government.

Legislation

For a Bill to progress through the UK Parliament it must be passed by both the House of Lords and the House of Commons before it is given Royal Assent by the Queen. Most of the House of Lords' time (60 per cent)

is spent on legislation. This may take the form of the Lords introducing legislation, or amending it.

Members of the Lords may spend many hours preparing information for the formal stages of legislation. For example, even before a Bill is introduced, the House of Lords will set up a committee. The committee will be made up of members of both Houses and will hear evidence from people who may be affected by the Bill. It will also identify any potential problems with the Bill and make any recommendations to the government.

It is argued that this will allow members of the House to debate the Bill in a more informed way, and will also save time in the long run when the Bill begins its passage through both Houses.

The Lords were involved in the Mental Health Bill, the purpose of which was to update the way people with a mental health condition are treated. The Bill introduced Community Treatment Orders (CTOs) so that the mentally ill could be monitored without being kept in a hospital. There were some concerns over this Bill regarding patient protection, and the Lords were able to recommend some changes regarding this. For example, changes made by the Lords included measures which stated that people could only be confined to hospital if hospital treatment was expected to improve their condition – or prevent it from getting any worse.

Many members of the Lords are professionals and have a lot of expertise in specific areas, meaning that they can offer invaluable insight at all stages of their examination of new legislation.

CASE STUDY

Corporate Manslaughter and Corporate Homicide Bill

The purpose of this Bill was to make it possible to prosecute companies and corporate executives when their negligence resulted in death. The Lords agreed with the Bill's principal provision but thought it should also apply to prisons and police cells. A former chief inspector of prisons, Lord Ramsbotham, gave the House examples of cases where people had died in custody. He argued that managers responsible for the care of these people would have taken their responsibilities more seriously if they knew they could face a charge of corporate manslaughter, and that it would be wrong for them to be exempt from the new law. The Commons continually rejected the amendment but the Lords voted to reinstate it four times. The Government eventually agreed to extend the provisions to deaths in custody within three to five years.

Delaying Laws

The House of Lords does not have the power to stop a new law that the House of Commons wants, but it can delay it. The Parliament Acts of 1911 and 1949 allow the House of Lords to delay a Bill for up to one year. There are, however, some Bills which it cannot delay e.g. a financial Bill.

A further restriction is the Salisbury Convention, which means that the House of Lords does not oppose legislation promised in the Government's election manifesto.

Committees

When considering a Bill, the committee of the whole House can be used i.e. the whole of the House of Lords or the Grand Committee. This committee can make speeches about a Bill or a motion. The Grand Committee is sometimes used, but needs everyone to vote unanimously for the Bill to pass so this is often used for uncontroversial Bills.

Scrutinising the Government

40 per cent of the time spent in the House of Lords is on scrutinising the activities of the government. The House of Lords also has a range of Select Committees. Most Select Committees are permanent, but the Lords may also set up *ad hoc* committees, which deal with particular topics and then disband when finished. The members of these committees are appointed by the House at the beginning of each parliamentary session and run for the duration of the session.

The main role of select committees is to scrutinise and investigate the work of the government. In order to do this, the committees will hold hearings and collect evidence.

Lords committees have experts from many fields and there is less 'party politics' because membership of committees is cross-party. Committees meet weekly, sometimes more often. There are also permanent committees investigating work relating to Europe, science and technology, economics and the constitution. Occasionally one-off committees are set up to deal with issues outside these areas.

The House of Lords Clashes with Government Anti-Terrorism Legislation

In October 2008, Gordon Brown's Labour Government proposed to raise the current limit for holding terror suspects in the UK from 28 days to 42 days as part of the Counter-Terrorism Bill. The Government's plan to extend the period for which the police can hold terrorist suspects before charging them passed through the House of Commons in June 2008 by just nine votes. The House of Lords rejected the plans by 309 votes to 118.

Home Secretary Jacqui Smith then told MPs in the Commons that plans to extend detention of terrorists to 42 days would be dropped from the Counter-Terrorism Bill. Ms Smith said that the measure would instead be contained within a separate piece of legislation to be brought to parliament at another time if needed.

A committee will write a report of its findings in an area or policy or Bill together with any recommendations to the government. These reports are available to the media and public for their information too. The Lord in charge of a select committee or an investigation into government affairs will often have a report named after them and make a statement in an investigation. One example is the Hutton Inquiry – the report which was released following the death of Dr Kelly and the alleged 'sexing up' of a government dossier.

Questions

Similarly to the House of Commons, members of the House of Lords can submit written or oral questions to Ministers. Oral questions take place for half an hour in the Lords chamber at the start of business each day. Four questions are allowed to be asked. Questions are directed at the government in its entirety rather than to specific departments.

Written questions from the House of Lords must be answered within 14 days by the government and, like the House of Commons questions, are published in Hansard. The number of written questions has grown over the years. In 2007 approximately 5,000 questions were asked.

Debates

The House of Lords debates a whole range of areas such as crime, education, justice and the environment. For example, in March 2009, the House of Lords debated the Postal Services Bill and the Borders, Citizenship and Immigration Bill. Often, members of the Lords will be experts in a particular area that they are debating about. You can view the most recent Lord's debates at: www.theyworkforyou.com/lords/

Reforming the House of Lords

One of the major criticisms of the House of Lords is that it is unelected. Almost half the time spent in the House of Lords is involved in passing legislation that affects the UK population, yet voters have no control over who is elected to make these decisions. The Labour Party, when elected to power in 1997, promised to introduce legislation that would make the House of Lords an elected second chamber. The 1999 House of Lords Act made some changes to the House of Lords but it still remains unelected.

Figure 2.8 A gathering of members of the House of Lords

In 2001, the Labour Government produced a White Paper calling for an appointed House of Lords by abolishing all Hereditary Peers and advocated the inclusion of elected members. On 4th February 2003, the House of Lords voted for this measure (335 votes to 110) but it was defeated in the House of Commons (323 votes to 245).

In 2007, the House of Commons voted in favour of an 80 per cent or a fully elected House of Lords by a majority of 113. The Lords rejected this plan by 361 to 121 votes and said they wanted a fully-appointed chamber.

After this, Justice Secretary Jack Straw set up a cross-party group and produced a White Paper in 2008 which set out plans for reform of the

The Labour Party manifesto for the general election on 1st May 1997 stated that:
    The House of Lords must be reformed. As an initial, self-contained reform, not dependent on further reform in the future, the right of hereditary Peers to sit and vote in the House of Lords will be ended by statute. This will be the first stage in a process of reform to make the House of Lords more democratic and representative. The legislative powers of the House of Lords will remain unaltered.

    The system of appointment of life Peers to the House of Lords will be reviewed. Our objective will be to ensure that over time party appointees as life Peers more accurately reflect the proportion of votes cast at the previous general election. We are committed to maintaining an independent crossbench presence of life Peers. No one political party should seek a majority in the House of Lords. A committee of both Houses of Parliament will be appointed to undertake a wide ranging review of possible further change and then to bring forward proposals for reform.

Source: (Labour Party, New Labour: Because Britain Deserves Better, April 1997, pp. 32–33)

House of Lords. This proposal suggested that members of the Lords should be elected and serve terms of between 12 and 15 years. The House would also be reduced in size to no more than 450 members. The Bishops would still be Lords, but the 92 hereditary Peers would be abolished. This will be part of the Labour manifesto at the 2010 general election.

The Changing Membership of the Lords

18th Century Acts of Union with Scotland (1707) and Ireland (1800) entitled Scottish and Irish Peers to elect representatives to sit in the Lords.

    1876 Appellate Jurisdiction Act creates Lords of Appeal in Ordinary (Law Lords) to carry out the judicial work of the House as the final court of appeal.

    1958 Life Peerages Act creates peerages 'for life' for men and women – women sit in the House for the first time.

    1963 Peerage Act allows hereditary Peers to disclaim their peerages, and allows hereditary peeresses (women) and all Scottish Peers to sit in the House.

    1999 House of Lords Act removes all except 92 hereditary Peers from the House.

    2005 Constitutional Reform Act removes the Law Lords and sets up a new, independent supreme court (from October 2009). It also changes the role of the Lord Chancellor, ending his role as a judge and as Speaker of the House of Lords.

    2006 House of Lords holds its first election for a Lord Speaker.

    2007: Commons votes for all elected House of Lords. Lords votes again the plans. Jack Straw sets up cross-party group and published white paper.

Source: www.parliament.uk/documents/upload/HofLBpmembership.pdf

How a Bill Passes Through Parliament

The procedure for passing Bills through the UK Parliament is similar in both Houses. A Bill must pass through several stages – in both Houses – to become a law. If the Bill started in the Commons it then moves to the Lords. If it started in the Lords it then moves to the Commons.

The only difference between what happens in each House is that, at the Third Stage, the House of Lords has the opportunity to suggest any further amendments but the House of Commons cannot do this.

Royal Assent

The final stage of the Bill's progress in Parliament is Royal Assent. This is when the Queen signs the Bill and authorises its progress into law. When the Queen signs the Bill, it becomes an Act of Parliament. The Bill may become law straight away or after a period of time if it has a specific date set.

The Queen signs the Bill because she is the Head of State. The Queen does not give assent in person, instead it is given by the Speaker in the Commons and the Lord Speaker in the Lords. Royal Assent is a formality. In reality the Queen is very unlikely to withhold consent. Queen Anne was the last monarch to do so, in 1707.

Powers of the Prime Minister

'**The Executive**' is the name commonly given to the UK Prime Minister and his Cabinet. The role of Prime Minister comes with many powers but there are checks in place to make sure that he/she doesn't become too powerful.

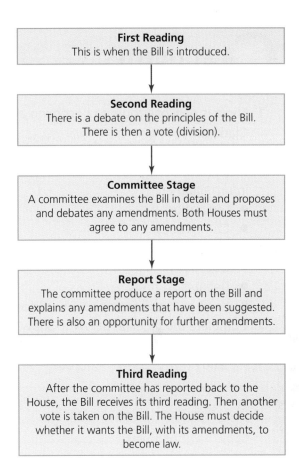

First Reading
This is when the Bill is introduced.

Second Reading
There is a debate on the principles of the Bill. There is then a vote (division).

Committee Stage
A committee examines the Bill in detail and proposes and debates any amendments. Both Houses must agree to any amendments.

Report Stage
The committee produce a report on the Bill and explains any amendments that have been suggested. There is also an opportunity for further amendments.

Third Reading
After the committee has reported back to the House, the Bill receives its third reading. Then another vote is taken on the Bill. The House must decide whether it wants the Bill, with its amendments, to become law.

Figure 2.9 The stages of a Bill moving through both Houses of Parliament

Power of Appointment and Re-shuffling

The Prime Minister is responsible for many government appointments. The Prime Minister will appoint the Cabinet, Government Ministers, senior civil servants, judges, Whips and senior military officers.

Appointing these roles gives the Prime Minister power because he/she can reward politicians in their political party who perform well and remain loyal. Some political party members will be ambitious and seek to gain a position in the Cabinet, so they will work well for the Prime Minister in the hope of being promoted. At any time, the Prime Minister can reshuffle the Cabinet. This means that he can

ACTIVITIES

1 There is only one route to becoming a member of the House of Lords. (View of Jane Clark)

To what extent can Jane Clark be accused of being selective in her use of facts?

2 Describe in detail the work of the House of Lords. In your answer, you should include information on:

- Legislation
- Committees
- Scrutinising the government
- Questions
- Debates

Remember to use examples where possible.

3 Complete the timeline below to show the events surrounding House of Lords reforms.

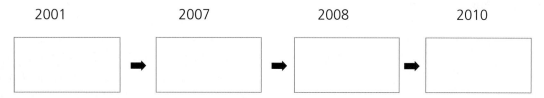

2001   2007   2008   2010

4 Briefly describe how a Bill passes through the UK Parliament.

sack a Minister or appoint them to another job. This often happens after a general election but it can happen at any time.

In June 2009, Gordon Brown re-shuffled his Cabinet to try and reassert his power as Prime Minister after four members of his Cabinet resigned in one week. For example, he appointed Yvette Cooper to take over at the Department of Work and Pensions, and Alan Johnson was appointed as Home Secretary.

However, as well as rewarding loyalty within the political party, the Prime Minister must also appoint Cabinet members that they do not necessarily personally like. Tony Blair needed to keep Gordon Brown in his Cabinet despite

reported disagreements and then Brown later replaced Blair as Prime Minister.

Leader of the Party

The Prime Minister is the leader of the largest political party in the House of Commons and most MPs from their own party will support them, but sometimes there are 'backbench' rebellions when their MPs may speak out against the government or the Prime Minister.

The Prime Minister uses Whips to try and make sure that MPs and their party members 'toe the party line' and remain loyal. The Chief Whip will report directly to the Prime Minister. Whips are particularly important

Figure 2.10 The Prime Minister and his Cabinet in 2009

held before this. It is the Prime Minister who decides when to ask the Queen to 'dissolve' Parliament, and consequently decides when the next general election will take place.

A Prime Minister will be most likely to hold a general election when opinion polls suggest that the government is popular and has a good chance of being re-elected. Tony Blair did this successfully in the 2001 and 2005 general elections.

when legislation is being passed. The government doesn't want to be seen to have members in their party who are not supporting policy, so sometimes Three Line Whips are issued when important votes are taking place. If an MP didn't turn up for a Three Line Whip, he/she would be seen to be rebelling against their party.

However, there are limits on the powers of a Prime Minister. If a Prime Minister loses the support from his party's backbenchers, their position becomes very weak. This happened to Tony Blair over a single issue – the Iraq war – and in mid–2009 Gordon Brown faced calls to step down over the MP expenses row as well as over the four resignations from members of the Cabinet on the day before the European Elections (4th June 2009). Backbench MPs may also turn against a Prime Minister and force a leadership challenge if they want a new leader for the party before the next general election.

The Power of Dissolution

The Power of dissolution is a power that solely lies with the Prime Minister. General elections must be held every five years but they can be

However, in the summer of 2009, Prime Minister Gordon Brown came under fierce pressure from opposition political parties to hold a general election. This pressure resulted from the controversy over MP expenses and Cabinet resignations just before the European Elections. For example, Communities Secretary Hazel Blears resigned the day before the elections, increasing pressure on Gordon Brown. These departures led to stormy Commons scenes at Prime Minister's Questions that week where Mr Brown denied his government was in 'meltdown' and rejected

Figure 2.11 Tony Blair arriving to arrange the dissolution of Parliament with the Queen in 2005

calls for an immediate general election. The latest that Gordon Brown could call the next general election is June 2010.

The last Labour Government was brought down by a Conservative 'no confidence' motion in 1979 after the SNP withdrew support for the government, although the then Prime Minister James Callaghan did not have a working parliamentary majority, unlike Gordon Brown.

Executive Head

The Prime Minister calls Cabinet meetings and controls the agenda and discussion giving him/her a lot of power to steer what is discussed and decided at these meetings. At the end of the meeting, the Prime Minister will summarise the views of the Cabinet at the meeting. This is recorded and becomes a policy document which all government members must support. The Cabinet is bound by **'collective responsibility'**, which means that all of its members must abide by and defend the decisions it takes, despite any private doubts that they might have. If a minister felt that they could not support a decision then they would have to resign. Robin Cook resigned from the Cabinet when Tony Blair was in power as he disagreed with the way that

Blair handled the Iraq war. As the Prime Minister is the head of the Cabinet, he also has a lot of power to influence the development of policies. For example, as Prime Minister and former Chancellor of the Exchequer, Gordon Brown has had a lot of influence over economic decisions.

International Role

The Prime Minister will represent the country internationally. This may mean taking foreign trips to places such as the White House or the UN Headquarters in New York to make international decisions. For example, Gordon Brown met with Barack Obama in 2009 in his Oval Office in the White House to further develop the relationship between the countries and to discuss national security. He also met other world leaders when he hosted the G20 summit in London in April 2009. The leaders met to discuss the world recession. The G20 is a group of the world's most powerful countries that together represent 85 per cent of the world's economy. It includes major industrial powers such as the US and Germany, and emerging economic powers such as Brazil and China.

Civil Service

The Prime Minister is also head of the civil service. The civil service is the 'administrative' part of the government. For example, civil servants work in the Cabinet Office at 10 Downing Street and their role is to inform the Prime Minister about what all the different government departments are doing to allow him/her to oversee their work and make sure s/he is aware of what is going on. The civil service is 'politically neutral' under the Civil Service Code and, therefore, has to be impartial,

THE **LONDON** SUMMIT 2009
STABILITY | GROWTH | JOBS

↑ Figure 2.12 The G20 gathering in London in April 2009

honest and objective. The research which it carries out for government departments must not be biased.

Civil servants also provide the Prime Minister and Ministers with research, information and advice to help make policy decisions. They tend to be experts on particular subjects. Other political parties do not have the advantage of these civil servants.

Media

The media can be a powerful tool for the Prime Minister, but it can also damage the reputation of the Prime Minister and his political party. For example, the public see Prime Ministers Questions every week and a good performance can raise party morale and display strong leadership to the media. Positive coverage can also attract voters. Mistakes are also widely publicised and can damage a Prime Minister's authority and reputation. This was seen in the 2009 expenses row when Gordon Brown was forced to apologise on behalf of MPs and also to change the system for MPs claiming expenses.

What is the Cabinet?

The Cabinet is a group of about 20 MPs (called Ministers) who are appointed to be in charge of particular government departments e.g. Health and also to plan and decide on government policy. The Cabinet meets at 10 Downing Street once a week.

Tony Blair was accused of having a 'sofa style' government, which meant that he sought advice from 'special advisers' outwith the Cabinet and made informal decisions without necessarily going through the Cabinet process. Gordon Brown has tried to make his mark as a different Prime Minister to Tony Blair through greater consulation with backbench MPs along with his Cabinet.

Prior to Cabinet meetings, Cabinet committees appointed by the Prime Minister will have met to discuss important and significant issues. The Cabinet will normally approve the decisions of the committees at whole Cabinet meetings.

ACTIVITIES

1 What is the Executive?
2 Write a report on the powers of the Prime Minister. You may wish to use some of the headings below to help you structure your answer:
   ● Appointment
   ● Leader of the party
   ● Dissolution
   ● Executive Head
   ● International role
   ● Civil service
   ● Media
3 What is the Cabinet and where do members meet?
4 Why did some people say that Tony Blair had a 'sofa style' government?

Participation in the UK Political System

The Decline in Participation

In the UK, the number of people taking part in political activity has fallen in recent years and is continuing to do so. However, the membership of pressure groups is increasing, showing that more people are taking part in some kinds of political activity. Political parties are concerned with broad policies, covering a range of issues. Pressure groups, however, are much narrower, campaigning either for a single issue, or for minor changes to policy. They do not seek to gain power in government but rather seek to influence it.

Turnout

In terms of voting, the Electoral Commission estimates that it takes 20 minutes to get to a polling station and mark a cross on the paper, but it would seem that two-thirds of the voting public cannot spare the time. According to the Electoral Commission, it would seem a growing number of people are not convinced that their views are heard, either on polling day or beyond. Overall, between 1999 and 2007, turnout at Scottish Parliament elections has fallen by 6.44 per cent, see Figure 2.13. Between 1997 and 2005, turnout at UK general elections fell by 10.2 per cent, see Figure 2.14.

Political Party Membership

It is argued that many people, especially younger people who are interested in politics, are more excited by 'single issue' politics as opposed to the ideology of a political party. Membership of all the major political parties in the UK has fallen overall in recent years and continues to do so. According to the *News of the World*, 40,000 supporters have left the Conservative Party since David Cameron took over as leader three years ago. When Tony Blair won the 1997 election the total number of members of the Labour Party stood at 405,000. In the decade after that victory, membership halved. However, since Gordon Brown became Prime Minister in July 2007, the decline has halted and Labour has managed to entice 10,000 new members according to the newspaper.

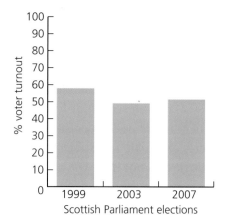

Figure 2.13 Turnout at Scottish Parliament elections

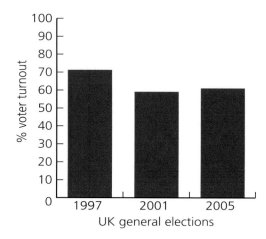

Figure 2.14 Turnout at UK general elections

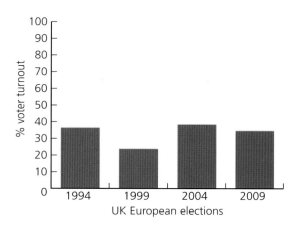

Figure 2.15 European election turnout in the UK

Why Don't People Participate?

Trust

One fifth of people in the British Election Study (2005) said that they do not vote because they do not trust politicians. This feeling was intensified in May/June 2009 when the scandal over the MPs claiming expenses for items that they shouldn't or claiming for overpriced items dominated the media for months. The report states: 'Three out of four people don't trust politicians to tell the truth.' (*Source: IpsosMori 2005*). But polls also suggest that people do not trust estate agents or journalists, but houses continue to be sold and papers to be read.

Time and Postal Votes

As mentioned previously, some people cannot find the time to get to the polling station. The government has tried to tackle this issue by allowing people to vote using a postal vote. Across Scotland in 2007, 11.2 per cent of the electorate received a postal ballot for the Scottish Parliament elections. This represents a sharp increase from 3.6 per cent in 2003. The number of people casting their votes by post in the 2005 general election tripled compared to 2001. Any UK citizen living in the UK or abroad can vote by post. The report on the Scottish Parliament and council elections suggested that postal voting may have slightly

increased the turnout in the 2007 elections. (*Source: www.electoralcommission.org.uk/ __data/ assets/excel_doc/0004/55561/Scotland-Parl-2007-Postal-Votes-Constituency.xls*)

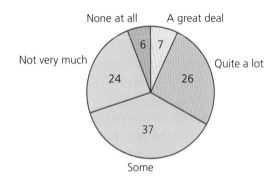

▲ **Figure 2.16** 2005 British Election Survey, responses to the question: How much interest do you generally have in what is going on in politics?

Interest

It could be that there is a general decline of interest in politics. Many see politics as boring and have no interest in it. They may feel that it has no impact on their lives or that nothing changes even if they vote or express a view.

Attempts to Encourage Political Participation

Non-participation in politics is a complex issue and there is no one reason for lack of participation, or one specific solution to

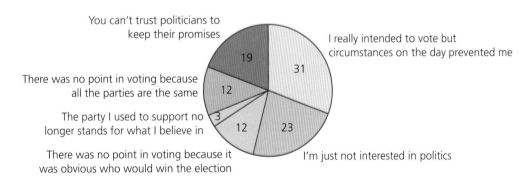

▲ **Figure 2.17** 2005 British Election Survey, responses to the question: Which of the statements comes closest to your reason(s) for not voting in the 2005 general election that was held on May 5th?

improve it. Members of all political parties have recognised the seriousness of low turnouts in elections and efforts have been made across the UK to encourage people to be involved in politics and vote. For example, the UK Government established the Electoral Commission with a remit which includes encouraging participation in elections in the UK. See www.electoralcommission.org.uk/

A report in 2004 by the Electoral Commission recommended that the age that an individual could stand as a candidate in any UK election be reduced to 18. The Commission found no reasonable argument why the candidacy age should not be brought into line with the current voting age and argued that there may be individuals aged under 21 who are capable of being effective representatives.

Alternative Voting System

Some people feel that their vote is wasted under the First Past the Post voting system used in UK elections. According to the Electoral Reform Society, 'only a change to our voting system, rather than our voting methods, is likely to promote the changes that are needed.' (Source: Turning Out or Turning Off www.electoralreform.org.uk/downloads/Turning%20out-3.pdf)

The Electoral Reform Society argues that the First Past the Post voting system does not encourage people to vote. This is because of its many faults, including the idea of wasted votes in safe seats and the two party race between Labour and the Conservative Party. There have been suggestions that First Past the Post should be replaced with a Proportional Representation system. However, the Additional Member System used in the Scottish Parliament is a mixed form of proportional representation, producing a more proportionally representative result, yet the turnout rate for Scottish Parliament Elections is lower than for UK general elections. (See pages 40–41 for more details on the arguments for and against First Past the Post.)

Other methods include considering the possibility of compulsory voting. Over twenty countries have some form of compulsory voting, which requires citizens to register to vote and to go to their polling place or vote on election day. Australia is one example where all citizens over the age of 18 (except those of unsound mind or those convicted of serious crimes) must be registered to vote and cast their vote at the polling station on election day. Australians who do not vote may be fined.

Text and internet voting has been suggested as a way of encouraging more young people to vote and there have been experiments in these areas. Less than 50 per cent of under 25s currently make the journey to the ballot box. The ease and popularity of text messaging may mean that more young people would vote. The appeal of text messaging has been spotted by companies such as MTV, BBC and ITV who incorporate the idea of 'text voting' into their TV shows.

Lower the Voting Age to 16

The concern over the fact that many young people in the UK do not vote has led to calls for the voting age to be lowered to 16. The Votes at 16 Coalition is a campaign to allow 16 and 17 year olds to vote in all UK elections. The coalition was launched in 2003, and is made up of over 40 leading youth and democracy organisations from across the UK (see www.votesat16.org.uk for details).

Jo Swinson is MP for East Dunbartonshire, and was the youngest Member of the House of Commons when she was elected in 2005. She supported the coalition and is leading a new call for MPs to lower the voting age to 16. Jo, supported by MPs from a range of political parties, tabled an Early Day Motion (EDM) calling on parliament to lower the voting age to 16.

Gordon Brown has said he wants to look seriously at lowering the voting age, and has launched a Youth Citizenship Commission to consider it. The Commission is working on a report looking at the advantages and disadvantages of giving 16 year olds voting rights. Some senior government ministers have said they support voting at 16, the Welsh Assembly also supports it, and a majority of members of the Scottish Parliament do as well. However, the power to implement this decision is retained by Westminster. Groups campaigning for this change include the National Union of Students, the Electoral Reform Society, the Children's Rights Alliance for England, British Youth Council and Children's Parliament in Scotland.

However, a review was carried out by the electoral commission in 2004 into whether the voting age should be lowered to 16. The Electoral Commission recommended that the voting age should not be lowered to 16.

In the European Parliament elections in June 2009, Ellen Soderberg from Sweden hoped to become Europe's youngest MEP at the age of 18. Astrid Lulling from Luxembourg was also a candidate, she was once the holder of the same title but, in 2009, she was attempting to become the Parliament's oldest member, turning 80 just four days after the election. One of the main reasons they were standing was to try and combat voter apathy. Ellen was not elected, but Astrid is now serving a new term in the European Parliament.

↑ **Figure 2.18** Astrid Lulling, MEP

Arguments in favour of lowering the voting age to 16

- *Fairness*: At 16, people become adults and take control of their own futures. If people are able to leave home, get a full time job, pay taxes, get married and join the armed forces at 16 then they should also be able to vote and have a say in how their country is run.
- *Young people want it*: Many young people want to vote and many politicians support the idea too. The Prime Minister has set up at commission to look into the issue. The Electoral Commission's public consultation on the voting age in 2004 found that 72 per cent of respondents favoured a voting age of 16. Young people want to be able to vote and it is possible that it would help engage young people in politics.
- *Other countries vote at 16*: For example, in Austria, all 16 and 17 year olds can now vote. Germany, Slovenia and Switzerland have also partially lowered the voting age to 16. In Germany, 16 year olds can vote in local elections. In Slovenia, 16 year olds can vote if they have jobs, and in Switzerland the constituent state Glarus has also lowered the voting age to 16 years.

Arguments against lowering the voting age to 16

- **Not mature enough**: Most 16 year olds are not mature or responsible enough to vote. Many do not know enough about politics and would not consider all the issues to make an informed decision. They would be impressionable by the media, friends and parents. The age at which to join the army and get married should be raised to 18 instead.
- **Young people wouldn't be engaged**: Lowering the voting age would not lead to more young people voting in elections. Young people find politics boring and wouldn't actually bother to vote. More 18–34 year olds voted during the 2004 season of *Big Brother* than the 2005 general election, so why should 16 year olds be able to vote?
- **Many other countries don't vote at 16**: Most of the 27 EU countries do not allow 16 and 17 year olds to vote, therefore why should the UK?

Source: MORI.

Table 2.4 Turnout at 2005 general election according to gender, age and social class 2005 (data sample of 10,986 British adults 'absolutely certain' to vote)

	2001 turnout (%)	**2005 turnout (%)**	**Change 2001–5**
Gender			
Men	61	62	+1
Women	58	61	+3
Age			
18–24	39	37	–2
25–34	46	48	+2
35–44	59	61	+2
45–54	65	64	–1
Social class*			
AB	68	70	+2
C1	60	62	+2
C2	56	57	+1
DE	53	54	+1
Ethnicity			
White	60	62	+2
Ethnic minority	47	47	–
Total	59	61	+2

*Notes:
A/B/C1 = Managers, administrators, professionals and clerical workers.
C2/DE = Skilled and unskilled manual workers, those on long-term benefit and the retired drawing a state pension.

One area of political activity which is increasing is membership of pressure groups. This could be related to the move towards more interest in single issue politics. Also, pressure groups do not seek to be in government but rather to influence the government (see pages 30–34).

ACTIVITIES

1 Voter turnout at UK general elections has fallen less compared to Scottish Parliament elections.' (View of Tamzin Khan)
   Using Figures 2.13 and 2.14, why could Tamzin Khan could be accused of exaggeration?
2 Which type of election has the highest turnout?
3 What changes have taken place in membership of political parties?
4 What are some of the reasons people give for not taking part in politics? You may wish to use Figure 2.17 in your answer.
5 What kinds of recommendations has the Electoral Commission made regarding participation in politics?
6 Look at the arguments for and against lowering the voting age to 16. Imagine that you are going to have a class debate on this topic. Choose the two arguments which you feel best support each side and explain why you feel that they are the best.
7 Using Table 2.4, what conclusions can be drawn about turnout at general elections? You should reach a conclusion about each of the following:
   ● age
   ● class
   ● ethnicity

The Media

What is the Media?

The media is an outlet for communicating information and news to the public. You may have heard of the term 'mass media' before. Mass media is basically any means or method used to communicate with a large audience e.g. the population of a country or the population around the globe.

The media is basically all information that is:

● broadcast through television, films or radio
● published through books, newspapers magazines etc.
● downloaded through the internet
● advertised in any of the above or through posters, billboards etc.

There are different types of media – print media (newspapers and magazines), audio media (radio), visual media (TV), and IT-based media (the internet).

Figure 2.19 The media exists in many forms

Role of the Media

The media carry many different types of
message: news, documentaries, music,
advertisements, dramas and quizzes are just a
few examples. These messages can all be
carried by different media types. Newspapers,
radio, TV and the internet, for example, can all
carry news. The media industry has many roles
in the democratic process. Many would argue
that its main roles in this area are to educate
and inform.

- **Informing**: The media is one of the main
  sources of information about the world of
  politics. Through the media, people gain
  information about politics whether it is
  local, national or international. It reports
  and broadcasts news, which keeps people
  informed about what is happening in the
  world. Regional newspapers and television
  channels will also broadcast news in the
  local area, for example, STV have news
  bulletins in regional areas of Scotland and
  the BBC have 'Scottish news' at 6.30pm
  every night. The *Edinburgh Evening News* is
  an example of a regional newspaper. The
  media also has the ability to act as a means

of encouraging political debate and
discussion. There are also local and national
newspapers reporting on political issues.

- **Educating**: The media has the
  means and ability to educate
  society. It can explain the
  significance of events
  happening around the world
  and the reasons behind such
  events. Some journalists will try
  and take an objective view
  when reporting to allow the
  public to make up their own
  minds

Influence of the Media

Whether it is directly or indirectly, television
broadcasts and newspaper articles are
arguably the most important source of
information about what the government and
politicians are doing. The media has a large
role in deciding what the public learns and
can shape and influence public knowledge
and attitudes.

In an elected democracy like the UK, 'free
press' is an important feature. 'Free press'
means that the government does not control
the media. This is important to ensure that we
learn about what is happening in the country
and the decisions that the government is
making. The media therefore has a
responsibility to be truthful and accurate in
the information it presents.

Television and radio have strict guidelines on
what they broadcast. Reporting must be
politically impartial and balanced under the
Office of Communications (Ofcom)
broadcasting code. Ofcom is the UK regulator
for both broadcasting and telecommunications
(www.ofcom.org.uk). However, newspapers (or
the 'print media') are slightly different. It is not
uncommon for newspapers to support or
oppose political parties in an open way via

their content. People can be influenced by the editorial view of a newspaper they read through headlines, opinions by columnists, cartoons etc. Over time, this may affect people's opinions about political parties and their policies. Many readers will not realise that the *Daily Record* favours the Labour Party and that the *Daily Mail* favours the Conservative Party unless there is an election taking place and the newspaper makes its political loyalties more obvious.

Due to its importance and influence, many political leaders now get lessons on how to deal with the media (e.g. looking and sounding good on TV). How the leader appears in the media is crucial – some would argue that image is now more important than policy and so less detail is given in interviews and more focus is placed upon likeability and personality.

Does the Media Influence Voting Behaviour?

The impact of the media, in terms of influencing how an individual votes, is a complex issue. It could be argued that the media is growing in influence as the effects of traditional factors such as social class lessen. Do many voters now use TV to form an opinion as to which party and leaders would best run Britain? Most would accept that TV can influence a person to varying extents, which is why news broadcasts are carefully balanced to give opposition as well as government points of view. Some would also argue that people are more influenced by what they see on TV than what they read in newspapers as TV has more visual and moving images which are more effective than printed words.

TV is also more up to date. Most people trust TV news more than newspapers, which are well known for bias. Many people buy newspapers to get racing tips, TV listings, celebrity gossip etc. or to get background knowledge on current affairs. However, over a period of time, readers may be influenced by the political line that a paper takes.

Despite the broadcasting neutrality rules regarding what is reported on TV, many politicians have argued that there can be bias shown in some TV reporting at some point in their career. Most political party leaders have also complained about the BBC during their time in government, suggesting bias in its coverage. A report commissioned by the BBC in 2007 concluded that, overall, the corporation's coverage of day to day politics is fair and impartial. However, it acknowledged that during the coverage of Live 8 (the 2005 anti-poverty concerts organised by rock star campaigners Bob Geldof, Bono (from U2) and writer Richard Curtis) the BBC failed to properly debate the issues raised by the concert. They suggested that, in effect, the BBC then became a vehicle for promoting Live 8, which was strongly supported by Tony Blair (then Prime Minister) and Gordon Brown. In this instance, the BBC was found to be unimpartial.

ACTIVITIES

1 What is the media?
2 Describe the four main types of media.
3 Explain how the media informs and educates the public.
4 Why is the concept of 'free press' important in a democratic country?
5 Why could it be argued that television can influence public opinion?
6 a) How is broadcasting neutrality ensured in TV and radio?
   b) Are neutrality rules always adhered to? Explain your answer.

Newspapers

There are many different newspapers available in the UK. Newspapers are normally split into two types: quality (sometimes called 'broadsheet') or tabloid (sometimes called 'red-top' or 'popular'). *The Sun* and the *Daily Record* are tabloid newspapers. *The Herald* and the *Guardian* are quality newspapers.

↑ Figure 2.20 Newspapers available in Scotland

Features of Tabloid and Quality Newspapers

Quality Newspapers

Size: large or compact

Photographs: few

Types of stories: informative, focused on big political and international issues

Language: more complex and sophisticated

Headlines: long and explanatory

Influence: not usually biased

Tabloid Newspapers

Size: small

Photographs: many

Types of stories: celebrity confessions, scandal

Language: more simplistic

Headlines: short and snappy

Influence: are biased

Newspaper sales in the UK are in a gradual, long term decline. The growth of the internet in particular has had an adverse effect on newspaper sales. However, it is still a large market and many millions of people still buy newspapers. British people are among the most avid newspaper readers in the world. 82 per cent of all British adults (40 million people) read a regional newspaper, compared with 61.5 per cent who read a national newspaper. (*Source: GB TGI 2008 Q3 (April 2007–March 2008)*)

The support of newspapers is very important to politicians. The 1997 British general election saw traditionally pro-Conservative newspapers switching their support to Labour. If British newspapers do have an influence on voting behaviour, it should be most apparent when newspapers change sides. On 17th March 1997, John Major (the serving Conservative Prime Minister) announced that the general election would be held on 1st May. The next morning, *The Sun* announced that it was backing Labour. The famous phrase: 'It's The Sun Wot Swung it' appeared when Labour won the general election that year. The traditional pro-conservative view amongst newspapers was dramatically broken for the first time in post-war British politics.

↑ Figure 2.21 This issue of *The Sun* was printed on 30th September 2009

During the 1992–1997 period, Labour took the potential influence of newspapers seriously and devoted a lot of time to convincing *The Sun*'s owner, Rupert Murdoch, that 'New Labour' was a party worth backing. Labour has won three successive general elections since then. However, there is concern that the ownership of the media is being concentrated in too few hands. News International has control of many news and media organisations. This company is owned by Rupert Murdoch and there are concerns that, as a result, he is able to have an effect on the opinions of the public and perhaps influence how people vote and view the political parties.

2009 can be seen as marking a change in support for Labour in the newspapers under Gordon Brown's leadership, culminating in the *Sun* announcing defection to the Conservatives, see Figure 2.21. Recession, Cabinet resignations and the scandal over MPs expenses have led to some unfavourable headlines for the Labour Party. Some newspapers who tend not to back a specific political party, also reported unfavourable headlines regarding Gordon Brown.

Is the Influence of Newspapers Declining?

CASE STUDY

The Media and the 2007 Scottish Parliament Elections

The May 2007 Scottish Parliament elections saw the SNP gain the largest number of seats (47) in the Scottish Parliament, one more than Labour, who gained 46. In this election, the largest party won despite not having the specific support of any conventional newspaper throughout the campaign. However, on election day some newspapers decided to run a negative campaign against the SNP.

- *The Sun* ran a front page image of a looped rope, inside which read the threat: 'Vote SNP today, and you put Scotland's head in the noose'.

- The *Daily Mail*'s front page warned: 'This man wants to destroy Britain' beside Mr Salmond's face.

- The *Daily Record* urged: 'Do not sleepwalk into independence. Do not let a protest vote break up Britain. Think about it.'

The SNP victory perhaps challenges the idea that newspapers have a great influence over voters. The negative campaigns did not prevent SNP success, albeit in a very marginal win. Some would argue that this result indicates a decline in the ability of newspapers to influence politics and elections and points to the increasing influence of alternative media forms like TV and the internet instead.

For example, the SNP chose not to conduct many newspaper interviews during the campaign and instead opted to use the internet to launch SNP TV. It also chose to focus mainly on one-to-one television interviews rather than newspaper interviews.

However, in several editorials prior to the election, a number of newspapers came out in favour of an SNP-led government. A SPICe briefing suggested that 'these were often heavily qualified endorsements suggests that this was possibly a case of public opinion and opinion polls influencing the press, rather than the other way around'. For example, the *Sunday Herald* editorial piece, entitled 'a vote for change is a leap of faith. It's a leap this newspaper is prepared to make' stated: 'It is our belief that the Scottish Labour Party has not earned the right to a third term... We could have reached that conclusion solely on the basis of its support for a war in Iraq, a conflict this newspaper has consistently opposed. But it is not just that error that has eroded our belief in the Labour Party. Their election campaign has been unremittingly negative.'

The Sunday Herald opinion was that the 'best outcome' would be: 'a coalition led by Alex Salmond. Like you, we can weigh up promises and add up economic policies, but in the end a vote for change is a leap of faith. It's a leap this newspaper is prepared to make.'

Source: SPICe Briefing, 8th May 2007, election 2007, Stephen Herbert, Ross Burnside, Murray Earle, Tom Edwards, Tom Foley, Iain McIver

New Forms of Media

One of the main developments in recent years in politics has been the increasing influence of new forms of media, in particular the internet. Blogs from well known journalists e.g. Brian Taylor of the BBC, and blog space for interactive messages at the bottom of articles posted on newspaper websites are now common. In the elections for the Scottish Parliament in 2007, many websites were set up to focus on the Scottish election campaign e.g. youscotland and Holyrood 2007. Youtube was also heavily utilised with interviews, blogs and party election broadcasts. Politicians are eager to use websites, blogs, podcasts and listings on social networking websites such as Facebook and Bebo as a way of reaching voters, especially young voters. Perhaps the next general election campaign will see more use made of new forms of media. Gordon Brown has already appeared on youtube.

Broadcasting Media

The laws which govern broadcasting (television and radio) in Scotland are currently reserved to Westminster. However, the Broadcasting Commission for Scotland was set up by Alex Salmond in one of his first acts after winning control of the Scottish parliament. Alex Salmond would like to see control over broadcasting devolved to Scotland as he thinks Scotland is underrepresented in terms of news, programmes and actors.

At the end of 2003, Ofcom replaced the Broadcasting Standards Commission and became the new communications sector regulator. Anyone, including the public and politicians, can complain if they feel they have been portrayed in an unfair way. For example, many people complained when Russell Brand and Jonathon Ross made inappropriate comments on a BBC2 radio programme. Jonathon Ross and Russell Brand were suspended and Russell Brand eventually resigned. The BBC confirmed that it had received over 27,000 complaints about their prank calls on the radio show.

Spin

The word 'spin' in politics is often associated with the act of trying to influence the public's opinion regarding government policy or public figures e.g. a politician. People who engage in spin are often called 'spin doctors'. The most well known spin doctor was perhaps Alistair Campbell who dealt with Tony Blair's public relations between 1994 and 2003. Many people believe that Tony Blair related well to the public for such a long time due to the advice and work of Alistair Campbell.

Spin techniques can often mean that people are selective in their use of facts – they don't present the whole truth. One spin technique involves the delay in the release of bad news so it can be hidden in the 'shadow' of more important or favourable news or events.

A famous quote was that of Jo Moore, a former UK Government press officer. She wrote 'It's now a very good day to get out anything we want to bury' in an email which was sent on 11th September 2001, following the attacks on the World Trade Centre. When this email was reported in the press it caused widespread outrage for which Jo Moore was forced to apologise. She was later made to resign when it was claimed she had sent a similar email following the death of Princess Margaret.

Internet

The internet is one of the fastest growing forms of communication and media. You will probably find that most people in your class use the internet on a regular basis. Most newspapers have an online website reporting daily news e.g. www.thescotsman.com and most TV and radio stations e.g. www.channel4. com and www.bbc.co.uk/radio1/ have online websites too.

The internet is a growing influence because so many people use it and access it so frequently. You can now submit petitions online to the UK Parliament (http://petitions. number10.gov.uk/) and at the Scottish Parliament (http:// epetitions.scottish.parliament.uk/).

Many politicians have acknowledged the influence of the internet and politicians are keen to engage with online networks to communicate with the public. The government in Scotland and the UK are increasing the amount of information available on the internet. The information available on the Scottish Parliament website (www.scottish. parliament.uk) highlights its commitment to its founding principles of openness, participation and accessibility. People can access a wide range of information including details of daily business. Holyrood TV provides archive and live versions of First Ministers Questions, committee meetings and debates. The UK Parliament website (http://www. parliament.uk/) has also been enhanced with a specific education section and you can now watch www.parliamentlive.tv, which carries live and archive coverage of all UK Parliament proceedings taking place in public, including debates and committee meetings of both the House of Lords and the House of Commons.

Controls on the Media – Newspapers and Magazines

The Press Complaints Commission is responsible for ensuring that a code of practice is followed by the media. The code of practice sets out guidelines to ensure that the rights of individuals are respected and that the media behaves in a professional manner. Editors and publishers are expected to apply the code of practice to their publications. If the code of practice is not adhered to, people are encouraged to write to the editor of the newspaper or magazine to resolve the issue. If it is not resolved, complaints can be made to the Press Complaints Commission who will investigate the enquiry. If the newspaper or magazine is found to be incorrect, they can be sued for libel damages.

In June 2009, David Beckham won undisclosed libel damages against Express Group Newspapers over an article which appeared in

the *Daily Star* in April. The front page stories: 'Becks and the Blonde Beauty' and 'Topless Model Claims She Was Chatted Up by Footie Star' were published on the newspaper's website. They had falsely suggested that David Beckham had 'made a play' for Ms Fogarasy after an AC Milan match in Hungary and that he had been emailing her with 'private party' invitations since they 'got close' after the match.

ACTIVITIES

1 Try to come up with the names of at least ten newspapers that are sold in Britain. They can be local, national, daily or weekly. Organise your list under the following headings:
   - Quality
   - Tabloid
2 Why is the support of newspapers important to politicians? Give examples.
3 Using the Case Study about the media's influence during the Scottish Parliament elections, explain why the influence of newspapers in politics may be declining.
4 Explain why the use of new forms of media such as the internet have grown in politics.
5 Explain the concept of 'spin.'
6 What controls are there to ensure that the media doesn't become too powerful?

3 Wealth and Health in the United Kingdom

The Development of the Welfare State

A welfare state is where a society has certain social and economic needs provided for by government. Individual governments might change policies affecting a welfare state, but the welfare state itself exists in the long term. The development of the welfare state in the United Kingdom was a gradual process which began in the late 18th and early 19th Centuries. In 1941, the government commissioned William Beveridge to write a report into the ways that Britain should be rebuilt after World War Two. He published his report in 1942 and recommended that the government should find ways of fighting the five 'Giant Evils' of Want, Disease, Ignorance, Squalor and Idleness.

In 1945, the new Prime Minister, Clement Attlee, announced that he would introduce the welfare state outlined in the 1942 Beveridge Report. This included the establishment of a National Health Service in 1948 with free medical treatment for all. A national system of benefits was also introduced to provide 'social security' so that the population would be protected from the 'cradle to the grave'. The new system was partly built on the National Insurance scheme that had been set up in 1911. People in work still had to make contributions each week, as did employers, but the benefits provided were now much greater.

Definitions of Poverty

There is no single definition of poverty. Two ways of defining poverty include **absolute** and **relative** poverty:

- Absolute poverty is a term used to describe the type of poverty experienced in very poor, lesser developed countries. This could be when people are living on the equivalent of $1–2 (US) a day. In recent years the government has defined absolute poverty in the United Kingdom as households living on less than half the average income.

- Relative poverty is defined in terms of the society in which a person lives. It applies in wealthy, developed countries such as the United Kingdom. A 'minimum income standard' is set, beneath which a person is said to be living in poverty. 'Households below Average Income' is a government report which is published regularly. This report measures levels of poverty in the UK, based on the number or proportion of people living on an income of below 60 per cent of the average income.

Another key term in defining poverty is **social exclusion**. This is about more than living on a low income, though it is connected to this. It is about being unable to take part in society and being able to purchase goods and services that most people in that society take for granted. The government currently defines it as:

'Social Exclusion is a complex and multi-dimensional process. It involves the lack or denial of resources, rights, goods and services, and the inability to participate in the normal relationships and activities available to the majority of people in society, whether in economic, social, cultural or political arenas. It affects both the quality of life of individuals and the equity and cohesion of society as a whole.'

Table 3.1 Adapted from Households below Average Income Report 2007–08

	Number (millions) living in UK households with below 60 % of average income (after housing costs deducted)		
	2007/08	Change since 2006/07	Change since 1998/9
Children	4.0	-0.1	-0.4
Working-age adults	7.5	-0.2	-0.8
Pensioners	2.0	No change	-0.9

ACTIVITIES

1   What is the difference between absolute poverty and relative poverty in the United Kingdom?

2   Write down as many ways as you can think of that individuals or groups can experience social exclusion.

Use Table 3.1 to answer the following three questions.

3   'Working age adults are more than twice as likely to live in households below 60 per cent of the average income than children.' Give one reason why this statement is exaggerated.

4   'The number of working age adults living in households below 60 per cent of the average income has fallen more than that for children and pensioners since 1998/9.' Explain why the person making this statement could be said to be selective in the use of facts.

5   'The number of people living in households with below 60 per cent of average income has fallen steadily since 1998/9.' Give one reason to oppose this statement.

The Causes of Poverty

The Link between Unemployment and Poverty

Unemployment is the biggest cause of poverty in the UK and causes people to rely on benefits for an income. Over 65 per cent of people living in poverty are not in work. A person could be unemployed because he/she lacks experience in the workplace. Employers are looking for workers with prior experience. If a young person leaves school at 16, they will lack experience because they have not had the opportunity to work before. An older person might be unemployed because they have been made redundant and lack experience in the types of jobs available. In this case there is a mismatch of skills.

Figure 3.1 shows that unemployment rates change over time. A downward trend in unemployment rates took place between 1992 and 2004. In 1992, unemployment peaked at 12.3 per cent and fell to 5.1 per cent in 2004. Between 2004 and 2008, unemployment rates rose slightly to 5.8 per cent. This graph also shows the difference between the unemployment rates for men and women. During the period 1988 to 2008, unemployment rates for women have been steadier than for men and also lower in all years. In the mid 1990s, the gap between men's and women's unemployment rates was at its widest for this period. This is because the recession in the mid 1990s affected manufacturing jobs, a higher proportion of which are filled by men than services, where a higher proportion of employees are women. We have once again entered a period of economic recession, fuelled by the 2008–9 banking crisis. Unemployment stood at almost 2.5 million in September 2009.

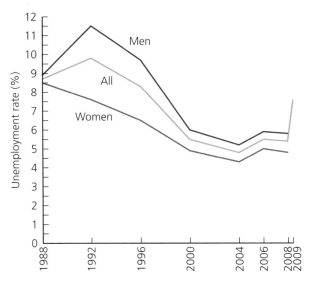

Figure 3.1 UK unemployment rates by gender 1988–2009

Source: Labour Force Survey, Office for National Statistics

In the Labour Force Survey, people who have been recently become unemployed were asked what their previous job was. Table 3.2 shows that, in 2008, unemployment rates were highest among those who previously worked in **elementary** occupations (9.1 per cent) and lowest among those who previously worked in **professional** occupations (1.3 per cent).

Elementary occupations are those that require the use of hand-held tools and also usually involve a high level of physical activity, for example, cleaning, labouring and refuse work.

Table 3.3 shows that this is an occupation which has a fairly even share of male and female workers and this could explain why the gap in male and female unemployment has reduced.

Table 3.2 UK Unemployment rates by previous occupation in 2008

Previous occupation	%
Managers and senior officials	2.0
Professional	1.3
Associate professional and technical	2.3
Administrative and secretarial	2.9
Skilled trades	3.7
Personal service	3.6
Sales and customer service	7.0
Process, plant and machine operatives	5.6
Elementary	9.1

Source: Labour Force Survey, Office for National Statistics

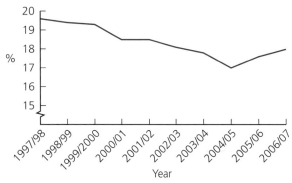

Figure 3.2 Proportion of people whose income is below 60 per cent of median household disposable incomes 1997/8–2006/7

On 15th July 2009 the Chartered Institute of Personnel and Development (CIPD) drew attention to the Labour Force Survey (LFS) which showed that so far 'blue collar workers – skilled and especially unskilled – have suffered far more than white collar workers from rising unemployment during the recession'. Therefore economic recessions can lead to some groups being more vulnerable to unemployment than others.

Table 3.3 Employment by gender and occupation, 2008

Occupation	Men			Women		
	Total (millions)	% full time	% part time	Total (millions)	% full time	% part time
Managers and senior officials	3.0	96	4	1.6	19	1.6
Professional	2.2	91	9	1.6	28	1.6
Associate professional and technical	2.1	91	9	2.2	32	2.2
Administrative and secretarial	0.7	85	15	2.6	42	2.6
Skilled trades	3.0	95	5	0.2	43	0.2
Personal service	0.4	81	19	2.0	47	2.0
Sales and customer service	0.7	60	40	1.5	65	1.5
Process, plant and machine operatives	1.8	92	8	0.3	25	0.3
Elementary	1.9	74	26	1.5	69	1.5
All occupations	15.8	89	11	13.5	42	13.5

The Link between Low Pay and Poverty

Although employment is the best way out of poverty, getting a job does not guarantee this. In 2008, 210,000 children in Scotland were living in relative poverty, with 90,000 of these children lived in households where at least one adult was in work. In the UK there are 1.8 million children living in in-work poverty. Regular, secure well paid employment is needed to lift families out of poverty in the long term.

Lone parents and their children are at more risk from living in poverty because of the problems lone parents face finding regular, well paid work that fits in with the daily routine of childcare arrangements.

The report 'Addressing In-work Poverty' states that in-work poverty has only been officially recognised in recent years. The Joseph Rowntree Foundation's report 'What Will it Take to End Child Poverty?' (Hirsch 2006) listed several factors that would reduce the risk of in-work poverty, including increased tax credits and in-work benefits, increased relative wages for the poor, and increased working hours in poor households.

The Benefit Trap

Some people find themselves caught in the 'benefit trap'. They find that it does not make financial sense to get a low paid job as they will lose out on essential benefits and actually be worse off. Returning to employment can cause stress and anxiety as the costs of travel to work, buying clothes and child care can mean that a family is no better off.

The Link between Family Structure and Poverty

The traditional family structure of a married mother and father with a child or children remains the most common family type in the United Kingdom. More than 8 million

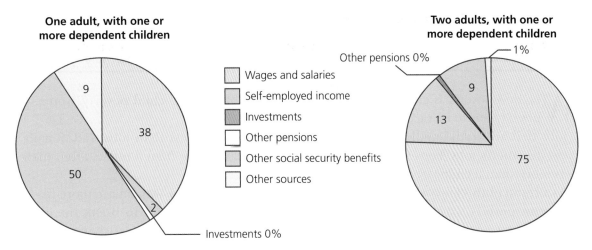

One adult, with one or more dependent children

- Wages and salaries
- Self-employed income
- Investments
- Other pensions
- Other social security benefits
- Other sources

Two adults, with one or more dependent children

Figure 3.3 Source of income in households with dependent children, 2008

(64 per cent) dependent children lived with married parents in the UK in 2008. The proportion of children living with lone mothers increased, from 19 per cent in 1997 to 22 per cent in 2008, while the proportion living with just their father remained stable, at around 2 per cent. Lone parents have the highest rates of unemployment. They also have the lowest employment rates. In 2008, the employment rate for lone mothers was 56 per cent and 64 per cent for lone fathers.

The Link between Gender and Poverty

Poverty in the UK has a female face

This stark fact can be clearly seen in the high rates of poverty amongst female-headed households:

- Over half (53 per cent) of all lone parent households are poor.
- Older, single women have a 24 per cent chance of living in poverty.
- The combination of racism and sexism makes black and ethnic minority women particularly vulnerable to poverty.

Much of women's poverty is hidden. In poor households, women often deny themselves basics such as food in order to protect their families from the consequences of poverty.

Women are more likely to experience persistent poverty. More than one fifth of women, 22 per cent, have a persistent low income, compared to 14 per cent of men. Living in persistent poverty denies women the opportunity to build up savings and assets to fall back on in times of hardship. This effect accumulates for older women and results in extensive poverty.

For men, economic inactivity is a major route into poverty. This is also true for women, but women face additional poverty risks as a result of their lower earning power, caring responsibilities and changing family structure.

Links to children's poverty

Women's poverty is closely linked to child poverty. To reduce child poverty, women's poverty has to be tackled.

Jobs that are traditionally viewed as women's jobs are paid less than jobs traditionally viewed as men's jobs. For example, a police officer is paid more than a nurse, a bin man gets more than a childcare worker.

As a result of this and other factors, there is still a gender pay gap, women are more likely to live in poverty, have less in savings and pensions, find it difficult to break the glass ceiling, experience discrimination at work, or to find flexible work that is satisfying and fits with their responsibilities in the home.

The Fawcett Society has also found that while women owe much less money than men, they are more likely to struggle with debt. Young women, mothers (particularly lone mothers), women who have been through relationship breakdown and black and mixed race women suffer most.

Women's Pensions

Because women are more likely to take time out of work to care for family and because they are more likely to be low-paid and therefore not earn enough to make contributions, their pensions are lower. Women tend to have less money in private and occupational pensions.

In 2005, the Pensions Commission report showed that thirty per cent of women reached state pension age on a full basic state pension, compared to over 80 per cent of men.

The report suggested this inequality between men and women at the point of retirement would erode over the next 20 years. By then, the average man or woman would then be eligible for over 90 per cent of the full basic state pension. This is because more women will have been working longer. The policy of crediting NI contributions to women who are at home will also have helped.

Source: Fawcett Society Report

The Link between Race and Poverty

Ethnic minority households are particularly at risk of poverty, especially Pakistani and Bangladeshi households. Around a third of working age Pakistani and Bangladeshi people are not in work and around a quarter of black Caribbean and black African are also unemployed. The proportion of people from ethnic minorities who are not in work but want to be in work has fallen over the last decade but is still much higher than for the majority white group. Of lone mothers amongst the most likely to stay in full-time work are black Caribbean women.

The reasons for ethnic minority households being more at risk from poverty include prejudice, discrimination, cultural and religious differences.

The Link between Disability and Poverty

In the UK, 30 per cent of disabled adults aged 25 to retirement are living in low income – around one and a half million people. This low-income rate is around double that for non-disabled adults and, unlike that for children and pensioners, is higher than a decade ago. In Scotland, just under a quarter of all individuals in households with at least one disabled adult or disabled child are living in relative poverty compared to 16 per cent of those in households with no disabled adult or disabled children. In Scotland, 68 per cent of disabled people have an income of less than £10,000. People with long term disabilities are particularly likely to live in poverty.

Reasons for diasabled people facing poverty are prejudice, discrimination, lack of access to training and poorly adapted buildings.

The Consequences of Poverty

Poor Housing

In recent years, buying a home has become very expensive. House prices increased by around 240 per cent between 1992 and 2007. This makes it very difficult for first-time buyers to get on to the property ladder. The economic

Figure 3.4 Poor housing in a high-unemployment area of Glasgow

ACTIVITIES

1 List the main causes of poverty.
2 Explain why some people find it difficult to get a job.
3 Using Figure 3.1, describe the trends in unemployment rates between 1988 and 2008 for both males and females.
4 Using Figure 3.2, describe the trend in the proportion of people living below 60 per cent of the average income in the UK.
5 What evidence is there that finding a job does not necessarily mean a route out of poverty?
6 What factors does the Joseph Rowntree Foundation's Report suggest would be a route out of poverty?
7 What is meant by the 'benefit trap'?
8 In what ways do the sources of income differ for one adult with dependent children compared to two adults with dependent children? Refer to Figure 3.3.
9 Explain the link between gender and poverty.
10 Explain why reducing the poverty of women is important for reducing child poverty.
11 Which ethnic groups are more likely to live in poverty?
12 How likely are people with disabilities to experience low pay and/or poverty?

downturn in 2008 made buying a new home or moving house even more difficult.

Lone parents with dependent children were more than twice as likely as couples with dependent children to live in a purpose-built flat or maisonette. People who live on benefits are more likely to live in 'non-decent' housing, suffer overcrowded conditions and live in poor neighbourhoods. Ethnic minority households are more likely to experience overcrowding than other groups.

Lone parents with dependent children spent almost one-quarter (24 per cent) of their monthly income on mortgage repayments compared with 16 per cent for couples with dependent children.

Homelessness

The homeless are among the poorest and most disadvantaged members of society. Almost half of homeless families are headed by female lone parents.

CASE STUDY

Homelessness in Scotland

In 2007–8, 56,609 households made homeless applications to their local council in Scotland. The number of households accepted as homeless or potentially homeless has increased by 24 per cent since 1997–8.

On 31st December 2008, there were 9,536 households in temporary accommodation across Scotland. 1,662 (17 per cent) of these households were in Bed and Breakfast hotels. The number of households in temporary accommodation increased by 10 per cent between 31st December 2007 and 31st December 2008.

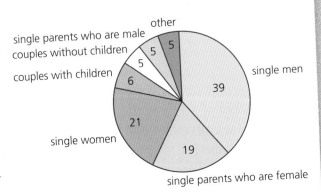

Figure 3.5 Who makes homeless applications in Scotland?

On 31st December 2008, there were 3,682 households with dependent children and pregnant women in temporary accommodation across Scotland. 91 (2 per cent) of these households were living in B&Bs. There were also 6,161 dependent children living in temporary accommodation across Scotland.

For those on low incomes, Housing Benefit is meant to help people afford their housing costs, but the system is very complicated. Shelter, a pressure group which campaigns on behalf of the homeless and on housing issues, has been successful in forcing improvements to the system to make it fairer and simpler. In 2008, a new flat rate Local Housing Allowance System was introduced for tenants in the private rented sector.

Mhoraig Green is a Research Fellow at the Poverty Alliance, Scotland's anti-poverty network. Here is a summary of her research results.

Living on a low income

People involved in this research described living on a low income and having to struggle to make ends meet. Getting by often involved making tough choices between things other people take for granted, including food and heating. Rising fuel prices led to difficult decisions for many participants:

'I now buy food and bring it home – cooked chicken and things like that, because I'm scared to use the oven because I know it costs too much money. I only use the washing machine twice a week because I'm scared of what it costs.'

'After bringing up kids and not working, then going back to work and being too old to take out a pension, there's no hope for me. I retire in a year and I've got nothing to look forward to. I'm going to be a poor pensioner and that's my future.'

'I'm scared to open the front door. If there's a knock, I'm on the nebuliser wondering how much he'll be looking for now.'

Barriers to work

'My husband works all night and then I'm out at college all day. All his money goes on council tax, rent and bills. We don't have a penny extra and I never see him. We'd be better off if he didn't work but he feels like he has to.'

'I gave up going to job interviews because employers were just playing the system. They interviewed you to tick a box. They knew they'd never employ you and they were just doing it for the stats.'

Quality of services

'GPs say: 'Go away, the only thing that's wrong with you is that you don't know how to cope. Now go away, I don't want to see you again.'

'The onus is on the claimant to know what to ask for.'

ACTIVITIES

1 What housing problems are faced by people on low incomes?

2 Explain why homelessness continues to be a problem in Scotland.

3 Read the statements made by people who are living on low incomes in the shaded box on page 79. Discuss in class the consequence of living in poverty.

4 Using examples from other sources, write a report on how poverty affects individuals and families, including:
 • the effect on physical health
 • the effect on mental health
 • the effect on relationships

Tackling Poverty in the UK

Central Government

Since 1997, successive Labour governments have implemented 'welfare to work' policies.

Jobcentre Plus

Jobcentre Plus helps people who are out of work to find work and also helps with making benefits claims. The Jobcentre Plus website gives information on how to go about this. People can make claims by phoning or texting. Claims for Jobseekers Allowance, Income Support and Incapacity Benefit can be made online.

Jobseekers Allowance

Jobseeker's Allowance (JSA) is the main benefit for people of working age who are out of work. If you're out of work or working less than 16 hours a week on average, you may be able to get Jobseeker's Allowance. To be eligible you must be capable of working, available for work, actively seeking work and below state pension age. **There are two types of JSA:**

• Contribution-based JSA is paid to those who have paid or been credited with National Insurance (NI) contributions in the relevant tax years. It is paid for up to twenty six weeks. After this period, a claimant moves onto income-based JSA. Income-based JSA is means-tested and based on income and savings and is also for those who do not qualify for contributions-based JSA.

• Unemployed 16 or 17 years old may be able to get income-based JSA for a short amount of time. For example, if somebody was forced to live away from their parents, they would find it very hard to live without JSA. Another example would be for somebody who was part of a couple with responsibility for a child. The current rates of JSA can be found on the Department of Work and Pensions website.

Some Opinions of Claimants

• 'The important thing to remember is that you must phone the job centre on the first day that you become unemployed. They will not begin processing a claim prior to that date, even if you know you will be out of work, and they tend not to back date a claim if you delay for a couple of days.'

• 'I found the whole process fairly easy to navigate and there were not any problems with my claim.'

• 'Although advisors may discuss with you other benefits that you may be able to claim, not all of them will do that, in my case I did not realise that I was exempt from prescription and dental charges whilst claiming JSA.'

• 'If you are polite to staff they are very helpful.'

• 'The Jobcentre Plus website is very useful and can be accessed at the Jobcentre Plus branch or at home.'

• 'They have produced a number of useful guides and there are links from the site to all of the different branches of the Benefits Agency as well as specific help for certain sections of the community like lone parents or the disabled.'

- 'After six months, you are likely to get a referral to what used be known as a Job Club, nowadays these tend to be run by charities who specialise in running specific programmes to help people.'

- 'If I have a criticism it would be that certainly there is a culture of one size fits all and you will be put on a programme after six months whether it is appropriate or not.'

Income Support

This is extra money to help people on a low income. It is for people who don't have to sign on as unemployed.

Employment and Support Allowance

Employment and Support Allowance (ESA) replaced Incapacity Benefit and Income Support on 27th October 2008. It is paid to those who cannot work because of an illness or disability.

ESA is a new way of helping people with an illness or disability to move into work, if they are able. There is evidence which shows that people are better off in work, not only financially, but also in terms of their health and well-being, their self-esteem and the future prospects for themselves and their family. ESA offers personalised support and financial help. Claimants are given support to help them manage and cope with their illness or disability while in work.

A Work Capability Assessment is carried out to assess what a person is capable of doing and identifies the health related support an individual might need.

Most people claiming ESA will be expected to take appropriate steps to help prepare for work, including attending a series of work-focused interviews with their personal adviser.

Under ESA, an individual who has an illness or disability that severely affects their ability to work will get increased financial support and will not be expected to prepare for a return to work.

Arguments for ESA

ESA will be fairer to new claimants as the practice of increasing benefits over time will be stopped.

ESA will cost less to the taxpayer – Incapacity Benefit was and still is very expensive.

It will help to get people back into work which will improve their health – Incapacity Benefit discouraged people from looking for work.

ESA will help to discourage welfare-dependency.

People who take up employment will qualify for extra benefits.

Arguments against ESA

ESA will increase hardship for vulnerable people with health problems.

The numbers receiving Incapacity Benefit were falling anyway so there was no need to change the system.

It will be very difficult to assess who is and who is not fit enough to work.

Many people will be forced to take on work when they are not fit enough.

This is more about saving money than helping people.

It will lead to an increase social exclusion which the government is supposed to be trying to reduce.

Disability Living Allowance

Disability Living Allowance (DLA) can be claimed if a person has severe difficulty walking, needs help getting around or needs looking after. This is a set rate of benefit and is not usually affected by savings or by other money coming in. A person may not get DLA if they are in hospital or a care home.

Tackling Fuel Poverty

Fuel poverty is when it would take more than 10 per cent of a family's income to heat a home to an acceptable standard. The Scottish Government has a target to end fuel poverty by 2016. A review of fuel poverty by the Scottish Government published in May 2008 stated that, although the existing fuel programmes the Warm Deal and the Central Heating Programmes had been quite successful, they were in need of reform.

More than one in four households in Scotland are fuel poor. The central heating programme has meant that there are now very few households in Scotland without central heating. Fuel poverty will be higher in areas where there are higher numbers of pensioner households, long-term sick and disabled households and single person households. Rises in fuel prices make the situation worse. Because fuel prices are a matter for the UK Government, the Scottish Government has to work along with Westminster on the fuel poverty issue.

Figure 3.6 The campaign against fuel poverty in Scotland

Cold Weather Payment

This is money towards extra heating costs during a week of very cold weather.

A person may get a Cold Weather Payment if they receive one or more of the following benefits:

- Income Support
- Jobseeker's Allowance (income-related)
- Employment and Support Allowance (income-related)
- Pension Credit

Winter Fuel Payment

This is a yearly payment made to households with any person aged 60+ living there, to help towards their heating bills in winter. This money is tax free. Most people do not need to claim this benefit, they will get this automatically, and do not need to be on other benefits to qualify for it. Winter Fuel Payments are paid to help with winter fuel bills each year. There is extra money for eligible households that include someone aged 80 or

Grandmother in fuel poverty fears

An Edinburgh grandmother has told how she is so worried about fuel poverty she only boils a kettle once a day.

Gwen Crystal, 63, from Pilton, is one of a group of residents from north Edinburgh campaigning for more help for vulnerable groups. Ms Crystal told the BBC Scotland news website she also lights candles every evening to avoid putting lights on. Fuel poverty is defined as spending more than 10 per cent of income on gas, electricity and heating oil.

Ms Crystal said she fills two thermos flasks every morning because it saves her having to boil the kettle again throughout the day and that lighting candles helped her feel better.

She said: 'It does give me a warm effect so I don't think I feel as cold. I sometimes put the hallway heater on if it's really cold and maybe for an hour in the sitting room then it goes off. I'm just frightened, I'm really, really frightened. You just think money, money, money. Money that I've not got.'

Source: http://news.bbc.co.uk/1/hi/scotland/edinburgh_and_east/7855812.stm

over in the qualifying week. The amount paid depends on household circumstances.

Sure Start Maternity Grant

This is a one-off payment for pregnant women who are on a low income, to help pay for things needed for a new baby. The grant is tax free and does not have to be paid back. Either the woman or her partner must be receiving benefits.

Community Care Grant

This is a tax free sum of money that does not have to be paid back. A Community Care Grant can help people to cope with special difficulties, such as returning to the community after being in care, or staying in their own home rather than going into care.

Social Fund

If a person is on a low income and faced with costs that are difficult to pay for out of their normal income, the Social Fund may be able to help. The Social Fund can give a payment (a grant or a loan) to help with items for the house, clothes, footwear, travel, items for a new baby, paying for a funeral or heating costs in very cold weather.

Tax Credits

Tax Credits are payments from the government. If an individual is responsible for at least one child or young person, they may qualify for Child Tax Credit. If a person works, but earns low wages, they may qualify for Working Tax Credit. Nine out of ten families with children get tax credits, but people don't need to have children to qualify. The amount of credit received is based upon:

- number of dependent children
- employment status – and how many hours are worked
- childcare costs
- if any of the dependent children have a disability
- if a person is aged 50+ and is coming off benefits

- income – the lower the income, the more tax credit that can be awarded

Example 1

Mr and Mrs Khan both work full time. Between them, they earn about £25,000 a year. They have three children. They get about £87 a week in tax credits. If their income was higher, and they earned about £50,000 a year, they'd get about £10 a week instead.

Example 2

Jon Barry is aged 30, not married and lives alone. He works full time and earns £10,000 a year. He gets about £24 a week in tax credits.

Tax Credits for Over 50s

If a person is over 50 and starting work again after being on state benefits, they may be eligible for extra tax credits. To qualify, a person has to be working for at least 16 hours a week. Further restrictions are that the claimant must:

- be starting work straight after coming off certain state benefits
- be aged 50 or over on the day of starting work
- be working for 16 hours a week or more
- have been on certain state benefits for at least six months

If a person has been on and off benefits for shorter periods, they may still receive the extra tax credits if:

- the gap between each period was no more than 12 weeks
- the total time on certain benefits adds up to at least six months

ACTIVITIES

1 What is meant by 'welfare to work' policies?
2 Describe in detail Jobseekers Allowance.
3 Choose three or four of the following benefits. Explain in detail how they help tackle poverty.
   - Income Support
   - Employment and Support Allowance (ESA)
   - Disability Living Allowance
   - Winter Fuel Payment
   - Cold Weather Payment
   - Sure Start Maternity Grant
   - Community Care Grant
   - Social Fund
   - Tax Credits
4 'Jobcentre Plus is an excellent service for unemployed people.' Give arguments for and against this view.
5 What proportions of families with children have tax credits?
6 'Tax Credits have been a great success.' Give one reason to support this statement.

Attracting Jobs to the UK

Scottish Development International

Scottish Development International is a government-funded organisation that can help businesses exploit Scotland's key strengths in knowledge-based industries, high-level skills, technology and innovation.

Scottish Development International's promotion of Scotland as a place to do business has created more then £500 million of planned investment while creating and safeguarding over 4000 jobs, including almost 2000 high value jobs, First Minister Alex Salmond announced today.

Announcing Scottish Development International's (SDI) annual results for 2008–09, Mr Salmond said the organisation's work to attract and maintain inward investment in Scotland from across the world is 'critical' in the current economic climate.

Results of the SDI performance report for the last financial year include:

- international companies committed more than £500 million to Scotland in capital expenditure and salaries
- nearly 2000 planned high value jobs were created or safeguarded for the period 2008–2009
- more than 4000 jobs in total have been created or safeguarded
- more than 80 per cent of jobs secured last year were from existing investors, highlighting Scotland's reputation as an excellent location for companies to consolidate their operations
- SDI has helped more than 800 Scottish companies to internationalise, 100 more than last year, highlighting the importance of exploring new markets during the downturn
- it is estimated that Scottish companies have generated more than £300 million in sales from exhibitions etc.

Source: Scottish Development International's annual results 2008–09 (published 14th June 2009)

Training and Education

Skills Development Scotland

In September 2007, the Scottish Secretary for Education and Lifelong Learning, Fiona Hyslop MSP, announced that Careers Scotland, Scottish University for Industry, and key skills elements in Scottish Enterprise and Highlands and Islands Enterprise would be brought together to form a new single skills body to take forward and deliver on the vision set out in the Scottish Government's skills strategy 'Skills for Scotland'.

Get Ready For Work

Get Ready for Work is a national training programme that has been developed to help people move into work, further training or college. It helps people to focus on what they want to do, learn new skills and give people the confidence to move into work either directly or via training or further education. The programme will help identify individual needs and develop the skills and confidence.

Participants will be involved in drawing up their own individual training plan. They will get help with interview techniques or advice on how to complete an application form or preparing a CV. Young persons aged between 16 and 19, not at school, college, employed or in training are eligible for Get Ready for Work.

Modern Apprenticeships

Modern Apprenticeships offer people aged over 16 the chance of paid employment, combined with the opportunity to train for jobs at craft, technician and management level. They are an exciting way of gaining skills and qualifications that will help to start a career without having to study full-time, and are available now across a wide range of industries.

They are supported by the Confederation of Business and Industry, the Trade Union Congress and a wide range of employers. All

↑ **Figure 3.7** A modern apprentice

the modern apprenticeship frameworks are developed by the industry or sector in which they will be implemented and therefore encompass all the skills required to become a craftsman, technician or manager in that area. Modern apprenticeship frameworks can also be used as the basis for training of more mature employees.

Skillseekers

Skillseekers is a vocational training programme for young people who want to develop skills and equip themselves for the world of work. It's open to people who have left school and have a job or who are looking for work. However, this programme is to be phased out.

Training for Work

Training for Work provides training support for people who are unemployed and actively looking for work. The programme – run by Skills Development Scotland (SDS) – allows people to undertake vocational training linked to local labour market opportunities, enabling individuals to secure and sustain employment.

Minimum Wage

There are three levels of minimum wage, and the rates from 1 October 2009 are:

- £5.80 per hour for workers aged 22 years and older

- A development rate of £4.83 per hour for workers aged 18–21 inclusive
- £3.57 per hour for all workers under the age of 18, who are no longer of compulsory school age

Scottish Parliament

The Scottish Government states, 'We recognise that poverty is much more than just low income. The factors that generate poverty are wide-ranging and encompass many aspects of day to day life such as health, housing, educational attainment, employability and access to services. We will reduce the inequalities between the least advantaged groups and communities and the rest of society by ensuring that support reaches those who need it most.'

The Government Economic Strategy includes the Solidarity Target: 'to increase overall income and the proportion of income earned by the three lowest deciles as a group by 2017'.

A report by Poverty Alliance was published in July 2008 and set out recommendations for tackling poverty based on discussions that had been held around Scotland. The key discussion areas were transport, health, housing, education and policing:

- **Key Recommendation 1:** The benefit system must be substantially simplified. People eligible for benefits must be able to understand what they are entitled to claim, when that entitlement starts and when it stops.
- **Key Recommendation 2:** The 'benefit trap' must be tackled and so to the disincentive to work it can engender.
- **Key Recommendation 3:** There must be free and universal access to childcare.

- **Key Recommendation 4:** The government must counter increases in fuel costs and food cost, especially in rural areas and especially in the lead up to winter.
- **Key Recommendation 5:** Support and encourage voluntary and community organisations, particularly those providing:
  - affordable alternatives to supermarket shopping (i.e. food co-operatives)
  - income maximisation advice
  - volunteering opportunities
- **Key Recommendation 6:** Improve the quality and quantity of Scottish social housing.
- **Key Recommendation 7:** Increase apprenticeship opportunities, especially amongst traditional trades.
- **Key Recommendation 8:** Politicians and policy-makers should improve their understanding of what it's like to live on a low income by 'trading places' with those living on low income.

As a result of the consultation process, a new Framework aimed at tackling poverty and income inequality in Scotland was launched by the Scottish Government on 24th November 2008. Supported by funding of £7.5 million, Achieving Our Potential sets out the joint approach of the Scottish Government and COSLA in the fight against poverty.

More Choices More Chances

The Scottish Government Strategy 'More Choices More Chances' focuses on giving young people under 16 and at the 16–19 years stage help and support to get into or back into education, employment or training. In Glasgow, a new strategic MCMC Partnership Group has been formed under the umbrella of Glasgow Works. The partnership is responsible for guiding the city's employability strategy.

Local Authorities

Housing Benefit and Council Tax Benefit

Housing Benefit and Council Tax Benefit can help towards paying rent and council tax. The local authority pays them for the claimant instead. People do not have to be receiving any other benefits to qualify for Housing Benefit or Council Tax Benefit. Housing Benefit does not cover all housing costs.

Housing Benefit and Council Tax Benefit Extended Payments

Extra help is given if a person has stopped claiming benefit because of:

- taking up full time work (of at least 16 hours a week) or 24 hours for a partner
- becoming self-employed
- increasing hours of work or wages

Voluntary Sector

Child Poverty Action Group

'Despite Scotland's undoubted wealth a staggering one in four of our children still live in poverty. What's more the latest official statistics suggest recent progress in reducing child poverty has stalled. CPAG in Scotland seeks to raise awareness of this scandal through the media and the publication, with partners, of Poverty in Scotland. We promote solutions to child poverty through policy and campaigning activity. We provide a wide range of high quality benefits and tax credits training courses. We produce Scottish handbooks and offer advice, information and support to advisers in Scotland about benefits and tax credits. We offer specialist advice on children and families, tax credits, students and benefits and black and minority ethic communities. We coordinate the Scottish Social Security Consortium (in partnership with Citizens Advice Scotland), a network of policy, parliamentary and rights workers from national and voluntary sector organisations based in Scotland. We work to maximise family incomes by helping to ensure those eligible for tax credits and benefits have access to their full entitlements.'

(*Source*: CPAG 7th May 2009)

Commenting on 2009 official child poverty figures, John Dickie, the Head of the Child Poverty Action Group (CPAG) in Scotland, said:

'The failure to make any real progress on child poverty for a third year running, despite promises from UK and Scottish government, is deplorable. You don't eradicate child poverty by doing nothing, but we've just had a 'do nothing' UK budget for the poorest children. The disgraceful Budget decision to give the poorest families less than the cost of a pint of milk per child to help them survive the weekly grind of the recession was a kick in the teeth.

But the Scottish Government also needs to ratchet up its action to meet its anti-poverty commitments. With so many families suffering ever greater pressure, commitments to extend free school meal entitlement to all Primary 1 to 3 children and to children in families receiving maximum Working Tax Credit are more important than ever. But we also need action to boost school clothing grants and remove the other additional charges that too often mean our poorest children miss out at school. It's also vital that government at all levels invests to ensure parents have access to the affordable childcare they need to take up work opportunities when they arise.

We need to remember these are not just statistics. These figures represent tens of thousands of children in Scotland being damaged by poorer health, lost opportunities at school and an inability to take part in the activities most children take for granted. These children are suffering now and need help now. A serious investment is urgently needed to support them. Even in the current economic situation it is not only affordable but one of the surest ways of boosting the economy.'

Shelter

Shelter is a charity that works to alleviate the distress caused by homelessness and bad housing. They do this by giving advice, information and advocacy to people in housing need, and by campaigning for lasting political change to end the housing crisis for good.

Shelter tackles the root causes of bad housing by lobbying government and local authorities for new laws and policies, and more investment, to improve the lives of homeless and badly-housed people.

Save the Children

Save the Children work to influence policy making in Scotland through:

- regularly briefing MSPs and decision makers on the issue of poverty
- actively campaigning to End Child Poverty in the UK
- developing solutions to provide more support for the poorest children in Scotland.

Key issues include the extension of entitlement to free school meals, child care and fuel poverty. Save the Children's Young East End Speaking programme in Glasgow supports young people take part in local decision-making. This programme has helped over 245 children make positive changes in their own communities. It takes place in Glasgow's East End – an area with widespread poverty,

Tunstall joins homelessness call

Singer KT Tunstall has called on the Scottish Government to help ensure homelessness is eradicated in Scotland by 2012. Tunstall, brought up in St Andrews, has joined a 'Hometime' campaign launched by charity Shelter Scotland which wants to ensure homeless targets are met. The campaign asks people to name which song reminds them of home.

Shelter Scotland aims to hand a list of songs over to politicians later this month. KT Tunstall has chosen Getting Some Fun Out of Life by Billie Holiday. She said: 'I love putting it on my old record player. It's the sound of a warm kitchen with a pot on the stove, a bottle of red wine open, and a dance with a good man.'

Edinburgh band Dirty Modern Hero have also been recruited to the campaign. They said: 'It is clear that the more people who are made aware of this campaign and the current Scottish Government promise, the more power we will have as a nation to ensure that this promise is met and that in only four years time we may have dramatically improved the lives of so many people currently homeless in Scotland.'

'Cannot fail'

They join indie-pop sensations The Wombats, DJ Calvin Harris, rock band Idlewild, Glasgow group The Haze and Scottish pop legend Dougie MacLean, who are among those to have already signed up to the campaign.

Graeme Brown, director of Shelter Scotland, urged people to support the campaign.

He said: 'We have an internationally acclaimed homelessness target to meet in 2012 and we cannot afford to fail. The eyes of many nations will be on this island that year, and not just because of the Olympics. Many nations have already shown an interest in our forward-thinking legislation and we must show it can work. He added that the most chosen song so far was a tie between Dougie MacLean's 'Caledonia' and '500 miles' by The Proclaimers.

deprivation, a lack of services and high unemployment.

How the Private Sector Helps to Tackle Poverty

Job Creation

Scottish Entrepreneur, Tom Hunter, set up the Hunter Foundation in1998. It has invested over £35 million in fostering an entrepreneurial spirit in Scotland since then. Positive Destinations is a £2 million grant programme that was undertaken by the Foundation in partnership with BBC Children in Need. The project has made grants to organisations to try out new approaches to help children and young people achieve a positive and sustained future in terms of education, employment or training. These projects are expected to generate learning and ensure sustainability of their work beyond the life of the programme.

Barnardos Youthbuild Paisley – supporting young people into employment

The Youthbuild Paisley project works to equip disadvantaged young people with the skills, experience and contacts to access sustainable employment. In particular, Youthbuild Paisley targets construction – an industry offering considerable opportunity created by local regeneration and investment. Youthbuild gets the best deal for its young people because it brings together partner agencies from all sectors, including partners from the industry itself.

The project addresses issues at the root of social exclusion. Young people are helped to overcome barriers such as homelessness and the impact of poverty.

ACTIVITIES

1 Describe in detail the ways in which each of the following help to tackle poverty and unemployment in Scotland:
2 Central Government
3 Scottish Parliament
4 Local Authorities
5 Voluntary organisations
6 Private sector

Health in the United Kingdom

The NHS came into operation on 5th July 1948. Aneurin Bevan was the Labour Government's Health Minister in charge of the process. This new health system was based on the principles of collective responsibility by the state for a universal and comprehensive range of services, with equal access for all citizens. At the heart of the development of the NHS were four founding principles: collectivism, universal provision, a comprehensive service and equality.

NHS: Health Care Provision

Primary Care

Primary care is a term which covers the services carried out within GP practices, where the GP would be the first point of contact for a patient. The primary care team involves not only the doctors, but also other staff such as district nurses, dentists, pharmacists, opticians and health visitors. Primary care in Scotland is arranged into **community health partnerships**. They provide an opportunity for health professionals in the wider community to work together to improve the lives of the local population which they serve. The Scottish Government is committed to providing a health service where the various health team members work together and there is good communication between them so that people get the complete package of care that they need. This was in response to criticism of care in the past when people had been left without appropriate care because of a lack of communication.

Community health partnerships (CHPs) and community health and care partnerships (CHCPs) have been introduced across Scotland to manage a wide range of local health services delivered in health centres, clinics, schools and homes. There are ten CHPs across the Greater Glasgow and Clyde area, six of these are called

CHCPs because they jointly manage both health and social care services.

Each CHP provides primary care services such as: health visiting, district nursing, speech and language therapy, physiotherapy, podiatry, nutrition and dietetic services, mental health, addiction counselling and learning disability services. Staff delivering these services work closely with other local health professionals, including GPs, dentists, pharmacists and opticians to plan and develop services across the CHP area.

CHPs will work closely with local councils, hospitals and community groups to breakdown the barriers that have traditionally existed between community health, social care and specialist health services. They will also develop partnerships with local education, leisure and employment services as these also have an important role to play in improving the health of local people.

Examples of Primary Care

District nurses:
- assess nursing needs and provide clinical care
- assist recovery
- promote and maintain health
- facilitate independence
- improve and maintain wellbeing and quality of life
- provide palliative and terminal care

Mental illness services for the elderly:
- assess, patients, both mentally and physically
- initiate and monitor a treatment programme
- assist/support patients to function fully in the community
- provide care to those who cannot be cared for in the community
- offer carer advice, education and support

↑ **Figure 3.8** District nursing

Optical services

Optometrists carry out eye tests to check the quality of your sight. They look for signs of eye disease which may need treatment from a doctor or eye surgeon and they prescribe and fit glasses and contact lenses. Opticians fit and sell glasses but they do not test eyes. They can give advice on types of lens, such as single vision or bifocal and help people to choose frames. Eye tests, glasses and contact lenses have to be paid for. But some people can get free eye tests and vouchers towards the cost of glasses or contact lenses. This includes:

- all children under 16
- some young people under 19
- people aged 60 or over
- people in Scotland (free sight tests only)
- people with certain eye conditions
- people entitled to certain benefits
- anyone else on a low income

Children's Services – Community Paediatrics

Examples of the kind of cases where community paediatricians would be involved include:

- developmental concerns
- special needs/neurodisability
- behavioural and emotional problems
- motor coordination problems
- communication problems
- health problems impacting on education
- child protection concerns

NHS Dental Treatment

Individuals can get free dental treatment if they:

- are under 18 years old
- are aged 18 and in full time education
- are pregnant
- have had a baby in the previous 12 months, or have had a stillborn baby in the previous 12 months
- are named on a valid HC2 or HC3 certificate
- are getting Income Support, income-based Jobseeker's Allowance or tax credits and meet qualifying conditions

The Prescription Charges Debate (see page 92)

Arguments for abolishing prescription charges:

- welfare to work policies move people into work, but this often means they now have to pay for prescriptions and this leaves them no better off
- there is an inequality in terms of which illnesses are exempt from charges
- most prescriptions are already dispensed free of charge and so to abolish charges would cost little more
- if prescription charges are abolished families will have more money to spend on better food and living conditions

Arguments against abolishing prescription charges:

- the income lost to the NHS will be equivalent to almost 200 full time nurses
- the income raised from prescription charges amounts to around £43 million per year
- people will demand drugs that they do not need – prescription charges were introduced to limit demand
- people who can afford to pay should do so

Health Improvement

Improving health and reducing health inequalities are key priorities for all staff in Renfrewshire CHP. There is a small team of specialist health improvement staff who lead and coordinate this work. The team also contributes to community planning, working alongside partners from the Local Authority, the police, the fire service and local communities. The key priorities of the health improvement team are to tackle smoking, obesity and alcohol.

Prescriptions

Doctors, dentists and some nurses can prescribe a range of drugs and appliances on the NHS. They can normally only prescribe a limited quantity of a drug at any time (usually one month's supply). In Scotland, people are entitled to get prescriptions free of charge if they:

- are on Income Support, income-based Jobseeker's Allowance, income-related Employment and Support Allowance or the guarantee credit part of Pension Credit. Their partner and children will also be entitled to free prescriptions.
- they may be entitled to free prescriptions, depending on income, if they are getting Working Tax Credit and/or Child Tax Credit
- are aged 60 or over
- have a listed medical condition and a valid medical exemption certificate
- are having treatment for cancer, the effects of cancer or of cancer treatment and have a valid medical exemption certificate
- are on prescribed medication to prevent a pandemic disease, for example, pandemic influenza
- have a continuing physical disability which means they cannot go out without help from another person and have a valid medical exemption certificate
- are under 16 in England or Scotland
- are a prisoner
- are pregnant, or have had a baby in the last twelve months and have a valid exemption certificate (this includes women who have had a miscarriage after the 24th week of pregnancy, or whose baby was stillborn)

The cost of prescriptions in Scotland has fallen from £5.00 to £4.00. The cost of prescription pre-payment certificates has also been reduced. A 12 month certificate now costs £38.00 and a four month certificate costs £13.00. Further annual reductions are planned to remove prescription charges altogether by 2011.

Mental Health Services

More than 20 per cent of adults are affected by mental health problems at any time – 30 per cent of GP consultations involve mental health problems. Ten per cent of adults are depressed, five per cent have anxiety disorders, 0.4 per cent of people living at home have schizophrenia (but many are not registered with a GP) and 0.5–1 per cent have bipolar affective disorders. 13 per cent of those with schizophrenia and 17 per cent with recurring major depressive illness will end their own lives. The suicide rate for young males has risen.

Improving Dementia Services in Forth Valley

Starting in 2007, 20 staff involved in providing care for people with dementia in Forth Valley took part in a two month project to identify ways to improve services and help meet local and national objectives for dementia care. Almost 200 proposals for change were identified, ranging from producing easy to understand literature to increase awareness of dementia, to developing rehabilitation services in people's homes. The Scottish Government provided £200,000 to support the project and the main resource provided locally was staff time. An evaluation of the project was unable to measure impact, such as reduced length of stay in hospital, but a staff survey highlighted more confidence in their capacity to deliver dementia-related services. Others involved in the project, such as the police, churches, libraries, voluntary organisations and members of the public, also reported better knowledge of how to support people with dementia.

Examples of Secondary Care (Acute Services)

Secondary Health Care is that which a patient receives when they have been referred to a hospital for specialist treatment. Each health board in Scotland is responsible for the delivery of secondary services.

Acute hospitals provide a wide range of specialist treatment for people in Scotland. These services include:

- appointments with consultants, nurses, dieticians, physiotherapists and a wide range of other professionals

- emergency treatment following accidents
- surgery and short-term care of patients with worrying health symptoms
- People attending hospitals can be seen in various hospital settings, such as hospital outpatient departments or health centres.

Table 3.4 Number of discharges by patient type, 2003/04–2007/08
Source: ISD Scotland

	2003/2004	2007/2008
Day cases	363,618	399,232
Elective patients	205,775	197,239
Emergency inpatients	471,823	524,872
Transfers	170,904	211,744
All	**1,212,120**	**1,333,087**

Maternity Services

Health professionals such as obstetricians and midwives help to make sure that any risks associated with pregnancy are reduced. The policy is to involve parents, support groups and a range of healthcare professionals in planning, so that the best service possible is provided. When they plan and review services they make sure the feedback they receive is used to change the way they provide services. Women are informed about the different options that are available to them, so they and their partners can make informed decisions about maternity care, including the decision about where to give birth. A maternity record is kept. The record must include relevant information about the pregnancy, birth and the time after the birth. All healthcare professionals involved must keep the maternity record up to date.

In 2008, a new initiative in maternity care was introduced in Scotland. Midwives are now supported by maternity care assistants. Some of the tasks to be undertaken by these workers include taking blood pressure, blood samples, temperature and pulse rates. The assistants receive thorough training. This frees up midwives to deal with the more complex and serious health issues facing pregnant women. This initiative is supported by the midwifery profession, but has come under some criticism from childbirth groups who say this is 'midwifery on the cheap' and could threaten the health of mothers and babies.

Scotland's maternity services have recently suffered a series of problems. In some cases, mothers have been moved to nearby hospitals because of a lack of beds and are often encouraged to leave hospital within hours of giving birth.

Greater Glasgow and Clyde Acute Services

Hospitals within the Greater Glasgow and Clyde Health Board include the Gartnavel Campus, Southern General Campus, Stobhill Campus, New Victoria Hospital and the new West of Scotland Heart and Lung Centre.

CASE STUDY

Southern General Campus

The Southern General Campus is being developed and the new South Glasgow Hospitals building is anticipated to be complete by 2015. With 1700 beds, this will be the biggest critical care complex in Scotland, catering for an estimated 110,000 A&E attendances per year. Existing facilities at the Southern General including the National Spinal Injuries Unit, the Institute of Neurosciences and the upgraded Maternity Unit.

A new children's hospital will also be built on the site. This means that this service will be close to the maternity and adult hospital services. The adult and children's hospitals will be built as a single integrated building. A new laboratory facility will also be built and haematology, biochemistry and mortuary services will be provided by these laboratories.

Accident and Emergency

A&E services have been undergoing change in recent years. One of the problems faced by A&E units has been that people with minor injuries have been dealt with by the same services as those dealing with serious emergencies. This can lead to very long waiting times for people with minor injuries if someone who is seriously ill arrives.

The decision has been made to separate care for each group. Two new A&E/ trauma centres at the new South Glasgow Hospital and the Glasgow Royal Infirmary will deal only with the most seriously ill and injured people on a 24 hours basis. Experts say this will save lives and improve recovery rates.

Emergency receiving units will be set up at the three main inpatient hospitals (at South Glasgow, Gartnavel and the Royal Infirmary) for heart attack victims to be admitted directly to hospital wards without having to stop at A&E. These patients will have been assessed and brought in by ambulance crews or have been referred direct by their GPs.

Figure 3.9 An A&E department

Five new minor injuries units (at the Victoria, Stobhill, Gartnavel, Royal Infirmary and South Glasgow hospitals) will offer 'nurse–led care for the lump, bump and sprain-suffering walking wounded who will no longer have to wait hours for attention'. A dedicated service for children under 13 years is to be based at the Royal Hospital for Sick Children.

ACTIVITIES

1 Define the following:
  ● primary care
  ● secondary care
2 Describe in detail at least three aspects of primary care services.
3 Describe in detail the types of health care provided by the secondary (acute) services.
4 Describe the changes that are being made to Accident and Emergency services in Glasgow. Explain why these changes are being made.
5 Why might some people be concerned about the changes to A&E services in Glasgow?

Care in the Community

Care in the community is about care and support in the home, rather than in institutions, for groups such as the elderly, physically or mentally disabled and mentally ill.

Background

There has been a growth in community care in recent years for the following reasons:

- allegations of low standards in long-stay hospitals
- difficulties in attracting suitably qualified staff
- concern that many stayed in care too long
- bed-blocking
- some argued community care would be cheaper

The National Health Service and Community Care Act was passed by the UK Parliament in 1990. In the 1990s there were many criticisms of community care as there was a lack of funding and a lack of cooperation between health and social care services. There were many examples reported of people being left without care.

The Scottish Government works in partnership with service users, carers, local authorities, the NHS, the Care Commission and the voluntary and independent sectors to improve community care services across Scotland.

Community Care for the Elderly in Scotland

By 2031 there will be around 1.31 million people of pensionable age in Scotland. The Community Care and Health (Scotland) Act 2002 is delivering major improvements in community care services. The Scottish Executive is committed to supporting carers as key partners in providing care, to help them to care as much or as long as they like. Many of

the changes outlined below have been implemented, taking account of the problems encountered in the past. On 1st July 2002 free personal care was introduced for people aged 65 and over in Scotland. This will mean an end to charging for personal care in the community.

The Care Commission

Care services have to follow rules and are inspected by the Scottish Commission for the Regulation of Care (the Care Commission). Its inspections are based on principles such as dignity, privacy, choice, safety, realising potential, equality and diversity. The intention is that users and carers can rely on the same standard of service wherever they live. Care homes, day care, independent hospitals, private psychiatric clinics and some independent clinics are among the services already being regulated.

The Care Commission regulates over 15,000 care services each year for adults and children. Over 320,000 people in Scotland use care services:

- 39.7 per cent are provided by childminders
- 29.2 per cent are in children's day care services
- 11.2 per cent are residential care homes

↑ **Figure 3.10** A residential care home

Care Home Services

These are services for vulnerable adults which provide accommodation together with nursing care, personal care or personal support. Types of adult care homes include facilities for:

- people with physical and sensory impairments
- older people
- people with learning disabilities
- people with drug and alcohol misuse problems
- people with mental health problems

Direct Payments

Direct Payments allow disabled people to purchase services to meet their community care needs instead of the local authority arranging services for them.

Joint Working

The Scottish Executive has asked health boards and local authorities to work together with the aim of delivering better and quicker services.

Delayed Discharge

The Scottish Executive's Delayed Discharge Action Plan was announced on 5th March 2002. This aims to reduce the number of people in Scotland waiting to move from hospital into care settings. The Scottish Government is continuing to try to make the transition from hospital care to a care setting easier for the people concerned.

The Care Commission carried out a review of the quality of care homes in 2004, for older people, children and young people. The Commission regulated 908 care homes for older people (with 34,240 residents) and 158 care homes for children and young people (with 1,022 residents). Together these groups form a substantial majority of the 45,000 people living in care homes in Scotland.

The Care Commission inspects all care homes at least twice a year and also investigates complaints received on a wide variety of issues. Complaints against care homes made up 64 per cent of all complaints dealt with by the Commission between January and March 2004.

The review analysed data from inspections and complaints-investigations carried out during the same year, together with questionnaires and interviews of older people and young people living in care homes.

When inspected, 45 per cent of care homes for older people and 36 per cent of care homes for children and young people were found to have breached at least one regulation, prompting the Care Commission to set out formal requirements for remedial action in their inspection reports. The requirements covered issues such as protecting residents' welfare, staffing, record keeping, improvements to facilities, and complaints procedures.

In a survey of more than 800 older people in care homes, 84 per cent said they were happy or very happy with their quality of care. Focus groups involving young people in care homes found that many had experienced good support and positive attitudes from staff, as well as improved living environments and better opportunities. However, two-thirds of the sample of young people said they were unhappy with some aspect of their care, and almost half believed they were not treated with respect.

Source: www.carecommission.com/index.php?option=com_content&task=view&id=103

ACTIVITIES

1 What criticisms were made of community care in the 1990s?
2 Produce a case study about Free Personal Care.
3 Describe the work of the Care Commission.
4 'The standard of care in care homes can no longer be criticised.' Give arguments for and against this view.
5 What other actions have been taken to improve community care?

Local Authorities Responsibilities in Promoting Health

Health Promoting Schools

Schools in Scotland are working hard to promote health as an important aspect of school life. Schools adopt a holistic approach which promotes physical, social, spiritual, mental and emotional wellbeing of all pupils and staff. The Schools (Health Promotion and Nutrition) (Scotland) Act 2007 placed a duty on local authorities to ensure that all of their schools are health promoting environments.

The Learning Teaching Scotland website (www.ltsscotland.org.uk) gives examples of what schools are doing to promote health. Activities taking place in schools include Fruity Fridays and Sporting Lunchtimes. Many Local Authorities have introduced practices such as:

- providing healthy packed lunch advice for parents in the form of leaflets, talking shops, demonstrations etc.
- changing portion sizes with monitoring of ratio of healthy to less healthy food stuffs
- stocking vending machines with healthy items

- stocking tuck-shops with healthy items
- promoting the importance of healthy eating as part of the curriculum (one secondary school introduced a 'healthy meals on a budget' class for pupils in their final year)

Human Papilloma Virus (HPV) Vaccine

Around 1000 women die from cervical cancer in the UK each year, and it is the second most common cancer in women worldwide. In Scotland around 100 women die from cervical cancer each year.

Although Health Protection Scotland is responsible for the coordination and delivery of the national HPV immunisation programme, the local authorities and schools also have an important part to play. It is through the local authorities and schools that the programme is administered.

Information about the HPV immunisation programme was issued to girls in schools during August and September 2008. The HPV immunisation programme started on 1st September 2008. All girls in Scotland who are in S2 are offered this vaccine. It will help protect them against the two main types of HPV that can cause cervical cancer. Girls aged 13 to 18 (born after 1st September 1990) are also being invited to receive the vaccine through a catch-up programme, phased over three years (2009–2010).

The Eco-Schools Programme

The eco-schools programme is an international initiative designed to encourage whole-school action for the environment. It is a recognised award scheme that accredits schools who make a commitment to continuously improve their environmental performance. It is also a learning resource that raises awareness of environmental and sustainable development issues throughout activities linked to curricular subjects and areas. The aim of the eco-schools programme is to make environmental awareness and action an intrinsic part of the life and ethos of the school for both pupils and for staff and to engage the wider community.

ACTIVITIES

1 What is the role of local authorities in promoting health?
2 Find out as much as you can about what your school does as a Health Promoting School. Use the information in this textbook and also your knowledge of your local area.

Tackling Inequalities in Health

National Geographical Inequalities

Table 3.5 Life expectancy by region
Source: ONS, Life expectancy at birth in the UK 2005–2007

Area	Life expectancy (yrs)	
	Males	Females
UK	77.2	81.5
England	77.5	81.7
North east	76.3	80.4
North west	76	80.4
Yorkshire and the Humber	76.9	81.1
East Midlands	77.6	81.6
West Midlands	76.9	81.4
East of England	78.7	82.6
London	77.9	82.4
South east	78.9	82.7
South west	78.7	82.9
Wales	76.7	81.1
Scotland	74.8	79.7
Northern Ireland	76.2	81.2

Table 3.6 Highest life expectancy by area
Source: ONS, Life expectancy at birth in the UK 2005–2007

Rank	Local area	Life expectancy (yrs)
1	Kensington and Chelsea (London)	83.7
2	Westminster (London)	81.5
3	East Dorset (South West)	81.3
4	Elmbridge (South East)	81.1
5	Hart (Sout East)	81.0
6	Fareham (South East)	80.9
7	Wokingham (South East)	80.8
8	Sevenoaks (South East)	80.7
8	Three Rivers (East of England)	80.6
10	Cotswold (South west)	80.6

Table 3.7 Lowest life expectancy by area
Source: ONS, Life expectancy at birth in the UK 2005–2007

Rank	Local area	Life expectancy (yrs)
432	Glasgow City (Scotland)	70.8
431	West Dunbartonshire (Scotland)	71.9
430	Inverclyde (Scotland)	72.5
429	North Lanarkshire (Scotland)	72.7
428	Eilean Siar (Scotland)	72.9
427	Blackpool (North West)	73.2
426	Manchester (Norh West)	73.4
425	Belfast (Northern Ireland)	73.6
424	Renfrewshire (Scotland)	73.7
423	North Ayrshire (Scotland)	73.7

There is a clear north-south divide in terms of average life expectancy. Figures for the years 2005–2007 show this divide. The average life expectancy for the UK is 77.2 years for males and 81.5 years for females. For Scotland the average life expectancy is lower than the UK average by 2.4 years for men and 1.8 years for women.

For both men and women the average life expectancy is lower in Scotland than in any other region of the UK. Seven of the ten areas with the lowest life expectancy are in Scotland.

Local Geographical Inequalities

'It is unacceptable in 21st Century Scotland that some people can expect to die earlier than others, simply due to an accident of birth or circumstance.' First Minister Alex Salmond.

Tackling inequalities at the national level would not take into account local differences. There are areas in Scotland which compare favourably with the south-east of England, while there are parts of London which have poor health profiles. Life expectancy is a useful way of getting an idea of inequalities in health.

The number of years a newborn child is expected to live varies across the Glasgow Health Board area in terms of gender and geography. It can be seen from Figures 3.11

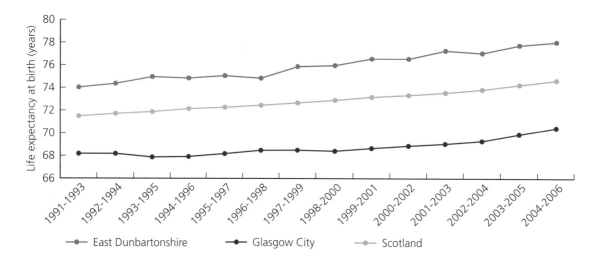

Figure 3.11 Greater Glasgow and Clyde Health Board: variations in male life expectancy

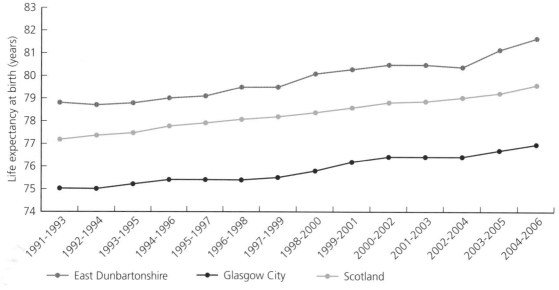

Figure 3.12 Greater Glasgow and Clyde Health Board: variations in female life expectancy

and 3.12 that life expectancy is increasing for males and females. However there are clear inequalities:

- there is a nine year gap in male life expectancy between East Dunbartonshire CHP (77.7 years) and North Glasgow CHCP (68.6 years)

- female life expectancy is higher than male life expectancy by six years across the NHS Greater Glasgow and Clyde area as a whole, but also varies by around 5.5 years across the CH(C)Ps

- the gap in life expectancy between the most affluent and deprived population communities has widened significantly in the last 20 years, particularly among males

- estimates of healthy life expectancy (years of life without a limiting long-term illness) show that across the west of Scotland there is a 12 year gap in male healthy life expectancy between Glasgow City Council (46.7 years) and East Renfrewshire (58.5 years) and there is an equally pronounced gap for women

Inequalities in Health, Life Expectancy and Social Class are Linked

The first report to acknowledge inequalities in health and the link between poverty and ill health was the Black Report (1980). This report had been commissioned by the Labour Government in 1979, but the Conservatives gained power before it was published. Very few copies were printed and it was suppressed: critics would argue that this was because it conflicted with their tax cutting policies and their policy of minimal government intervention 'rolling back the state'. The report concluded that class inequalities in health could be traced from childhood and continued through life. According to the report, the

government should take a more active role in encouraging changes 'in people's diet, exercise and smoking and drinking behaviour. Greater emphasis should be given to preventing ill health rather than curing it and a first step should be a ban on smoking in public places.'

Tackling Health Inequalities: Ten Years On

The Acheson Report was published in 1998 and its findings agreed with the Black Report. To tackle the effects of poverty, issues such as social inclusion in education, poor housing, unemployment and low pay had to be addressed. In 2009 the UK Department of Health published a report called 'Tackling health inequalities 10 years on: a review of developments in tackling health inequalities in England over the last 10 years'. This report (carried out by Sir Michael Marmot) shows significant improvements since the Acheson Report:

- Average life expectancy for all groups in England increased significantly between 1995–1997 and 2005–2007: for males by an extra 3.1 years and for females by an extra 2.1 years.

- For disadvantaged areas (a group of 70 local authority areas with the worst health and deprivation indicators) there has been an increase in life expectancy of only very slightly less than for the whole population – 2.9 years for men and 1.9 for females.

- Infant mortality rates have fallen to an historically low level, having fallen from 5.6 infant deaths per 1,000 live births in 1995–1997 to 4.7 per 1,000 in 2005–2007.

Health inequalities between different groups and areas and the whole population, however, persist in both of these areas.

The Glasgow Centre for Population Health

The Glasgow Centre for Population Health was established in 2004 to find out more about how to improve health and tackle inequality. As a result, the Equally Well Report was published. This report highlights the fact that a large number of Scots suffer ill health and have their life expectancy shortened by the circumstances they were born into.

This report found that much more was needed to be done about children's health and development in the very early years. Other areas requiring more focus were mental health, alcohol, drugs and violence. The necessity to improve physical and social environments was also acknowledged.

The GCPH has also created community profiles for the Greater Glasgow and Clyde Area. One of the purposes of the profiles is to highlight health and social inequalities.

CASE STUDY

A Comparison between North Glasgow and East Dunbartonshire

North Glasgow

Population

North Glasgow has a population of nearly 100,000 people, of whom 17 per cent are children, 68 per cent are young and middle-aged adults and 15 per cent are older people. There has been a small drop in the size of the overall population in the last ten years. Approximately 1,700 asylum seekers live in the area and the proportion of the population from a minority ethnic community (4.6 per cent) is more than double the national average. There were over 1,200 live births in 2006. There are 47,600 households in North Glasgow, of which over 20,000 (43 per cent) are single adult households. Single parent households, of which there are 5,300, make up 41 per cent of all households containing children.

↑ **Figure 3.13** North Glasgow

Life expectancy and mortality

For men, life expectancy (at birth) is estimated to be 68.2 years, more than five years lower than the Scottish average, and has only risen by approximately 1.4 years in the period 1994–1998 to 2001–2005. Female life expectancy (75.4 years) has risen only slightly (by less than a year) in the same period and is nearly four years below the Scottish average. Mortality and mortality rates from cancer, coronary heart disease and cerebrovascular disease (in the under 75s) are all above the Scottish average but have all fallen to a varying degree in recent years.

Behaviour
Over 1,300 patients are admitted to hospital annually for alcohol related or attributable causes and there have been over 270 deaths due to alcohol in the last five years. An estimated 30,000 of adults smoke: 37.5 per cent (compared to 27 per cent nationally). There have been 204 drug related deaths in North Glasgow over the last ten years.

Hospitalisation/Social Work
Approximately 580 new cancer cases are registered annually and 900 heart disease patients are admitted to hospital each year. There are over 8,000 patients admitted as a medical emergency annually. There are nearly 10,000 Social Work clients, 2,000 of whom are children and 3,000 of whom are older people.

Mental health and function
There were over 130 suicides in the period 2001–2005 and there are nearly 400 new in-patient admissions to psychiatric specialties annually. Community Health and Wellbeing

Prosperity/poverty
Nearly 28,000 people, 28 per cent of the population, are defined to be income deprived, and over 14,000 adults, 22 per cent of the working age population are employment deprived. There are nearly 2,000 workplaces, employing nearly 35,000 people.

Crime
In recent years over 260 serious assaults have been recorded in the area annually, as well as over 1,000 domestic abuse incidents and around 220 assault episodes (for residents) requiring overnight hospital treatment.

Child and maternal health
30 per cent of women smoke during pregnancy, compared to 24 per cent nationally, and 33 per cent of mothers breast feed for six to eight weeks following birth (36 per cent nationally). Primary immunisation rates are

slightly below the national average. The rate of low birth-weight babies is 56 per cent above the national average, while the infant mortality rate is 27 per cent above the overall Scottish rate. The teenage pregnancy rate (under 18s) is 61 per cent above the Scottish average. The rate of admission for dental conditions among children is 55 per cent above the national average. Child road accident casualty rates are 30 per cent higher than the national average.

East Dunbartonshire

Population

East Dunbartonshire has a population of approximately 105,000 people, of whom 19 per cent are children, 63 per cent are young and middle-aged adults and over 17 per cent are older people. There has been a fall of over 3,800 in the size of the overall population in the last ten years.

Figure 3.14 East Dunbartonshire

The proportion of the population from a minority ethnic community (3.1 per cent) is above the Scottish average. There were over 922 live births in 2006.

Life expectancy and mortality

For men, life expectancy (at birth) is estimated to be 77.4 years, 3.5 years higher than the Scottish average, and has risen by 2.4 years in the period 1994–8 to 2001–5. Female life expectancy (80.9 years) has risen by 1.6 years in the same period and is approximately 1.8 years higher than the Scottish average. All-cause mortality and mortality rates from cancer, coronary heart disease and cerebrovascular disease (in the under 75s) are all below the Scottish average and have all fallen considerably in recent years.

Behaviour

Over 650 patients are admitted to hospital annually for alcohol related or attributable causes and there have been over 100 deaths due to alcohol in the last five years. An estimated 16,000 adults smoke: 19 per cent, compared to 27 per cent nationally. There have been 32 drug related deaths in East Dunbartonshire over the last ten years.

Hospitalisation/Social Work

Approximately 560 new cancer cases are registered annually and nearly 850 heart disease patients are admitted to hospital each year. There are approximately 5,800 patients admitted as a medical emergency annually. There are over 5,400 Social Work clients, 670 of whom are children and over 2,400 of whom are older people.

Mental health and function

There were 65 suicides in the period 2001–5 and there are nearly 200 new in-patient admissions to psychiatric specialties annually.

Prosperity/poverty

Over 7,800 people, 7.4 per cent of the population, are defined to be income deprived and 5,250 adults, 8.2 per cent of the working age population, are employment deprived. There are over 2,700 workplaces, employing over 25,000 people. House price sale values in 2006 were approximately 30 per cent above the national average.

Crime

In recent years on average 80 serious assaults have been recorded in the area annually, as well as over 300 domestic abuse incidents and around 60 assault episodes (for residents) requiring overnight hospital treatment.

Child and maternal health

Compared to 24 per cent nationally, 16 per cent of women smoke during pregnancy, and 47 per cent of mothers breast feed for six to eight weeks following birth (36 per cent nationally). Primary immunisation rates are close to or slightly above the Scottish average. The rate of low birth-weight babies is 21 per cent below the Scottish average, while the teenage pregnancy rate (under 18) is 34 per cent below the national average. Over 170 children are admitted to hospital for dental conditions annually.

Source: Greater Glasgow and Clyde

Dental Disease

Scottish children have very poor oral health compared to other EU countries. Dental disease is strongly associated with poverty. It is a very shocking fact that 29 per cent of three year olds in the Greater Glasgow and Clyde Health Board area have decayed, missing or filled baby teeth.

Children in the most disadvantaged communities have the highest levels of decay. This could easily be prevented. GGCHB distributes toothpaste and toothbrushes to children from the time their first teeth appear. Programmes of tooth-brushing are established in local nurseries.

The Scottish Government set dental health targets in 2006:

Children

- five year olds (Primary 1): 60 per cent of children should have no signs of dental disease
- 11–12 year olds (Primary 7): 60 per cent of children should have no signs of dental disease in permanent teeth

Adults

- 90 per cent of adults should have some natural teeth
- 65 per cent of adults aged 55–74 years should have some natural teeth

Oral Cancer

- current declining trends in oral cancer should be reversed, with a five-year survival expectation for males by 2015

Figures for the school year 2007–8, show that 57.7 per cent of Scottish five year olds showed no obvious dental decay experience. This is an improvement compared with 54.1 per cent in 2005–6 and 50.7 per cent in 2003–4. However, the figures vary across Scotland, with the least deprived areas already meeting the target of 60 per cent and much higher levels of decay in the most deprived areas.

Tackling Inequalities in Maternal and Neo-natal Health

In the Greater Glasgow and Clyde area, a range of services supports vulnerable children and families in the early years, for example, the Special Needs Pregnancy Service. In this service, health and social work services work together to assist pregnant women who have special social or psychological needs. Midwives are dedicated to vulnerable women including asylum seekers, homeless and teenagers. Women in deprived areas are encouraged to breastfeed with the help of peer supporters. Parents and Children Together Teams (PACT) have been set up to provide support for families with young children who face multiple health and social problems. These teams include social workers, health visitors, nursery nurses, family support and money advice workers. Special support is given to women who may be victims of abuse.

Lifestyle and Health

Obesity is a growing problem in the western world and in Scotland particularly. A reduction in levels of exercise contributes to this problem. Average energy expenditure per day has fallen by 800 calories since the 1950s, while the proportion of fat in the diet has increased by 50 per cent. In 1996, ten per cent of children in the UK were obese with the figure increasing to 16 per cent by 2004.

Social Class and Obesity

The lowest social class has levels of obesity which match American levels, while the highest social class has the lowest levels. The proportion of unskilled women who are obese is 28 per cent, double the figure for professional women. Nutritionists agree that inactivity, rather than diet, is the key element in rising levels of obesity.

Studies show the big increases in health risks due to obesity, such as diabetes, heart disease, breast, bowel, prostate and other cancers, osteoarthritis and dementia. Evidence to link obesity and socio-economic circumstances is unclear, but there is a definite relationship between obesity and health inequality. Obesity threatens to cancel out the positive benefits of many of the health advances made in recent years.

Lifestyle and Smoking

In recent years, the number of 15 year old girls who say they smoke has doubled. Glasgow has one of the worst records for lung cancer among women. Smoking is one reason that explains the different mortality rates between the social classes.

The Scottish Government estimates that:

- smoking accounts for about 24 per cent of all deaths in Scotland, rising to as much as 34 per cent in some areas
- lifelong smokers die on average about 10 years younger than non-smokers
- smoking also causes a great deal of long-term ill-health due to diseases of the heart, lung and arteries and a long list of cancers and other conditions

The report states that there is a clear relationship between smoking and deprivation. The most recent Scottish Household Survey shows adult smoking rates vary from 12 per cent in the least deprived fifth of the population to 41 per cent in the most disadvantaged fifth. This is a huge change from the situation fifty years ago when around 80 per cent of men and 50 per cent of women were smokers across the whole population. The good news is that the decline in smoking rates can explain much of the decrease in rates of coronary heart disease and almost all the decrease in rates of lung cancer among men.

However, because smoking rates have fallen faster in the more affluent area, there is a widening gap in health inequalities related to smoking. Smoking explains at least half the health inequalities related to socio-economic circumstances in Scotland. This is why discouraging smoking is on of the most important ways of reducing health inequalities.

Alcohol Abuse

Alcohol contributes to 8500 hospital admissions in Glasgow each year. Glasgow has 14,000 problem alcohol users. A 2006 report of alcohol trends in Scotland painted a depressing picture. Between 1980 and 2005, deaths related to alcohol consumption increased from 200 to 500 per year. There are gender and regional differences in alcohol problems. The Western Isles, followed by Glasgow and Inverclyde, have the highest figures, whilst East Dunbartonshire and Aberdeenshire the lowest. Alcohol-related liver damage is becoming increasingly common in under-40 year olds. The youngest person found to have alcohol related liver damage was a 17 year old boy who started drinking aged 12.

- Alcohol consumption has increased in the United Kingdom for at least the last 25 years as it has become more affordable. At the same time, the strengths of the two most popular alcoholic drinks – table wine and beer – have increased.
- 72 per cent of men and 58 per cent of women in Scotland drink regularly.
- Among them, 63 per cent of men and 57 per cent of women exceeded the recommended maximum daily amount at some point in the week, although a smaller number exceeded the maximum weekly recommended total consumption.

- Men's consumption of alcohol has fallen slightly over time, while women's continues to rise. Three quarters of men and women drink at home rather than in pubs, clubs, or restaurants.
- Sixteen to 24 year olds drink most heavily compared with other adults. In Scotland, amongst 13 year olds, 56 per cent of boys and 59 per cent of girls have drunk alcohol at some point in their lives. Seven per cent of 13 year olds and 18 per cent of 15 year olds reported having been drunk more than 10 times.

Source: Report by the Director of Public Health of Greater Glasgow and Clyde

The report says that 'Socio-economic deprivation is associated with increasing alcohol consumption, but the harm it causes people in more deprived circumstances cannot be attributed solely to the quantity of alcohol consumed. There is little evidence to explain why alcohol and deprivation make such a damaging combination, but it is likely to be due to a mixture of individual risks (such as poor diet or drug use) and environmental risks (such as drinking on the street).'

Alcohol and Society

A health study into masculinity and alcohol concluded that using alcohol was central to young men's understanding of what it means to be a man in Glasgow.

Violence is linked to poverty. The death rate from assault in our most deprived areas is more than ten times that in our more affluent areas. The major gap in life expectancy between the most and least deprived areas is partly due to this statistic.

Greater Glasgow and Clyde health services have joined together with Strathclyde Police to tackle alcohol misuse. One aim is to introduce an early detection programme to identify and support people who may be unaware that they are at risk of developing alcohol-related health problems. Over one hundred GP surgeries are helping to deliver the programme. Health staff are being trained in alcohol awareness. Money is being invested in Community Addiction Teams (CATS) to create extra medical, nursing and social care posts. A new addiction unit is also being planned. (*Source: Neil Hunter from Glasgow Addiction Services*)

Medics Against Violence (MAV) aims to raise awareness of the short and long term impact of violence-related injuries and to prevent young people from becoming victims. Healthcare workers see the results of violence every day. Scars caused by knives and other weapons are more than physical, the damage is also psychological. MAV is running an educational programme aimed at 14 year olds. The aim is to reduce the number of young people attending hospitals with serious injuries caused by violence.

Unemployment and poverty can have a huge influence on health. Often mental health is affected. Being out of work and feeling worthless can cause physical ill health too.

Work and self-esteem are key ways to tackling health inequality. GPs in the south east of Glasgow have been given the power to prescribe jobs to unemployed patients. Doctors identify patients whom they believe would gain health benefits from worthwhile work. Experts from the special employability service help the patient to link with some of the city's groups designed to help people back into work.

Single mum Katy Cooper felt isolated in her new home. She wasn't sleeping and had little confidence. She was offered a place on the Prescription for Work Scheme by her GP. She is now training in childcare and attending reflexology classes. She feels she has got a lot of her energy back and is using her brain again.

Health Inequalities Related to Gender

Life expectancy is higher for women than men. Women also have a longer 'healthy life' expectancy. According to the Scottish government, males in the least deprived fifth of the Scottish population are expected to live

94 per cent of their life in good health – compared with 85 per cent in the most deprived fifth. Females in the least deprived fifth are expected to live 93 per cent of their life in good health – compared with 84 per cent in the most deprived fifth of the population.

Mortality rates among young men in disadvantaged areas have been increasing when rates across the rest of the population have been decreasing. Diseases related to drug abuse such as Hepatitis C, which can lead to liver disease, are partly the reason for this trend.

Health inequalities Related to Ethnic Groups

Compared with the white population, the incidence of heart attacks in Scottish South Asians is 45 per cent higher in men and 80 per cent higher in women. Scots of Caribbean, Asian and African extraction are more at risk of strokes that the white population. Asians have a higher risk of tuberculosis. Diabetes rates are higher in the West Indian population. Some diseases are rarely seen outside certain ethnic groups, for example, sickle cell anaemia is almost exclusively found in the Afro-Caribbean group. All ethnic minority groups are less likely to drink alcohol and therefore suffer less of the effects. Racism can have a direct effect on health. If certain groups are denied equal opportunity, such as jobs and housing, then this will result in higher levels of poverty and ill health. People of African origin formed just over five per cent of the minority ethnic population in Scotland in 2001, but represented 33 per cent of the psychiatric patients in hospitals who were from ethnic minorities.

Putting New Initiatives to the Test

Govanhill has significant health and social inequalities. It has a large black and ethnic minority population. This area is involved in testing a new initiative to tackle health inequalities. A programme of social, economic and physical regeneration is being developed in order to address problems such as alcohol, drugs and community safety.

Whitecrook (in West Dunbartonshire) is piloting a programme to tackle high levels of smoking prevalence. Whitecrook has a smoking prevalence of 40.2 per cent compared to the national average of 24.7 per cent. The programme will focus on prevention and education, smoking cessation services and targeting tobacco sales.

East Lothian is looking at health inequalities in the early years. Lanarkshire is targeting sustained employment and decent work. Fife is targeting anti-social behaviour in relation to alcohol and underage drinking. Dundee is focusing on ways of improving wellbeing.

ACTIVITIES

1 List and describe the main factors which are linked to inequalities in health.
2 Using Tables 3.5, 3.6 and 3.7, describe national inequalities in life expectancy.
3 Read through the whole section on inequalities in health and list all of the government reports mentioned.
4 Describe what is outlined in each of the reports you have mentioned in as much detail as you can.
5 What evidence is there of reductions in inequalities in recent years?
6 What is the nature of the work of the Glasgow Centre for Population Health?
7 Why did this organisation develop community profiles for the Greater Glasgow and Clyde Health Board?
8 Summarise the most important issues within the Case Studies of East Dunbartonshire and North Glasgow.
9 'Lifestyle is the main factor influencing a person's health.' Give two reasons to support and two reasoning to oppose this statement.
10 Describe the links between:
   ● gender and ill health
   ● ethnic groups and ill health
11 Describe three initiatives and policies to tackle inequalities in health.
12 Find out more about each (and others) on the internet.

In a democracy people have rights, but they also have responsibilities. In order to ensure that people's rights are respected, rules and laws are necessary. In our private lives, we may have rules at home to help the smooth running of the household. At school, standards of behaviour are set out to ensure that all young people receive their right to be educated in a safe environment.

Scots Law

Scotland has its own distinct legal system. Scots Law comes from many different sources. Some of these sources date back to Roman times. The courts in Scotland are an important source of law as they can change the law. The UK Parliament makes laws called Acts of Parliament, often called statutes. Working out what the law means is complicated as the details are contained within small sections of these statutes. Many different sections may have to be studied to interpret the law.

⬆ **Figure 4.1** The High Court in Glasgow

The Scottish Parliament was given powers by the UK Parliament to make laws on devolved matters.

Why Rules and Laws are Necessary

Most people accept that rules and laws are necessary in order to prevent a complete breakdown of law and order; anarchy.

Crime takes place when somebody breaks one of the laws of the country. It is the job of the police to prevent people from breaking the laws and to investigate cases when the law has been broken.

Criminal Law

Criminal law deals with identifying when the law has been broken and then with prosecuting people who have broken the law. Some offences are less serious than others, such as driving a car without proper lights or committing a breach of the peace, but other offences are much more serious. Murder, rape and assault are all serious crimes and are dealt with severely.

Civil Law

Civil law is used to settle disputes between individuals. It sets the rules for civil procedures such as buying and selling a house or for divorce. Civil law is about the rights and obligations of individuals and organisations. The principles of civil law were influenced by Roman law. Civil law aims to sort out arguments and problems between people, and other organisations, such as businesses. Civil law affects our daily lives, personal relationships within families, with neighbours and members of communities, in our work, at home or in our leisure time.

ACTIVITIES

1 Why are rules and laws necessary to keep law and order in our society?
2 Give examples of rules and laws from your daily lives at home and in school.
3 What is the role of the following in making laws for Scotland?
   ● The Courts
   ● The Scottish Parliament
   ● The UK Parliament
4 Describe the following:
   ● Criminal Law
   ● Civil Law

Scottish Courts

The Scottish legal system has various different courts. There are three main criminal courts in Scotland: the High Court of Justiciary, the Sheriff Courts and the Justice of the Peace Courts. All courts are administered by the Scottish Courts Service (SCS) which is an executive agency of the Scottish Government. There have been changes to the Scottish Courts system. This is as a result of the Criminal Proceedings etc. (Reform) (Scotland) Act 2007. Under this legislation, the process of creating **Sheriffdoms** (a group of courts) took place.

There are now six Sheriffdoms in Scotland and each Sheriffdom contains one or more Sheriff Courts. Each Sheriffdom now also contains a number of Justice of the Peace Courts, which replace the District Courts previously operating. This change was phased-in and, by the end of 2009, all District Courts were replaced by

Justice of the Peace Courts. District Courts had been the responsibility of the local authorities but now all courts are administered by the SCS. This was intended to streamline the system. Some Justice of the Peace Courts will be run from the same site as the old District Court. For example, in Paisley, the Justice of the Peace Court is operated from the Renfrewshire Council building where the District Court had been operated from.

The Prosecution of Crime

There are two types of criminal procedure: solemn and summary. In **solemn procedure**, a trial takes place before a judge sitting with a jury of fifteen members of the public. All cases in the High Court of Justiciary are tried by solemn procedure. Solemn procedure is also conducted in Sheriff Courts. The alleged offence is set out in a document called an **indictment**. The judge's role is to make decisions regarding questions of the law itself and how it applies to the case. The jury's role is to make decisions regarding questions of fact and they may reach a decision by a simple majority vote. In **summary procedure** in Sheriff and District Courts, the judge sits without a jury and decides questions of both fact and law. The alleged offence is set out in a document called a **summary complaint**.

The Crown Office is the head office of the Procurator Fiscal Service, which is a civil service department. The Lord Advocate is the head of this department and the chief public prosecutor for Scotland. When the police write a report, giving details of alleged crimes, this goes to the Procurator Fiscal who decides whether or not to prosecute. All prosecutions in Scotland are conducted by the Crown Office. Prosecutions are conducted in the High Court of Justiciary by the Lord Advocate, Elish Angiolini, or by the Solicitor General for Scotland, or by Advocates Depute (also know as

Crown Counsel) of whom there are thirteen. In all other criminal courts they are conducted by the Procurator Fiscal or, in busy areas, one of his deputes, all of whom are legally qualified.

Figure 4.2 Lord Advocate Elish Angiolini

High Court of Justiciary

The High Court of Justiciary is Scotland's supreme criminal court. It has jurisdiction over the whole of Scotland and over almost all crimes. This court sits in cities and larger towns throughout Scotland. The High Court has unlimited sentencing powers. Edinburgh and Glasgow have permanent High Court buildings. In other areas the High Court sits in the local Sheriff Court building.

Lord Justice General and the Lord Justice Clerk preside over the High Court. Other full time judges are known as Lord Commissioners when sitting in the High Court. The High Court deals with the most serious crimes such as murder, rape, culpable homicide, armed robbery, drug trafficking and serious sexual offences, particularly those involving children. A single Judge presides over each case and defendants are tried under solemn procedure by a jury of fifteen men and women.

Sheriffdoms: Sheriff Courts and Justice of the Peace Courts

There are 49 Sheriff Courts in Scotland, each representing a particular Sheriff Court District. These Districts are grouped into six wider Sheriffdoms. The Sheriffdoms are shown in Table 4.1 alongside each of the courts in their area. Sheriff Courts deal with most cases that go to court across Scotland. They deal with both civil and criminal cases. Examples of criminal cases the Sheriff Court can deal with are: theft, assault, possession of drugs, soliciting or appeals from a Children's Hearing. Examples of civil cases the Sheriff Court can deal with are: separation, divorce or dissolution of a civil partnership, custody or aliment (financial settlement) disputes and adoption.

Table 4.1

Sheriffdom	Sheriff Court
Glasgow and Strathkelvin	Glasgow
Grampian Highland and Islands	Aberdeen; Banff; Dingwall; Elgin; For William; Inverness; Kirkwall; Lerwick; Lochmaddy; Peterhead; Portree; Stonehaven; Stornoway; Tain; Wick
Lothian and Borders	Duns; Edinburgh; Haddington; Jedburgh; Linlithgow; Peebles; Selkirk
North Strathclyde	Campbeltown; Dumbarton; Dunoon; Greenock; Kilmarnock; Oban; Paisley; Rothesay
South Strathclyde, Dumfries and Galloway	Airdrie; Ayr; Dumfries; Hamilton; Kirkcudbright; Lanark; Stranraer
Tayside, Central and Fife	Alloa; Arbroath; Cupar; Dundee; Dunfermline; Falkirk; Forfar; Kirkcaldy; Perth; Stirling

Sentencing in Sheriff Courts

In Sheriff Courts, the Sheriff has jurisdiction in both summary and solemn criminal cases. In summary court procedure, a Sheriff may impose prison sentences of up to 12 months or a fine up to a maximum of £10,000. Under solemn procedure (that is a trial with a jury) the Sheriff may impose an unlimited fine or a maximum custodial sentence of five years. The maximum sentence in Sheriff Court solemn procedure was only three years until 1st May 2004; so for cases that were first called before that date, the maximum prison sentence is three years. The Sheriff also has a range of non-custodial sentences available, for example, community service and probation.

Justice of the Peace Courts

Justice of the Peace Courts have replaced District Courts and they are run by the Scottish Courts Service. A Justice of the Peace Court is a **lay court** where a Justice of the Peace (JP) who is not legally qualified sits with a legally qualified Clerk. The Clerk provides advice to the JP on matters of law and procedure. Examples of cases the Justice of the Peace Courts can deal with are: some traffic offences (for example driving through a red traffic light), being drunk and disorderly, assaulting a police officer.

Table 4.2 Percentage of summary court cases dealt with within 26 weeks in Scotland

2005–06	2006–07	2007–08
65 %	65 %	67 %

Source: Crown Office

Sentencing in Justice of the Peace Courts

The maximum sentence that a JP may impose is 60 days imprisonment or a fine not exceeding £2,500. The sentencing powers of the JP Court are the same as those that were in the District Court. In Glasgow District Court only, some courts are presided over by a legally qualified Stipendiary Magistrate. The maximum sentence that a Stipendiary Magistrate may impose is 12 months imprisonment or a fine not exceeding £10,000.

Court of Session

The Court of Session is Scotland's supreme civil court. This court sits in Parliament House in Edinburgh and acts as a **court of first instance** and a **court of appeal**. An appeal can be referred from the Court of Session to the House of Lords. Each judge takes the courtesy title of 'Lord' or 'Lady' followed by their surname or a territorial title. The court is headed by the Lord President.

Figure 4.3 A Lord of the Court of Session, Edinburgh

Range of Sentences Available

The most lenient outcome for someone who has been found guilty in a Scottish court would be an absolute discharge or an admonition (a warning). An order to find caution might also be imposed – this is when the accused is ordered to pay money to the court as security for her/his good behaviour over a certain period. This can be for up to one year in the Sheriff Court. At the end of the period, if the accused has been of good behaviour, they can apply to the court to have the money repaid. A range of other sentences can be imposed by the Judge/Sheriff.

Custodial Sentences and Non-Custodial Sentences

A custodial sentence is where a person's liberty is restricted. This could be in either a prison or in a young offenders institution. There are two types of prisoner: a **sentenced** prisoner will have been convicted, whilst a **remand** prisoner has not been convicted but is being held in prison until charges are heard in court. A non-custodial sentence is one which does not involve imprisonment.

Figure 4.4 Time in prison is known as a custodial sentence

Supervised Attendance Order

As an alternative to serving time in prison for failing to pay a fine, the court may impose a Supervised Attendance Order (SAO). This requires the accused to carry out constructive activities under supervision, such as unpaid work for between 10 and 100 hours, depending on the amount of the unpaid fine. Some arguments in favour of SAOs rather than custodial sentences include:

- The average cost of a SAO is £733 compared to the average cost of a prison sentence which is £837.
- A large proportion of the prison population is made up of people who do not pay fines and less serious offences.
- Re-conviction rates reduce significantly after offenders are on SAOs compared to serving time in prison.
- Offenders are given advice on how to handle money problems and prepare for employment.
- There is an opportunity for SAO recipients to study educational courses and do unpaid work in the community.
- Some have taken on voluntary work as a result or have gone on to full time study.
- Patterns of offending are more likely to be broken when people feel useful and accepted in their local communities.

Probation Order

A probation order requires the accused to be under the supervision of a local authority officer for a fixed period of between six months and three years

Community Service Order

A community service order requires the accused to undertake between 80 and 300 hours of unpaid work in the community, under the supervision of a social worker. This is a direct alternative to a period of imprisonment.

There was a 30 per cent rise in the use of community service orders between 2004 and 2009. Some argue that CSOs are a 'soft-option' but others believe that they do more good than prison sentences. Justice Minister Kenny McAskill, argues that he wants to see criminals pay for their crimes through the 'sweat on their brow' rather than serving short prison sentences of six months or less.

Concerns about CSOs:

- Some say that it is very difficult for social workers to force criminals to serve their CSOs.

- Opponents of CSOs say that the streets of Scotland's towns and cities will not be safe as criminals can walk around freely.

Community-based Projects

In 2009, a community-based project opened in Paisley to tackle persistent offending. The Turnaround Project offers intensive support over an eight-week period for young men between the ages of 16 and 30. The project aims to break the cycle of short custodial sentences followed by further offending, typical of many repeat offenders. Such projects intend to reduce the number of short-term prison sentences.

Imprisonment

The type of court in which the trial was held determines the length of the period of imprisonment that may be imposed. If the accused is aged between 16 and 21, they will be detained in a Young Offenders Institution rather than a prison.

There are schemes in prison to tackle re-offending, such as education, training and drug rehabilitation. There need to be enough resources to meet the needs of the prison population (See Case Study: Six Days in Cornton Vale).

Arguments in favour of prison

Depriving someone of their freedom is a good form of punishment.

It can act as a deterrent.

It keeps people locked up who might otherwise be committing crimes.

Arguments against prison

Prisoners are eventually released and can re-offend.

Over 50 per cent of adults and three-quarters of young offenders are reconvicted within two years.

Four out of five shoplifters are reconvicted within two years of leaving prison.

Compensation

Either in addition to, or instead of, most other sentences, the court may order the accused to pay compensation to their victims for loss or injury resulting from the crime. In fixing the amount, the court will consider the accused's financial circumstances. This money is paid to the court, which then forwards the money to the victims.

Juvenile Courts

Scotland has a very distinctive system of care and justice for children and young people.

The system was implemented in 1968, following the Kilbrandon Report and is now part of the Children (Scotland Act) 1995. It was decided that children who were appearing in front of courts had common needs and that they were better served by a separation of courts and welfare service. The facts were to be established by the courts but the welfare needs were to be the responsibility of the Children's Hearings. In 1971, Children's Hearings took over most of the responsibility for young people under 16 and in some cases under 18 who had committed offences and needed care and protection.

CASE STUDY

Six Days in Cornton Vale

It was only six days. Less than a week of my life. But every one of the 144 hours I spent behind bars opened my eyes just a little bit wider. I knew that I would not be in Cornton Vale women's prison for long. I knew I had family and friends on the outside and I knew I would leave to a warm home and fulfilling job. I had more to hold on to than practically every other prisoner in there – but it was still one of the saddest experiences of my life.

Don't think for a second that I am looking for sympathy. I had a choice. I could have paid a fine instead of going to jail. But the £300 penalty was for an anti-nuclear protest I do not consider a crime. I made my choice and I'd make the same one again. But the other women in Cornton Vale were born with few options and have less with every year that passes.

The opportunities went with every drink, every fix of heroin, every petty theft, every spell inside. Hundreds of women clatter back and forth through the gates of that miserable place like they are on a baggage carousel at the airport. If a society can be judged by how it treats prisoners then we are a cold, empty and bleak place.

Figure 4.5 Rosie Kane

I thought I was prepared when I was sentenced to 14 days on Friday, October 27.

But I was a fool for thinking I was ready. Nothing can prepare you for the cell door slamming behind you.

I arrived at the prison in Stirling just after 2pm but the radio had already been reporting I was on my way. So within five minutes of my arrival, three of my 269 fellow inmates were at my cell to greet me. They were welcoming and kind and I was grateful. I was already Prisoner 99451 and in my jail clothes. I'd rather have had a suit with arrows up it than those black, torn trackie bottoms.

Despite stories about prisoners enjoying hot and cold running luxury, I wasn't expecting the Hilton. Just as well, really. After just six days, I came out a stone lighter despite eating every meal. The hunger was constant. So was the cold. Locked in the cell at half past seven at night – six o'clock at the weekend – wearing every scrap of clothing I had and the quilt wrapped around my feet, I was still freezing. I had £5 a week to spend but coffee was a luxury only allowed at weekends.

Morale is rock bottom, for guards and prisoners. There is a culture of bullying and aggression. It is hellish. I had been told conditions in men's prisons are better than in women's because men wouldn't put up with it. Women don't riot, you see. Particularly women whose lives have almost always been lived in the shadow of abuse. They have been given nothing and they expect nothing. They have already been stripped of dignity, hope, and any belief in themselves or a better life.

Most seem to be in for drugs, drink, petty thefts, or unpaid fines. One 27 year old women was typical. She seemed gentle, articulate and educated but when she goes on a bender she turns from Jekyll into Mrs Hyde. Her raging drunken spells often end in arrest and prison. This time, she had thrown some candles and a James Blunt CD out of a window during an argument. Drugs are the reason why other women are there. Shaking and shivering, these poor wee lassies detoxing are the most pathetic sight.

I watched tiny, pinched women who looked like children suffering in agony – knowing that, even if they manage to stay clean in Cornton Vale, they'll be going back to homeless hostels awash with heroin. Twelve women have taken their own lives in this jail since 1995. What is the point of spending £300 a day keeping prisoners behind bars, when they do not pose a risk of violence, if we do nothing to stop their swift and inevitable return to jail?

Locking them up and throwing away the key is not a penal policy. It's a nonsense sanctioned by politicians desperate to look tough by picking on the easiest targets. If we spent less of our taxes on prisons, we could fund properly effective residential rehab programmes. If cash was ploughed into social work and solid support structures, our jails would be emptier and our streets safer.

We need to intervene early. Many of the women behind bars could have been identified by their teachers before they even left primary school. By the time they reached adulthood, they had already been in and out of trouble and in and out of jail. I'm sure plenty of people will be queuing up to accuse me of gesture politics, of wasting taxpayers' money. They're wrong. My week in jail was harrowing but enlightening.

Source: Rosie Kane, *Sunday Mail* www. scottishsocialistparty.org/pages/rosiejail.html

A young person may be called to a Children's Hearing if they:

- are beyond the control of parents or carers
- are at risk of moral danger
- are (or have been) the victim of an offence, including physical injury or sexual abuse
- are likely to suffer serious harm to their health or development through lack of care
- are misusing drugs, alcohol or solvents
- have committed an offence
- are not attending school regularly without a reasonable excuse
- are subject to an antisocial behaviour order and the Sheriff requires the case to be referred to a children's hearing

A young person will only go to court if the offence is very serious. The Procurator Fiscal decides if prosecution is in the public interest. However, even then, the Procurator Fiscal may refer this to the Children's Reporter to decide whether a Children's Hearing would be more appropriate.

The Children's Reporter

A referral may be made to the Children's Reporter by the police or a social worker as well as by health or educations services, a member of the public or the child themselves. The Reporter could come to one of the following decisions:

- They can decide that no further action is required. The Reporter will write to the child/young person and usually the parent
- They may refer the child or young person to the local authority so that advice, guidance and assistance can be given on an informal and voluntary basis. This usually involves support from a social worker.

- They can arrange a Children's Hearing because they consider that compulsory measures of supervision are necessary for the child.

The Children's Panel

↑ **Figure 4.6** A Children's Hearing panel meeting

The Children's Panel is made up of members of the community, aged 18 or over, who have volunteered in this important work. Even though they are volunteers, they go through important training. There must be both men and women on the panel.

The Children's Hearing

The whole philosophy of a Children's Hearing is to support the child. The child must be there during the meeting. The layout of the room is informal and the young person can have a person of their choosing at the hearing with them. The parents/carers involved will also attend. The Children's Hearing will receive a report from social workers and possibly from the child's school, which all participants are entitled to see.

The Hearing will take place in the young person's home area. Every Children's Hearing has three panel members, one of whom chairs the meeting. They must decide if compulsory methods of supervision are needed and what methods would be the most suitable. The Hearing can only go ahead if the young person accepts the grounds for referral. If the grounds for referral are not accepted then the Hearing may be discharged or referred to the Sheriff to establish the grounds and another Hearing called.

It could be decided that a child who has committed a relatively minor offence should be given a Compulsory Supervision Order in their own interests. On the other hand, if a more serious offence has been committed, a CSO may not be used because the young person could stay at home with support from the community.

Supervision Requirements

A supervision requirement will be made if it is deemed necessary. In most cases the child will remain at home but will be placed under the supervision of a social worker. In other cases the decision will be made to place the child in care. This may be with other relatives, foster parents, children's homes or secure accommodation. Under the Anti-Social Behaviour etc. (Scotland) Act, Hearings can put restrictions on where a child can go. This will involve an electronic tag and a thorough package of support to help moderate the child's behaviour. A supervision requirement must be reviewed at a hearing within a year.

Scotland's Youth Justice System: Continuing Research and Reform

Even though the Children's Hearing System has many strengths and has been praised internationally, the system is still not perfect. Read these brief extracts from various research papers.

Scottish Youth Justice Baseline

THERE ARE STILL TOO MANY GAPS: TOO MANY SPACES OFFENDERS CAN FALL THROUGH...

IT TAKES TOO LONG FOR BEHAVIOUR TO BE CHALLENGED...

No single agency meets all of its standards...

WHERE THERE IS REAL JOINT WORKING, BETTER RESULTS ARE EVIDENT...

Better data analysis is helping to improve decisions about where resources are targeted...

Strengthening For the Future: A Consultation on the Reform of Children's Hearing Systems

In 2008 Scottish Ministers said:

'Scottish Ministers support the fundamental principles underlying the Hearings system, but want to look at whether they can be developed and improved. It is important that we confirm what those principles are, that they are understood and that you are happy to endorse them. We also wish to consider whether they can be enhanced.

We believe that the principles of the system are:

- that the child is at the centre of the system (i.e. that it is the future wellbeing of the child which is most important)
- that the process is integrated, independent and looks at the whole needs of the child

(i.e. offending is considered alongside care and protection within a single process)

- that unacceptable behaviour and offending is addressed first and foremost through the Hearings system and that children should only be dealt with through the criminal justice system in exceptional circumstances

- that the system is locally-based and community-focused (panel members are drawn from, and represent, the local community)

- that where facts cannot be agreed, the Sheriff Court resolves these points, not the Hearing.'

However, the Scottish Government felt that it could be improved further:

- because so many agencies are involved in the decisions surrounding each child there can be confusion in terms of roles, responsibilities and when to take action

- Children's Panel members could specialise in certain issues

- it should be more clear that children who need to be referred are being referred

- children's services should be evaluated and inspected on a regular basis

- the Children's Hearing System should have more powers to influence parental behaviour and actions

- there should be a consideration of how to make services more relevant to young people and involve them in decision making.

ACTIVITIES

1 Explain why the Scottish Government made changes to the Scottish Court System.
2 Describe the process of bringing a case to court.
3 Describe in detail the following adult criminal courts, giving examples of sentencing powers and types of crimes heard in each court:
   - Justice of the Peace
   - Sheriff Court
   - High Court
4 Describe summary and solemn procedures.
5 Study Table 4.2. 'The Scottish Government is making progress towards its target in terms of the increase in the percentage of criminal cases disposed of within 26 weeks.' Give one reason to support this statement.
6 Describe the civil court system in Scotland.
7 What are the main principles of the Children Hearing system in Scotland?
8 Why might a young person be called to a Children's Hearing?
9 When might a juvenile case go to court?
10 Describe the membership of the Children's Panel and the actions it can take.
11 Why could it be said that the Children's Hearing system is not perfect?
12 Explain, in detail, why some people believe that non-custodial sentences are better than custodial sentences for all but the most serious crimes.

Types of Crime

The most serious crimes, such as murder, serious assault, rape and indecent assaults make up only five per cent of all crimes recorded.

Table 4.3 Crimes recorded by the police, Scotland 2007–8

Crime Group	Number of crimes recorded 2007–8	% change 2006–7 to 2007–8
Non-sexual crimes of violence	12,874	–9
Crimes of indecency	6,552	–3
Crimes of dishonesty	166,718	–9
Fire-raising/ Vandalism	118,025	–9
Other crimes	81,340	–4
Total crimes	385,509	–8

Source: Scottish Government Statistics

Anti-Social Behaviour

Anti-social behaviour affects people living in their communities. These crimes can make people feel uncomfortable and unsafe in their own neighbourhoods. Crimes of the anti-social behaviour type can include noisy neighbours, graffiti, intimidation, and vandalism.

Mugging

Most muggings take place in the street or on public transport. They usually happen in the evening. Muggers use physical force to make people hand over their belongings and they may carry weapons such as bottles or knives. Because most young people carry around expensive items such as mobile phones and MP3 players, muggers take advantage of this.

Assault

When someone is beaten up or threatened with violence this is known as assault. People found guilty of assault will face serious punishments and may have to spend time at a young offender's institution or in prison. If the assault is found to be motivated by racism or homophobia or if someone was attacked because of their religious beliefs then the sentence will be more severe.

Drug Crimes

There are three categories of drugs, as classified by the government, and each category has different sentencing penalties attached to it if you are caught in possession of them.

Table 4.4 Categories of drug and maximum sentences for possession

Category of Drug	Description	Maximum Sentence
Class A drugs	These drugs include heroin, cocaine, ecstasy and LSD.	Up to seven years in prison or an unlimited fine (or both).
Class B drugs	Class B drugs include speed, cannabis and some amphetamines.	Up to five years in prison or an unlimited fine (or both).
Class C drugs	Class C drugs include ketamine, GHB and some tranquilisers.	Up to two years in prison or an unlimited fine (or both).

Possession of Drugs

Possession of illegal drugs can result in a person being charged. The punishment is dependent on the type of drug. A person may receive a harsher punishment if they have committed a crime before. If a person has no criminal history and is found in possession of a Class C drug then a formal warning will be given. Possession of Class A or B drugs carries harsher punishments. If anyone under 17 is caught in possession of drugs, the police are allowed to inform their parents. If anyone over 18 is caught in possession of cannabis then the police will consider arrest and confiscate the drugs. The police are also likely to give a warning for a first offence of possession or give a Penalty Notice for disorder (an on-the-spot fine of £80) for a second offence. If it is the third time they have been caught with cannabis then will be arrested – this could lead to conviction and a criminal record.

⬆ **Figure 4.7** Illegal drugs

If a young person between 10 and 17 years is caught in possession of cannabis, the police will confiscate the drug and possibly arrest them or refer them to a Youth Offending Team (YOT).

Supplying and Dealing

Offences related to supplying and dealing drugs carry much tougher punishments. Sharing drugs with friends is considered supplying. The maximum sentences for intent to supply drugs are:

● up to life in prison or an unlimited fine (or both) for a Class A drug

● up to 14 years in prison or an unlimited fine (or both) for a Class B or Class C drug

Other restricted substances:

● it's against the law for a shop to sell solvents, cigarette lighter refills and some glues to under 18s if they believe that they will use them as a drug

● if you're under 18, you will not be allowed to buy alcohol, cigarettes, cigars or tobacco

Domestic Violence

Domestic violence includes violent and aggressive behaviour between people in a family or in a relationship, including child abuse. Child abuse can take the form of physical or emotional abuse. This type of abuse can have very long-term effects and impact on a person's chances of living a normal adult life with good mental health. Sadly, many victims of abuse think that the violence they experience is their own fault and often feel too ashamed to seek help.

Table 4.5 Gender breakdown of incidents of domestic abuse 2000–1 to 2007–8

	2000–1	2001–2	2002–3	2003–4	2004–5	2005–6	2006–7	2007–8
Female victim, male perpetrator	91%	90%	89%	89%	88%	87%	87%	85%
Male victim, female perpetrator	8%	8%	9%	9%	11%	11%	11%	13%
Same gender victim and perpetrator	1%	1%	1%	1%	2%	2%	2%	2%

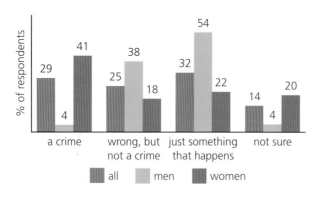

Figure 4.8 Perceptions of domestic violence

Knife Crime

This includes:

- carrying or trying to buy a knife if you're under 18
- threatening people with a knife
- carrying a knife that is banned
- a murder where the victim was stabbed with a knife
- a robbery or burglary where the thieves carried a knife as a weapon

While there has been a lot of news coverage of knife crimes recently, this type of crime still makes up a small percentage of the total crimes committed every year in the UK. However, the extent of injury possible makes it a serious issue.

Knife Crime Law in the UK

There are a number of different rules that apply to knives:

- it's illegal to buy most types of knife if aged under 18
- anyone over 16 can be charged and taken to court if they're caught with an illegal knife
- if aged under 16 and caught carrying a knife, a community sentence or a detention and training order will be given
- a person could be searched at any time if a police officer or a teacher thinks they may be carrying a knife

- even if carrying a knife and legally allowed to (like a penknife with a blade that's shorter than three inches), it becomes illegal if you use it as a weapon to threaten or harm anyone

The maximum sentence for anyone found guilty of carrying an illegal knife is now four years.

Gun Crime

Gun crime can cover any crime that involves the use of a gun or other firearm. This also includes carrying or using an imitation gun. Incidents involving guns make up less than one per cent of the total number of crimes committed every year. However, the number of reported offences has been growing steadily over the past few years.

Legislation on gun laws is a reserved matter, that is, it is decided at Westminster, not in the Scottish Parliament. There is disagreement as the Scottish Government wants tighter laws than Westminster. Recently sentencing for convictions involving guns has been toughened. Illegal possession can lead to a minimum custodial sentence of five years. The minimum age to buy an air rifle is now 17 years.

Racial Hate Crime

Race crime is described as 'racially aggravated' or 'racially motivated' and includes crimes committed on the basis of race, nationality, culture and language. This type of crime can cause a lot of fear in communities.

Race crime does not necessarily involve violence or physical injury. It could be in the form of threatening or abusive language. If a crime is racially motivated it can carry a stiffer sentence than if the same crime was committed with no racial motive.

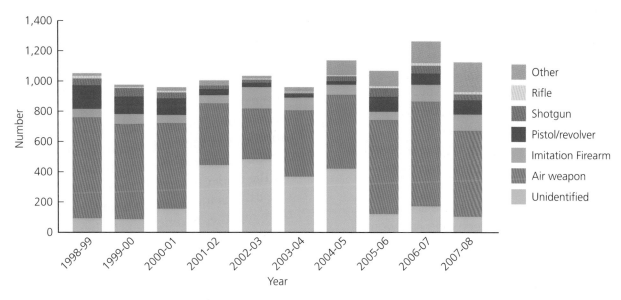

Figure 4.9 Crimes involving a firearm in Scotland 1998–9 to 2007–8

Religious Hate Crime

If a person is a victim of a crime because of their religion, then they should report it to the police as soon as possible. Discrimination laws means that employers must make sure that all their employees are treated in the same way as each other, regardless of their religious beliefs.

Rape and Sexual Assault

Rape is when someone forces another person to have sex against their will. Most rape victims are women, but men can also be the victims of rape. Sexual assault covers any sort of sexual contact and behaviour that is unwanted. Rape is not always committed by a stranger to the victim, it can be committed by a family member or an acquaintance. When a victim is under 18, rape can often be referred to as child abuse. Sometimes a person's drink can be 'spiked' with a date rape drug.

White-Collar Crime

White-collar work is a term which broadly describes office work or work in business. It has been defined as 'a crime committed by a person of respectability and high social status in the course of his occupation'. White-collar crimes include fraud, bribery, insider trading, embezzlement, computer crime, and forgery.

Blue-Collar Crime

People employed in relatively unskilled environments and living in inner-city areas have fewer advantages or opportunities to exploit than those who work in situations where large financial transactions occur and where people live in areas of relative prosperity. Blue-collar crime tends to be more obvious and attract more police attention, for example, housebreaking, vandalism and shoplifting. White-collar crimes are less obvious because they are usually connected with legitimate business, for example, tax fraud.

ACTIVITIES

1 Describe in detail the types of crime that are more likely to be committed by young people.
2 Why do you think knife crimes and gun crimes are causing so much concern in the media?
3 Study Figure 4.8. 'There is no difference between men and women in perceptions of domestic abuse.' Give one reason to oppose this statement.
4 Study Table 4.5. 'There has been a significant fall in the percentage incidents of domestic abuse between 2000–1 and 2007–8.' Give two reasons why this statement is exaggerated.
5 Study Figure 4.9. 'There has been no improvement in the volume of crimes involving firearms in recent years.' Give reasons to support this statement.
6 Discuss the classifications of drugs crime. Do you agree with the classifications?
7 What is the difference between white-collar and blue-collar crime?
8 Why are blue collar crimes likely to be more visible?

Important Note

Often when explanations are given for why crime is committed, the reasons given are too simplistic. This can lead to stereotyping, prejudice and discrimination. For these reasons, this section has been written under one heading. It will then be for the reader to identify some individual causes. It is important to be able to link them together in order to get a better understanding.

Causes of Crime

People are responsible for their own behaviour and accountable for their actions. However, societies need to provide the conditions for people to have the best possible chance of being able to act responsibly.

When a young person or groups of young people commit crimes, there are usually **social reasons**. It can often be partly to do with some young people not having access to leisure facilities, for example, not being able to take part in sports or go to the cinema very often due to **poverty** and **social exclusion**. Young people from well-off families are more likely to be able to afford such leisure and sports activities. Therefore young people from poorer socio-economic backgrounds may be more likely to get involved in criminal activity for material gain or for amusement and thrills.

Poverty can lead to a lack of educational opportunities, poor housing and the social exclusion and stigma attached to being poor. Many young people who commit crime have been excluded from school. They may feel abandoned by their teachers and perhaps their families too. Some young people are unable to get work when they leave full time education and cannot afford to progress to further education. Young people in this position often find comfort and a sense of belonging in gangs and gang culture. Because our society attaches so much importance to material belongings, this can lead some young people to commit crime to be able to acquire electronic goods and fashionable clothes.

Figure 4.10 Young people experiencing social exclusion may have few options in how and where to spend their leisure time

Long-term **unemployment** can cause a lack of self esteem and frustration, especially in young males. The effects of failure at school and insecure employment can combine to increase the risk of a person committing crime. Unemployed men who have served long-term prison sentences are more likely to re-offend.

There is not a direct link between poverty and crime. However, the conditions associated with crime can mean that people who live in poverty may be more susceptible to getting involved in crime. The **social environment** a young person is brought up in can influence their behaviour. Neglect, criminality in parents, parents arguing or unable to cope, family violence and abuse are all factors which can lead a child into crime. Children require good care and resources to be able to cope in the modern world. Children who require support from social services and mental health services are more likely to be vulnerable to becoming involved in crime.

Many people with **mental health problems** end up in the criminal justice system. Research has been carried out in Canada measuring the links between mental health, youth delinquency and criminal behaviour. It was found that the level of a young person's self esteem and their ability to handle stress was linked to whether or not a young person would display delinquent behaviour. The report concluded that understanding these links is very important as this will encourage governments to develop policies for intervention and to reduce re-offending. The report also found that experiences at home, school and in the community were very important. In a survey it was found that 65 per cent of youth who reported being highly involved with their school reported no aggression, compared to 47 per cent of those not highly involved with school.

The British Crime Survey 2003 reported that: 'in nearly half (48 per cent) of all violent incidents, victims believed offenders to be under the influence of alcohol. This figure rose to 60 per cent in cases of 'stranger violence'.

Alcohol abuse is linked most strongly to crimes of violence. Nearly half of all violent crimes are committed while under the **influence of alcohol**. It has been found that 'frequency of drunkenness' was strongly linked to 'general offending and criminal and disorderly behaviour during and after drinking'.

However, research shows there is no single direct causal link between alcohol and violent or abusive behaviours, it is more of a complex mix of factors. There are also indirect links to crime. Alcohol and drugs may create the sort of dysfunctional family from which children are more likely to turn to crime.

In 2007 the Scottish Government conducted a review of the law on alcohol-related crime. The intention of this review was to make it clear to offenders that alcohol will not be seen as a mitigating factor in criminal activity. The Justice Secretary Kenny MacAskill said:

'We in Scotland have a cultural problem with alcohol. Too many Scots think it acceptable to get drunk. Abused partners. Random assaults. Stabbings. Vandalism. The impact is there for all to see – on the streets in the police stations, in hospital emergency departments, and in the courts.

The most recent statistics show that seven out of ten of those accused of murder in Scotland had been drinking or on drugs. Nearly half of Scotland's 7,000 prisoners say they were drunk at the time they committed their offence.

The Scottish government is developing a long-term strategic approach to shifting attitudes and changing behaviour towards alcoholism. The misuse of alcohol does much more harm to our society than violence and crime alone – it is a significant factor holding back the health of the nation.'

There is much evidence to support the idea that those with a dependency on **drug use** are more likely to be arrested for crimes such as burglary or shop theft, or for robbery and handling stolen goods – crimes that will help to pay for the drug habit. However, the question of whether drug use leads people into criminal activity, or whether those who use drugs are already predisposed to such activity, is debatable.

Crime is committed in some areas more than others. Evidence shows that criminal activity is not evenly distributed geographically. Some areas suffer higher crime rates than others. These areas are sometimes called '**hot spots**'. The economic status, or wealth of an area is an

important factor. Studies have found that robbery rates are higher than average in poorer areas with higher levels of social problems. The highest rates of violent crime also occur in the poorer areas.

However, social and economic inequality might have a greater effect than poverty alone. Poverty might have a greater effect on crime in urban rather than in rural areas. Taking inequality into account, studies have shown that urban areas tend to be more mixed than rural areas and therefore have higher levels of inequality.

There may also be more victims of crime in disadvantaged areas. Some studies have found that demand for police services is higher in more disadvantaged areas. Victims in disadvantaged areas are more likely to suffer crime closer to their own homes and repeated number of times in their own neighbourhood. It has also been found that people in disadvantaged areas may be the target of crime because they are more likely to carry cash.

Areas which suffer higher rates of long-term **unemployment** are also likely to suffer more crime. Young people who are not in school or employment may be more likely to get involved in crime. The lack of provision of suitable apprenticeships for young people is a contributory factor. Densely populated cities with large populations and concentrations of drug users will also produce higher crime rates and victim rates. This type of crime may not be reported if the victim is a drug user.

There are differences between **men** and **women** in terms of criminal behaviour and their experiences of the criminal justice system. By far the majority of crime in Scotland is committed by men – when women offend they tend to commit low-level, non-violent offences and pose little risk to society.

Table 4.6 Local authorities in Scotland, crime statistics

Council area	Population (000s)	Unemployment rate 2009 (%)	Non-sexual crimes of violence	Crimes of indecency	Crimes of dishonesty	Fire-raising, vandalism etc.	Other crimes	Total crimes	% of crimes cleared up
Aberdeen City	210	3.6	554	520	12,200	5,050	3,579	21,903	47
Aberdeenshire	241	2.5	185	242	3,428	3,138	1,500	8,493	47
Angus	110	4.4	142	131	2,302	1,965	1,007	5,547	57
Argyll & Bute	91	4.3	117	108	1,709	1,743	1,374	5,051	50
Clackmannanshire	50	5.4	119	81	1,540	1,487	1,345	4,572	68
Dumfries & Galloway	149	4.6	153	130	2,961	2,974	2,171	8,389	61
Dundee City	142	6.3	332	203	7,602	3,471	2,859	14,467	55
East Ayrshire	120	6.0	330	99	3,556	2,795	1,885	8,665	47
East Dunbartonshire	105	3.9	120	47	1,769	1,542	718	4,196	37
East Lothian	96	3.5	144	91	1,810	1,667	665	4,377	45
East Renfrewshire	89	3.5	108	22	1,540	1,369	604	3,643	32
Edinburgh, City of	477	4.4	1,325	610	23,817	12,483	6,857	45,092	42
Eilean Siar	26	4.4	47	18	304	299	302	970	72
Falkirk	152	4.4	215	276	4,150	3,012	2,020	9,673	57
Fife	362	5.7	501	584	11,436	8,690	4,151	25,362	55
Glasgow City	584	7.1	3,715	1,196	29,538	16,708	18,364	69,521	46
Highland	210	3.4	417	330	4,991	4,420	3,829	13,987	62
Inverclyde	81	6.2	299	47	2,265	2,190	1,705	6,506	45
Midlothian	81	4.1	139	76	2,010	2,258	855	5,338	46
Moray	88	3.8	106	191	2,073	1,897	1,025	5,292	45
North Ayrshire	136	7.3	412	172	3,342	3,616	2,200	9,742	50
North Lanarkshire	326	5.9	821	338	10,656	9,234	5,393	26,442	40
Orkney Islands	20	2.6	3	15	178	167	55	418	64
Perth & Kinross	144	3.6	134	71	3,399	1,841	1,445	6,890	57
Renfrewshire	170	5.5	589	155	5,800	3,634	2,459	12,637	40
Scottish Borders	112	3.6	119	70	1,633	1,497	1,141	4,460	66
Shetland Islands	22	2.4	15	18	266	255	202	756	71
South Ayrshire	112	5.2	239	103	2,861	2,395	1,606	7,204	48
South Lanarkshire	310	4.4	731	169	7,311	7,131	4,638	19,980	43
Stirling	88	4.5	131	122	2,489	1,669	1,169	5,580	58
West Dunbartonshire	91	6.8	330	117	3,077	3,055	2,290	8,869	46
West Lothian	170	4.7	282	200	4,705	4,373	1,927	11,487	40
SCOTLAND	**5165**	**4.9**	**12,874**	**6,552**	**166,718**	**118,025**	**81,340**	**385,509**	**48**

Economic recession and crime: burglaries and knife robberies up

Robberies at knife point have risen by almost a fifth, according to official figures for England and Wales. Domestic burglaries jumped 4 per cent – the first significant rise for some years. The Home Office figures for the three months to September 2008 indicate that total recorded crime continues to fall – down 3 per cent over the quarter.

The figures come after the Home Office named 18 police forces involved in a row over the miscounting of some serious violence. According to the British Crime Survey – a mass study of the experience of those surveyed rather than reports to the police – the risk of being a victim of crime remained at 23 per cent. Within that, the level of overall violent crime was said to be stable.

Rises in recorded crime:
- Knife/sharp instrument robbery: 18 per cent
- Fraud/forgery: 16 per cent
- Drugs: nine per cent
- Home burglary: four per cent
- Other burglary: three per cent

(*Source*: Home Office)

But crimes recorded by the police showed significant increases in some key areas, including home break-ins, violence related to knives or sharp instruments, and drugs. The rise in burglaries was the largest for seven years.

Separate Home Office figures showed that the total of 270 knife killings in 2007–8 was the highest since records began three decades ago. The nine per cent rise in recorded drug offences was related to the police's increased use of powers to issue cannabis warnings, said the Home Office.

Recorded firearms offences fell by 29 per cent between July and September 2008.

Downturn link denied

Responding to the figures, Home Secretary Jacqui Smith denied that there was an inevitable link between an economic downturn and a rise in break-ins.

'It's a fact that there's been an increase and that's worrying,' she told the BBC News Channel. 'That's why last September we started work in the department [asking] if we are facing tough economic times, what will be the impact on crime.'

But Shadow Home Secretary Chris Grayling said: 'These statistics show the harsh consequence of Gordon Brown's economic downturn. This is made worse because the Home Secretary clearly has no idea how to deal with this credit crunch crime wave. It is particularly alarming that robberies involving knives have soared and that fatal stabbings are at an all-time high. There's no rocket science about this.'

Source: Dominic Casciani, BBC News

Crime statistics for Scotland are collated and released separately from those in England and Wales. The latest figures showed that recorded crime in Scotland had fallen to its lowest level in more than a quarter of a century, down eight per cent on the previous year.

ACTIVITIES

1 Create a memory map of the different causes of crime. Make as many connections as you can between the different factors.

2 'People are responsible for their own behaviour and have only themselves to blame if they get involved in criminal activities.' Explain why some might agree with this statement and why some would disagree with it. In your conclusion, mention whether you agree or disagree with the statement.

3 Study Table 4.6. Give reasons to support and oppose the view that crime rates are higher in densely populated cities than in less populated areas.

4 Give reasons to support and oppose the view that higher crime rates are linked to low income and unemployment.

5 Read the BBC News article. According to this article, did crime rates rise or fall in the three months to 8th September 2009? Answer in detail.

6 What did Jacqui Smith say about the link between economic downturn and break-ins?

7 What was the view of opposition politicians in 2008?

Scotland's Laws on Buying and Selling Alcohol

Alcohol is a legal drug, but misuse can lead to health problems and disorderliness. Scotland's laws on alcohol are a mixture of Scottish laws and those that apply across the UK. There are a number of laws governing its sale, purchase and consumption. The Licensing (Scotland) Act 2005 came into force on 1st September 2009. This Act intends to:

- secure public safety
- prevent public nuisance
- protect and improve public health
- protect children from harm

The licensing system involves licensing of premises and personal licences. All premises where alcohol is served and sold require a premises licence. A personal licence is issued to an individual and allows that person to authorise the sale of alcohol.

Figure 4.11 It is an offence to be drunk in a public place

Public Drunkenness and Nuisance Behaviour

It's an offence to be drunk in a public place, even though most people won't have to answer in court because of it. The Criminal Justice (Scotland) Act 1980 designated places where the police can take drunk and incapable people to sober up. Holders of licences to sell alcohol have to undergo training on their duties and obligations to sell alcohol responsibly. This includes not serving drunken people. People who are already drunk should not be allowed to buy alcohol.

Preventing Nuisance

The Local Government (Scotland) Act 1973 gives local authorities the power to introduce byelaws designed to stop the drinking behaviour of some being a nuisance to others. Many local authorities have used this power to make byelaws banning drinking in public, in areas where there had previously been problems.

Age Limits

- People who are 18 years of age or older can buy alcohol in the same way as other adults. However, the licence holder can refuse to allow anyone under 21 on the premises if they wish (they can refuse entrance to anyone they like so long as it's not on the grounds of race, gender or disability).

- People over the age of 16 can buy beer, wine or cider as long as it's served with a meal and consumed in an area used solely for eating meals. It is illegal for people under the age of 18 to buy or be sold alcohol in any other circumstances.

- Children who are 14 or over are allowed on licensed premises but can't buy alcohol or have it bought for them.

- From 2009, Scotland's new laws mean that buying alcohol for anyone under 18 is an offence punishable by a fine up to £5000 and/or a prison sentence of up to 3 months.

Under-age Drinking

59 per cent of Scottish 15 year olds drink alcopops and 24 per cent claim to have bought alcohol from a shop. Meanwhile, three quarters of 15 year olds who have had alcohol say they've been drunk and, in 2002, 17 per cent of 15 year old girls and 12 per cent of 15 year old boys reported having had unprotected sex as a result of alcohol.

No Proof – No Sale

Many licensed premises already operate a policy whereby young people must produce proof of their age before being served. From 2009, this applies to all licensed premises in Scotland. At the same time, all licensed premises will be required to display a notice stating this.

Alcohol and Driving

In 2002, there were an estimated 820 drink-drive accidents in Scotland. These resulted in 1270 people being injured and 50 deaths. The 'Blood Alcohol Concentration' (BAC) limit is the amount of alcohol we are legally permitted to have in our blood while in charge of a vehicle. However, it is far safer to have none at all. The Road Traffic Act 1988 sets the blood alcohol limit for driving on public roads. Currently, the maximum BAC is set at 80mg per 100ml of blood.

Legal Consequences

If someone is killed through careless driving while under the influence of drink or drugs, it can lead to up to 10 years in prison, an unlimited fine and automatic disqualification from driving (Road Traffic Act, 1991).

Driving or attempting to drive while unfit due to alcohol consumption leads to automatic disqualification (a driving ban), a large fine and the possibility of a prison sentence. How much a person is fined and the length of any prison sentences or disqualifications will depend on circumstances and any history of similar offences.

Drugs

Under the Misuse of Drugs Act 1971, it is an arrestable offence for any person:

- to import or export a controlled drug
- to produce controlled drugs
- to supply or offer to supply a controlled drug to another person
- to be concerned in the supplying of such a drug to another person
- to be involved in making an offer to supply such a drug to another person
- to have a controlled drug in their possession
- to have a controlled drug in their possession, whether lawful or not, with intent to supply it to another
- to cultivate any plant of the cannabis family

For the occupier or any person concerned in the management of any premises, it is an arrestable offence to knowingly permit or suffer any:

- production or attempted production of a controlled drug
- supply, attempt to supply or offer to supply, of a controlled drug
- preparation of opium for smoking
- smoking of cannabis, cannabis resin or prepared opium
- to smoke or otherwise use prepared opium
- to frequent a place used for the purpose of opium smoking

Dangerous and Careless Driving/Riding

Under the Road Traffic Act 1988 it is an arrestable offence for a person:

- to cause the death of another person by driving a mechanically propelled vehicle dangerously on a road or any other public place
- to drive a mechanically propelled vehicle dangerously on a road or any other public place
- to drive a mechanically propelled vehicle on a road or any other public place without due care and attention or without reasonable consideration for other persons using the road or public place
- to ride a cycle on a road dangerously to ride a cycle on a road without due care and attention, or without reasonable consideration for other persons using the road
- to refuse to give or to give the police a false name and address

The remaining offences are normally by way of summons:

- a person driving a mechanically propelled vehicle on a road must stop the vehicle if asked to do so by a constable in uniform
- a person driving a mechanically propelled vehicle on a road, or who a constable has reasonable cause to believe has committed an offence in relation to the use of that vehicle on a road, must produce his licence so as to enable the constable to ascertain the name and address of the holder
- a person required by a constable to produce his licence must, on being so required by the constable, state his date of birth

Minimum Ages for Driving

Table 4.7 Minimum age for driving by category of vehicle

Category	Class of vehicle	Minimum age
A1	Motorcycle not exceeding 125cc and power output not exceeding 11kw.	17
B	Motor vehicle, maximum authorised mass not exceeding 3500kg and not more than 8 passenger seats. Can draw a trailer of maximum authorised mass not exceeding 750kg or larger trailer provided the combined weight does not exceed 3500kg and the authorised mass of the trailer does not exceed the unladen weight of the towing vehicle.	17
D1	Motor vehicle used for the carriage of passengers, more than 8 but not more than 16 passenger seats. Can also draw a trailer of maximum authorised mass 750kg.	18
P	Moped	16

ACTIVITIES

1 In what ways has legislation on buying and selling alcohol changed since the Licensing (Scotland) Act 1976?

2 Describe the law in relation to alcohol and driving and the legal consequences of drink driving.

3 'It is illegal for any person to consume alcohol if under the age of 18 years.' Explain fully why the person who made this statement could be accused of exaggeration?

4 Draw up a table of drug offences and police powers in relation to each drug.

5 Try to find examples of convictions for dangerous driving in national and local newspapers and from the internet. Write an account of three convictions and what punishment was given in each case.

The Structure and Organisation of Scottish Police Forces

There are eight police forces in Scotland, each covering a different region.

The largest force is Strathclyde Police, which has its headquarters in Glasgow. The smallest is Dumfries and Galloway. The Police (Scotland) Act 1967 states that the police authority, the Chief Constable and the Secretary of State for Scotland are all responsible for the Scottish Police Force. Each force is maintained by a police authority or joint board. Northern Police, Central Scotland Police, Grampian Police, Lothian and Borders Police, Strathclyde Police and Tayside Police are maintained by joint police boards. Dumfries and Galloway and Fife Constabularies are directly administered by the councils for their geographical areas.

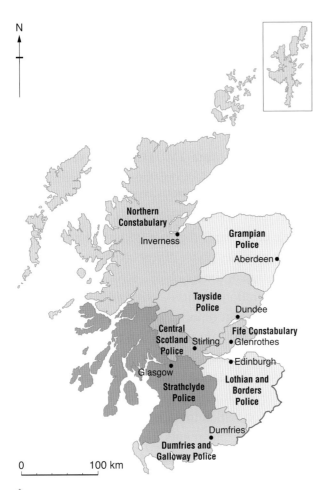

Figure 4.12 Police forces in Scotland

annual report on the statistics and performance in policing of the force area to the police authority. A copy of this report is also sent to the Scottish Parliament. This report is available to the public.

Men and women between 18 and a half and 40 years old can apply to join the police. In some forces, cadet schemes are in place to prepare candidates between 16 and an 18 and a half for a career in the police service. The majority of those entering the police come in at the rank of constable. To be considered for promotions to sergeant and inspector, a pass in the appropriate qualifying examination is required. There are opportunities for accelerated promotion for a small number of police constables.

Uniformed Branch

Members of the uniformed branch have a particular responsibility for preserving the peace, preventing crime, protecting people and property and maintaining public order. This involves both foot and mobile patrols, making best use of modern technology for communications.

Criminal Investigation Department (CID)

The CID investigates crime. It also deals with the checking and classification of crime reports, collects all kinds of information relating to crime in a district, prepares crime statistics and advises on crime prevention. There are CID officers in most of the departments of each police force and they work closely with their uniformed colleagues. Specialist drugs units operate in each force.

The main responsibilities of the police authorities are to set the budget for the force and provide the Chief Constable with the resources (manpower, buildings and equipment) necessary to police the area adequately and efficiently. They appoint officers of the rank of Assistant Chief Constable and above. The ranks within the police service, in descending order of seniority, are Chief Constable (most senior police officer), Deputy Chief Constable, Assistant Chief Constable, Chief Superintendent, Superintendent, Chief Inspector, Inspector, Sergeant and Constable.

The Chief Constable is responsible for police operations. The Chief Constable must comply with instructions from the Lord Advocate, the Sheriff Principal or the appropriate prosecutor in relation to offences and prosecutions. The Chief Constable is required by law to submit an

Traffic Department

Officers of the Traffic Department enforce road traffic laws, traffic management, road safety and other related matters.

Each police force is divided into at least three branches – uniformed, criminal investigation and traffic. Some forces have other specialist units, such as underwater units, mounted (horse-riding) and handlers of police dogs. Most Scottish police forces today also have a community relations branch. This branch deals with advising the public, organises community projects and works with schools.

The Role of the Police

Maintaining Law and Order and Crime Prevention

Foot and mobile patrols not only help to prevent crime and respond quickly to crimes reports, they also help to reassure the public. Police officers will patrol 'hot spots', responding to information from the public in relation to youth disorder, public drinking, irresponsible driving or street noise outside licensed premises. The Central Scotland Police Force has a high profile initiative called Operation Reassurance. This initiative helps to allay public fears about the threat or the perceived threat of crime. This initiative hopes to reduce crime rates in relation to violent crime, crimes of disorder and dishonesty.

Modern Technology

Strathclyde Police was the first force in Scotland to try out a new mobile computer system allowing police to provide a more efficient service. It reduced the amount of time spent filling in forms. The new system consists of mobile data terminal (MDT) in police vehicles and a hand-held electronic note book (called a PDA) for foot patrol officers. The MDT is a digital touch screen which is mounted on the vehicle dashboard. Together with the hand held PDA, it provides police officers with key information at the touch of a screen. The PDAs allow operational officers to record crime and vehicle accident reports, take witness statements and notes. The information can then be downloaded onto a computer when the officer returns to the station without them having to complete any further paperwork. The information will automatically be forwarded to the relevant departments. This saves, on average, one hour per officer, per eight hour shift.

Police in Renfrewshire have been wearing body-mounted CCTV cameras to record incidents of anti-social behaviour. This new

Table 4.8 Operation Reassurance performance in Central Scotland 2005–06

	Target	Actual	Performance
Satisfaction with police visibility	> 40%	41 %	++
Crime clear up rate	> 60%	65 %	++
Racist crime clear up rate	> 83%	84 %	++
Vandalism cleared up	> 630	570	–
Number of residential housebreakings	< 190	146	++
999 calls answered within 10 seconds	> 88%	87 %	+
Urgent call attendance	> 88%	88 %	++

Symbol	Key
++	Target achieved or surpassed
+	Improvement on three year average, but target not fully met
–	Worse than three year average, target not met
>	Denotes figure being greater than
<	Denotes figure being less than

technology is intended to deter crime, gather evidence, provide corroboration and show openness and accountability. It also protects officers while allowing them to carry on with their duties. It also helps to prevent false allegations and therefore increases police accountability. Any photograph not required for evidence will be destroyed within 31 days.

Community Policing

Community policing has been defined as 'the provision of designated officers to cover a specific area of a town or city or, in rural areas, several villages or hamlets. Those officers will be seen as part of the community rather than as a separate entity. They will probably patrol on foot or on bicycle and will communicate with members of the public while they are on patrol. They will not just keep themselves to themselves; they will talk to the public.'

Central Scotland Police have increased the number of community police officers. Working within eight teams, they cover the whole area under the force's boundaries. This new community policing policy emphasises the need for police and communities to work together. Operation Ultraviolet is an example of a community policing initiative in Central Scotland.

↑ **Figure 4.13** Body-mounted CCTV camera

↑ **Figure 4.14** Central Scotland community policing

CASE STUDY

Operation Ultraviolet Throws Spotlight on Dealers in Community

A series of raids targeting drug dealers operating in the heart of Central Scotland communities have been conducted. Twelve addresses across Clackmannanshire, Stirling and Falkirk Area Commands were searched as part of Operation Ultraviolet and more than 20 people are now facing 100-plus charges in relation to drug supply and possession. The enforcement action was taken by police in partnership with health agencies and voluntary sector groups whose aim is to encourage anyone seeking routes out of drug abuse to find help.

The raids were the force's response to a series of incidents in recent months involving near-miss overdoses and a number of fatalities in 2008 linked to drug taking. There were five confirmed fatal drug overdoses last year in Central Scotland and toxicology results are awaited for nine others. There were 95 known incidents of overdoses which resulted in drug users being resuscitated since October 2007. Heroin was the most commonly used drug in many of these cases.

Quantities of heroin and other drugs were recovered during the raids which took place in Alva, Tillicoultry, Sauchie, Tullibody, Cambus, Stirling, Bannockburn, Falkirk and Camelon. Heroin and cannabis were recovered along with cash during the three day operation.

Chief Constable Kevin Smith said: 'Drug dealing is about earning money on the back of the misery of others caused by addiction. The abuse of illegal drugs like heroin, as we have seen in this area, has led to the loss of life and in other cases has come within moments of someone dying. These are the results of dealing activity. Each person who loses their life to drugs is someone's son or daughter – that's the true and very sad cost of this criminal activity to families and communities. That's what Central Scotland Police is absolutely committed to stopping in conjunction with our partners, through rigorous enforcement as well as intervention.'

Fiona Mackenzie, NHS Forth Valley Chief Executive and Chair of the Forth Valley Substance Action Team, said: 'Forth Valley SAT is committed to working with our partners to reduce the health and social harm caused by substance misuse. We have a wide range of services to support those affected by drugs and alcohol, and their families. Reducing the availability of illegal drugs is vital and we value the role which the police play in supporting our remit.'

Source: Central Scotland Police, Thursday, 12th February 2009, www.centralscotland. police.uk/articles/operation_ultraviolet.php

An inquiry focusing on the effectiveness of community policing in Scotland was launched on 18th March 2008 by the Scottish Parliament's Justice Committee. The Committee's Convener, Bill Aitken MSP, said: 'At the conclusion of the Justice Committee's wide-ranging inquiry into the effective use of police resources last year we expressed concern that there was no common definition or approach to community policing in Scotland. It is of such fundamental importance to the people of Scotland that we made a commitment to carry out a second phase inquiry to examine in more detail how effectively community policing is currently being delivered.'

Some of the key questions to be considered by the Committee include:

● What level of priority do the police and other stakeholders give community policing compared with other elements of police work?

● Does more emphasis need to be placed on community policing (with more resources being directed to that area)?

● How do services other than police forces contribute to community policing?

● What examples are there of good practice in relation to community policing (both within Scotland and elsewhere)?

● What examples are there of good practice in relation to community warden schemes and other local initiatives which assist in the policing of communities?

● What impact have community policing initiatives had on: a) community–police relations; b) the prevention and detection of both crime and antisocial behaviour and c) perceptions of crime and antisocial behaviour within communities.(e.g. the 'fear of crime')?

● What challenges face communities in articulating their policing needs and what are the views of communities about participating in policing?

Investigating Crime

Strathclyde Police has a dedicated Criminal Investigation Department (CID), which is responsible for investigating a wide range of crimes. Officers who are particularly interested in the investigation of crime, and demonstrate an aptitude for it, can choose to specialise in CID work. Officers working in CID have the title 'detective' added in front of their rank.

CID is split into three areas:

● Operations
● Intelligence
● Counter Terrorist Intelligence Section

Operations
CID Operations is made up of several sections which work together to tackle all aspects of criminal activity. This includes serious crime, family protection, fraud and computer crime amongst others.

Intelligence
Units within CID intelligence include:

● the Drug Squad and Surveillance Units which target those involved in serious crime
● the Force Intelligence Bureau which gathers, assesses and passes on criminal intelligence to the police service and acts as a point of contact with other law enforcement agencies
● the Statement of Opinion Unit which provides expert drug opinion to the courts and also contributes to the Force drugs education and awareness

Counter Terrorism Intelligence Section
The Counter Terrorism Intelligence Section (CTIS) has a key role in protecting communities and maintaining order. They

work with other agencies within the police and external agencies. They collate, assess and disseminate intelligence related to terrorism, espionage, subversion, serious crime and threats posed to public order.

An article in *The Scotsman* on 21st June 2009 reported that 'Scotland's army of full-time police counter-terror experts has tripled since the Glasgow Airport attack, new figures revealed last night. The Scottish Government said it had now funded almost 170 police and civilian specialists to protect the nation from Islamic and other extremists, compared with just over 60 two years ago.'

The article reported that the Scottish Government confirmed that it would work with the Association of Chief Police Officers in Scotland and other key agencies to develop a programme to prevent terrorism.

CASE STUDY

Strathclyde Police

- Scotland's largest police force
- 8,000 police officers and 2,700 police staff work around the clock
- provides a vast range of policing services on behalf of 12 local authorities
- protects nearly 2.3 million people
- covers 5,371 square miles of Scotland from Glasgow's lively urban areas to the rural remoteness of the Inner Hebrides
- a number of specialist units complement traditional policing

Air Support Unit

- based at the City Heliport, ideal providing the best air support coverage
- available 365 days a year
- can be requested by any Strathclyde Police officer
- initial response time of just two minutesto any incident in the Greater Glasgow area
- each crew consists of two police officers and a civilian pilot
- the pilot drives, the front-seat observer is responsible for navigation, communication with Force Control and the operational control of the aircraft and the rear-seat observer communicates with divisional control rooms, takes aerial photos and operates various items of equipment
- all crew members are equipped with flying helmets, flame-retardant flying suits and life vests
- all crew are trained in underwater escape techniques

Mounted Branch

- horses provide specialist support where the particular strengths of officers on horseback can allow Strathclyde Police to carry out its duties more effectively
- officers of the mounted branch are supported by 'strappers' who are responsible for the day-to-day maintenance of the stables, and a saddler who deals with the repair and maintenance of the saddles, bridles and harnesses
- from their new base at Blairfield Farm, Stewarton, officers and horses cover the entire Force area from Oban to Girvan and from Islay to Forth

Dog Branch

- headquarters are located at Pollok Country Park, Pollok, Glasgow
- the Regional Dog Training Centre is the operational headquarters for the deployment of police dogs throughout the Strathclyde area
- specialises in training general purpose, drugs detection and explosive detection dogs, as well as dogs for offender detection and tactical firearms support
- the Dog Branch consists of two inspectors, six sergeants, 54 constables, five force support staff and 80 dogs, assisting Strathclyde Police divisions on a 24-hour basis, seven days a week

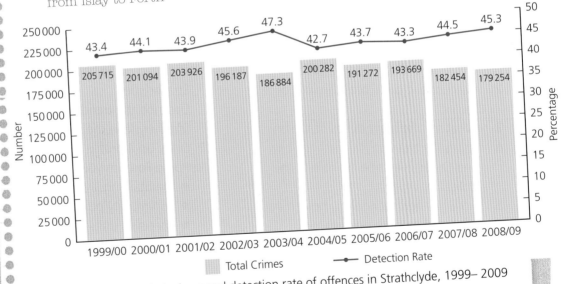

Figure 4.15 Recorded crimes and detection rate of offences in Strathclyde, 1999– 2009

Detection rate definition

A crime is 'detected' if a suspect has been identified and interviewed and there is sufficient evidence to bring a charge. There does not have to be a prosecution.

Table 4.9 Number of police officers (Strathclyde) by rank, gender, ethnicity and detached, March 2009

	Total	Male	Female	Of which are BME*
Chief Constable	1	1	0	0
Deputy Chief Constable	1	1	0	0
Assistant Chief Constable	3	2	1	0
Chief Superintendent	18	16	2	0
Superintendent	62	56	6	1
Chief Inspector	97	86	11	0
Inspector	421	366	55	1
Sergeant	1063	873	190	7
Constable	6285	4493	1792	93
Special Constables	455	291	164	18
Total	7951	5894	2057	102

*BME = Black and Minority Ethnic groups

Source: Strathclyde Police

ACTIVITIES

1 Construct a flow chart to show the structure of the police in Scotland.

2 Describe the three branches of police forces.

3 What are the main duties of the police?

4 Using the heading 'Maintaining Law and Order', describe the role of the police.

5 How has new technology helped and improved modern policing?

6 Write a paragraph on what is involved in Community Policing.

7 Using the heading 'Investigating Crime', give a full account of the work of CID.

8 Study Figure 4.15. Describe the trend in recorded crime between 1998–2009 in Strathclyde.

9 Describe the trend in detection rates in Strathclyde in the same period.

10 Draw up a profile of the work of the Police Force in your area. Include:
   ● maintaining law and order
   ● community policing
   ● specialist units

11 'There is no longer gender or ethnic inequality within the police force.' Study Table 4.9 and give reasons to oppose this statement.

5 The Republic of South Africa

South Africa is the fourth largest country in the continent of Africa. It is roughly five times the size of the UK. It remains one of the least populated countries in Africa with a population of just under 49 million in 2009. The UK has a higher population than South Africa.

Provinces

South Africa is divided into nine main regions known as provinces: Western Cape, Eastern Cape, Northern Cape, North West, Free State, KwaZulu-Natal, Gauteng, Mpumalanga, and Limpopo. Each province has its own government, making decisions about local issues, while national issues are dealt with by the national parliament. Provinces vary hugely in terms of size, population density, concentration of ethnic groups and natural resources. For example, Gauteng is tiny and crowded in comparison with the vast, arid and empty Northern Cape. Mpumalanga is the second smallest province after Gauteng, with the rest all taking between eight and 14 per cent of South Africa's total land area.

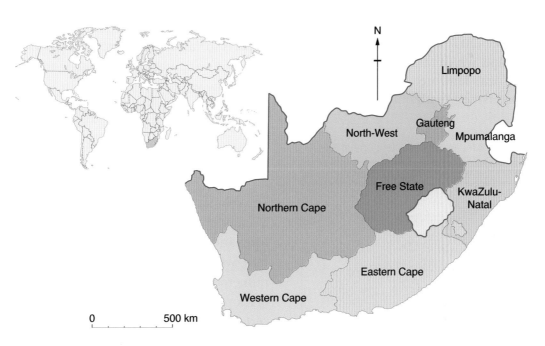

Figure 5.1 Location and provinces of South Africa

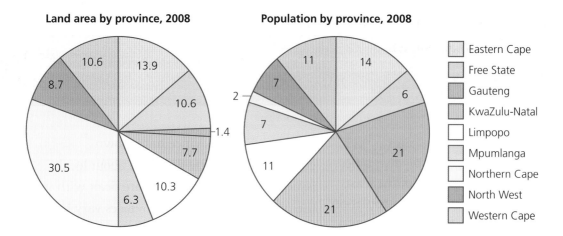

Figure 5.2 Land area and population by province, 2008

Source: Statistics South Africa, mid-year population estimates, 2008

The number of people living in the provinces also varies considerably. Despite being the smallest in land area, Gauteng has the largest share of the South African population. Approximately 10.4 million people (21.4 per cent of the population) live in this province. KwaZulu-Natal is the province with the second largest population, with approximately 10.1 million people (20.7 per cent). By contrast, the Northern Cape, which takes up nearly a third of South Africa's land area, has by far the smallest population (with only 1.1 million people).

This variation translates into huge differences in population density. Gauteng has an average of 576 people per square kilometre, while the Northern Cape is extremely spacious, with only three people for each square kilometre.

Different provinces contribute to wealth in South Africa through its main industries and exports to varying degrees. Nearly two-thirds of exports originate from Gauteng making it one of the wealthiest provinces in South Africa. This may explain why it remains one of the most populated provinces.

Table 5.1 South African provinces by population, 2008

Province	2008 (millions)
Eastern Cape	6.5
Free State	2.8
Gauteng	10.4
KwaZulu-Natal	10.1
Limpopo	5.2
Mpumalanga	3.6
Northern Cape	1.1
North West	3.4
Western Cape	5.3
Total	48.7

Source: Statistics South Africa, Mid-Year Population Estimates, 2008

Ethnic Groups

The colonial history of South Africa has created a nation made up of four ethnic groups: the black indigenous population, people of mixed race, whites and Indians/Asians. There are numerous tribal groups which form part of the black population, these are concentrated in certain provinces. For example, the Zulu tribe in Kwazulu-Natal forms the largest tribal group in South Africa, numbering just over 10 million people in 2009.

Table 5.2 Main industries in the provinces of South Africa, 2009

Province	Main Industries
Eastern Cape	car manufacturing, farming
Free State	mining: gold, coal, uranium and diamonds
Gauteng	commerce, research, manufacturing
KwaZulu-Natal	coal mining, sugar cane plantations, fruit farming
Limpopo	cattle ranching, fruit growing, coal mining, iron ore mining
Mpumalanga	fruit production, forestry, coal mining, paper production
Northern Cape	diamond mining, sheep farming, horticulture, iron ore mining
North West	coal and uranium mining, wheat production, cattle ranching
Western Cape	clothing/textiles, printing/publishing, farming, iron and steel production

Table 5.3 Population of South Africa by ethnic group, 2008

Population Group	Number	Percentage of total (%)
Black	38,565,100	79.2
White	4,499,200	9.2
Mixed race	4,379,200	9.0
Asian/Indian	1,243,500	2.6
Total	48,687,000	100

Source: Statistics South Africa, mid-year population estimates, 2008

Figure 5.3 South Africa is made up of a variety of diverse ethnic groups

Table 5.3 shows that the population of South Africa in 2008 was nearly 49 million. Black Africans are in the majority (approximately 38.6 million) and make up about 79 per cent of the total population. The white population is estimated at 4.5 million, the mixed race population is 4.4 million and the Indian/Asian population is 1.2 million.

ACTIVITIES

1 List the nine provinces in South Africa.
2 What conclusions can be drawn about the differences in population and land area by province?
3 'Well over half of all exports originate in Gauteng.' (Ceril Tsoti) Give one reason to support the view of Ceril Tsoti.
4 Draw a pie chart showing the main ethnic groups in South Africa.

Apartheid

While this part of the course is not specifically examined, it is important to have some understanding of apartheid. It will help you to gain a deeper understanding of why social and economic inequalities continue to exist.

Descendants of white settlers (Afrikaners), mostly from the Netherlands, set up a system based on 'separate development' known as apartheid. The main idea behind it was to ensure that whites (in particular Afrikaners) would have the best possible standard of living. This was done by the governing party at the time, the National Party, who initiated a range of measures designed to concentrate power in their hands and restrict what non-whites could do.

Dividing South Africa

These measures were introduced by the National Party between 1948 and 1990 to support apartheid. The Population Registration Act 1950, Mixed Marriages Act 1949 and the Immorality Acts 1950 and 1957 tried to make sure that the 'purity' of the whites was maintained. White people, who were the minority ethnic group in South Africa, received about 87 per cent of the land. The rest was divided up amongst the black tribes, who were each given a 'homeland'. For example, the Zulu tribe's homeland was KwaZulu-Natal. This allowed the government to claim that black people were not really South African citizens, but were rather citizens of their homeland. It also gave the government the excuse to forcibly remove black people from 'white' South Africa.

Controlling South Africa

The Government hoped to weaken any attempts from the population to unite against apartheid. It relied on harsh and oppressive laws to control black people. The Pass Laws meant every non-white person had to carry identity documents, which were proof that they were entitled to be in 'white' South Africa. The Terrorism Act and Internal Security Act gave the police and security forces enormous powers. Opposition political parties like the African National Congress (ANC) were banned and many members, like Nelson Mandela, were arrested. Schools were segregated on the basis of race, as was employment and housing. This created huge gulfs of inequality between whites and non-whites.

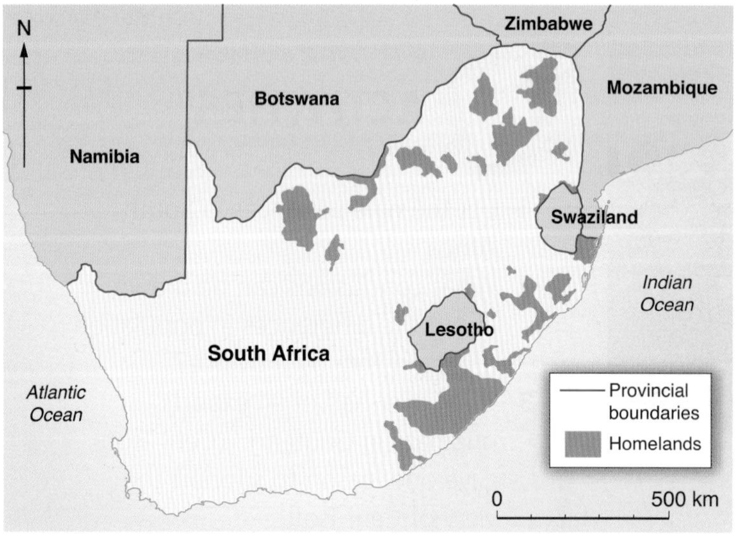

Figure 5.4 South Africa's 'homelands'

⬆ **Figure 5.5** Racial segregation during apartheid

⬆ **Figure 5.6** Nelson Mandela and F.W. De Klerk celebrating the end of apartheid

The Truth and Reconciliation Commission (TRC) was set up after the end of apartheid to allow people the opportunity to discover the truth about past events and forgive perpetuators. The spirit of forgiveness allowed a new fresh beginning in post-apartheid South Africa. The TRC was concerned with activities that happened in the period 1960 to 1994, ending with the year of President Mandela's inauguration. Archbishop Desmond Tutu chaired the hearings which began in April 1996. The Commission received over 6,000 applications for amnesty. This means that people who committed crimes such as murder for political reasons during the apartheid years could be given freedom.

Reform

Mounting international condemnation and economic **sanctions** (where countries refused to trade goods and services with South Africa) led F.W. De Klerk, the Afrikaner leader of the National Party and President of South Africa, to come to the conclusion that apartheid had no future and that Nelson Mandela was the key to peace.

In 1990, the ban on activities of the ANC was removed and Nelson Mandela, its leader, was released from prison. From 1990 to 1994 the ANC and National Party held negotiations and discussions to decide the future structure of the South African Government. They agreed to a written set of rules known as a Constitution. In 1994, the first ever multi-racial elections took place in South Africa. The ANC won the election and Nelson Mandela became the first black President of South Africa.

ACTIVITIES

1 What is meant by the term 'apartheid'?
2 Why did Afrikaners enforce separate development?
3 Briefly describe the main measures introduced to support apartheid.
4 Why do you think opposition political parties were banned?
5 Why were schools segregated?
6 What led to the overhaul of apartheid?
7 Do you agree or disagree with the main aims of the Truth and Reconciliation Commission? Give reasons to justify your answer.

Social Inequalities

After apartheid ended in 1994, the government was confronted with the huge social and economic problems faced by non-whites. On the whole, social inequalities in health, education, housing, crime and justice and economic inequalities in employment and land ownership needed to be addressed. The gulf between whites and non-whites, particularly blacks, was huge.

The ANC government (elected in 1994 under Nelson Mandela) introduced a number of policies to improve social and economic conditions for non-whites. The Reconstruction and Development Programme (RDP) later replaced with Growth, Employment and Reconstruction Programme (GEAR) set targets on a number of social and economic areas.

Health

Free universal access to primary health care (doctors, dentists, pharmacists) was introduced in 1994 for all South Africans. This forms the basis of healthcare delivery programmes and has had a major impact on the South African population.

South Africa's health care system consists of a large public sector and a smaller, but fast-growing, private sector. Health care varies from the most basic primary health care, offered free by the state, to highly specialised hi-tech

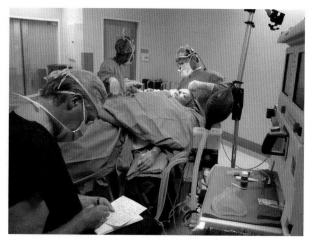

↑ Figure 5.7 A modern, private hospital in South Africa

health services available in the private sector for those who can afford it.

80 per cent of the population, mostly black people, rely on free health care to meet their basic needs. On the other hand, the growing private sector, run largely for profit, caters to high-income earners who tend to be white and members of medical schemes. Foreigners looking for top-quality surgical procedures at relatively affordable prices also rely on private health care in South Africa.

Each year, eight per cent or more of the Gross National Product (an indicator of the wealth produced by the country) is spent on the national health system, including both the public and private health sectors. On average 60 per cent of this is spent in the private sector, which provides care to 20 per cent of the population.

Table 5.4 Inequalities in health in South African provinces, 2009

Health Indicator	KwaZulu-Natal	Western Cape
Life expectancy (years)	43	60
Under five mortality rate (%)	88	37
Adult mortality rate	72	38
HIV positive rate (%)	16	6

↑ Figure 5.8 Awareness of HIV/AIDS and its prevention is increasing in South Africa

The standard of health care varies from province to province. With fewer resources and more poor people, cash-strapped provinces like the Eastern Cape face greater health challenges than wealthier provinces like Gauteng and the Western Cape.

Table 5.4 suggests that provincial health indicators are, to a great extent, determined by the number of HIV/AIDS infections in the province. Of all the challenges that face provincial health departments, controlling the effect of the HIV/AIDS pandemic is crucial to improving the lives, and life span, of their people.

If you take South Africa as a whole, the adult HIV prevalence rate (the proportion of adults who are infected with HIV) was estimated at 11 per cent in 2008, an estimate of 5.35 million people.

The problem of HIV/AIDS is one of the most serious problems facing South Africa today. The high level of infection and the resulting high death rate place a huge strain on health services and the economy. The loss of workers and impact on productivity is costing the South

African economy millions every year. In addition, the high number of orphans (estimated at 1.6 million) created as a result of deaths continues to increase. The government is coming under increasing pressure to increase its spending on treating people with HIV/AIDS. This is because the life expectancy by 2010 is estimated to be about 45 years for people with HIV/AIDS.

In the past, former President Thabo Mbeki was heavily criticised for denying a connection between the HIV virus and AIDS. He publicly stated his belief that anti-retroviral drugs (ARV) are dangerously toxic. This view, which receives little support within the medical community, resulted in the government's refusal to increase the availability of Nevirapine, an ARV that is believed to cut mother-to-child transmission of HIV by 50 per cent. South Africa has slowly moved forward from this hard line approach.

Consequently, the Department of Health developed the National Strategic Plan (NSP) for HIV and AIDS for 2007 to 2011. The plan places new emphasis on treatment and prevention. It also spells out clear, measurable targets, and places a high priority on tracking its progress. The primary goal is to reduce the rate of new HIV infections and to minimise the impact of AIDS on individuals, families and communities.

In 2009, the government set itself the target of getting 80 per cent of HIV-positive South Africans on antiretroviral treatment by 2011, while bringing the rate of new HIV infections down by 50 per cent. Over 630,000 people are currently on the government's anti-retroviral programme, and the spending plan announced in the 2008 budget provides for an increase to 1.4 million people by 2011/12.

Other diseases also continue to plague South Africa. Since 2001, the number of tuberculosis (TB) cases has increased rapidly. The South African cure rate is about 56 per cent, with wide differences between provinces – some districts in KwaZulu-Natal and Mpumalanga have a cure rate below 40 per cent. They have equally failed in trying to reduce the spread of malaria. Although there are fewer cases now that then were during the late 90s, the number of cases has increased since 2005.

Over the years, the health system has had to deal with the loss of experienced health professionals, mainly to developed countries. In President Zuma's State of the Nation address in 2009, he stated 'salaries, working conditions and management skills need to be improved. Expat health and managerial professionals must be attracted back to South Africa.' As a result, in 2009, South Africa's government offered doctors (who were on strike) salary increases ranging from 10 to 60 per cent. Rural allowances were offered to doctors to attract them to remote areas. The government also plans to increase the number of healthcare workers in the country by about 30,000 over the next five years (2009–2014).

Over and above improving the status of health professionals, the Zuma Government also plan to improve the network of clinics, which form the backbone of primary and preventive healthcare in South Africa. The Hospital Revitalisation Programme entered its seventh year in 2009. The programme includes improving infrastructure, health technology (equipment), and quality of care within targeted hospitals in the programme. Four new hospitals were officially opened during 2006–7. In 2007–8, there were 39 active projects. Free primary health care has expanded and 1,600 more clinics have been built. By 2009, about 248 out of 400 public hospitals have been revitalised and refurbished.

Opposition leaders and several interest groups specialising in health have argued that some public hospitals are worse now than they had been during the apartheid era. Helen Zille, leader of the Democratic Alliance, opposes ANC health reform. She argues that 'bad management, not lack of funding, is the main reason for the deteriorating state of South Africa's public health system'. She suggests that hospital manager appointments should be based on qualifications, experience and record.

Education

The South African Constitution of 1994 sets out the vision of education in South Africa. Article 29 states that education is a universal right and it is the duty of the state to make it available and accessible.

The Department of Education is responsible for education across the country as a whole, while each of the nine provinces also has its own education department. Power is further passed down to grassroots level. Each school has a governing body that is elected. They have a significant say in the running of their schools. Compared with most other countries, education receives a large budget – usually around 20 per cent of total government expenditure.

However, more money is always needed to address the huge backlogs left by 40 years of apartheid education. Under that system, white South African children received a quality schooling virtually for free, while their black counterparts had only 'Bantu education' (regarded as inferior). Although today's government is working to reduce the inequalities in education, the apartheid legacy remains. The greatest challenges lie in the

⬆ **Figure 5.9** Contrasting schools in the wealthy and poor provinces of South Africa

poorer, rural provinces like the Eastern Cape and KwaZulu-Natal. Schools are generally better resourced in the more affluent provinces such as Gauteng and the Western Cape.

Literacy rates in South Africa are low. According to official government statistics, just over a quarter of adults are illiterate. One of the basic causes of this is the lack of money to fund education. Although up to 20 per cent of the nation's budget is spent on educational programmes, this is not sufficient to provide every learner with the opportunity to become a confident reader and writer.

In addition, despite clear references to 'equity' and fairness in the Constitution, provinces receive different levels of funding. This inequality between provinces is highlighted in Table 5.5. Other problems include disparities (differences) in the costs of school fees, a lack of teacher training, a shortage of materials in indigenous (local) African languages, and an absence of access to books. While these are certainly key factors in the low literacy rates, specialists also point out that South Africa does not have a 'reading culture'.

Inequality also exists between different groups of people. Many children in South Africa attend private schools. Their parents are the ones who have good jobs e.g. in offices, banks and factories, or they are landowners. They are able to afford high quality education for their

Table 5.5 Inequalities in education between provinces, 2009

Indicators	Western Cape	Gauteng	Limpopo	Mpumalanga
Level of education				
No schooling	3%	4%	16%	15%
Literacy rate	97%	94%	82%	83%
Level of education				
Matriculation pass rate	78%	76%	54%	52%
university entrance pass rate	33%	31%	13%	13%

Source: Adapted from Government Statistics, 2009

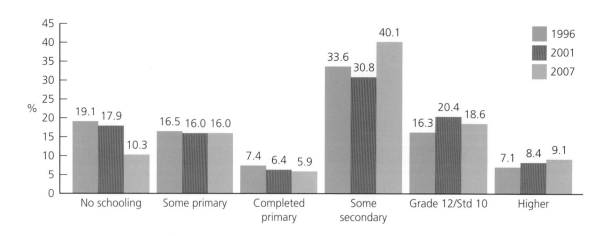

Figure 5.10 Highest level of education amongst population aged 20 years and above

Source: Statistics South Africa, Statistical Release, Community Survey 2007

children. Private schools have the latest resources – interactive whiteboards, computers, laptops and even multi-purpose fitness suites. On the other hand, schools in townships are literally crumbling. Teachers are over worked, ill trained and have high rates of absence. Many teachers are exhausted from 'moonlighting', teaching evening classes in another school to make ends meet. In some cases, violence and drug dealing spill into the classrooms. Sometimes teachers are too scared to confront pupils and their families, even for the most serious breaches of discipline.

However, between 2001 and 2007, there was a notable growth in some secondary schooling among persons aged 20 years and older (from 33.6 per cent in 1996 to 40.1 per cent in 2007). There was also a decrease in the percentage of those with no schooling in this age group since 1996. In 1996, for those aged 20 years and above, no schooling accounted for 19.1 per cent and steadily decreased to 17.9 per cent in 2001 and to 10.3 per cent in 2007. For those with primary education, there was no change since 1996, In 2007, 9.1 per cent of persons aged 20 years and above had completed higher education, against 8.4 per cent in 2001 and 7.1 per cent in 1996.

There are success indicators, including the increasing rate of matriculation pass rates – they have risen from 58 per cent in 1994 to 65 per cent in 2007 (although 2008 figures witnessed a decrease in pass rates). Overcrowding in classrooms has been reduced: by 2006 there was one teacher for every 32 learners, an improvement from one teacher for 43 learners in 1996. In higher education, 140,000 students have been supported through the national financial scheme, which is helping to improve participation of the poor in higher education.

The Zuma Government aims to expand the number of schools where students will pay no fees – the target is that 60 per cent of schools will eventually be no-fee schools. They also aim to ensure that South Africa is completely literate by 2014 through mass literacy campaigns, known as Kha ri Gude.

Zuma's ANC Government will also prepare and employ 15,000 teacher trainers per year and strengthen support for crèches and pre-schools in rural villages and urban centres. They also aim to improve the quality of schooling, particularly the performance in mathematics, science, technology and language development.

CASE STUDY

The poorest schools in terms of resources and results are the all-black schools in urban and rural areas. The government is targeting education for the poorest of the poor in particular, with two notable programmes.

One is '**fee-free schools**', institutions that receive all their required funding from the state and so do not have to charge any school fees to students. These have been carefully identified in the country's most poverty-stricken areas, and will make up 40 per cent of all schools in 2010.

The other is the national '**schools nutrition programme**', which feeds 1.6 million school children every day, including all those attending primary schools in 13 rural and eight urban poverty hot-spots. Over 400 of the poorest high schools in KwaZulu-Natal provide a hot meal to their impoverished learners as a result of the government's school nutrition programme. The total amount the education department will be spending for the nutrition programme in the high schools is 555 million Rand (approximately £4.5 million) for the 2009–10 financial year.

Measures will include provision of incentives for mathematics and science teachers. This basically involves giving extra income to teachers that deliver results.

This is part of a wider drive to promote the status of teachers, by ensuring there are enough available, and improving their pay and training. The government is keen to ensure that quality teaching becomes the norm, rather than the exception.

South Africa's Department of Education launched the Teacher Laptop Initiative in July 2009, making teachers (who are permanently employed by the state) eligible for a monthly allowance to buy a laptop computer. This initiative is part of its strategy to improve ICT in teaching and learning in South Africa. Software loaded on the laptops includes Windows XP or higher, Microsoft Office 2007, anti-virus software, school administration and national curriculum software, and teacher development materials.

Housing

The legacy of the apartheid years is still visible in terms of segregated (separate) residential housing patterns between the races. While the former white, middle class suburbs have welcomed the new prosperous black elite, the formal townships and informal townships (shanty towns) have experienced limited progress. In the formal townships such as Soweto, shopping malls have been built and homes have electricity and inside toilets. But a different picture emerges in the informal communities established on undeveloped land nearby towns and cities. These **shanty towns** or squatter camps tend to be on land that nobody else wants – areas of swampland or disused land along railway lines. Sometimes a shanty town starts as just one or two houses and then grows into a community over time. The settlements range in size from clusters of approximately thirty houses to sprawling areas containing several thousand of these homemade huts, tightly packed together.

Resourceful residents in shanty towns have created makeshift homes using any building materials that they can scavenge, such as broken bits of board, old car tyres, plastic sheeting, corrugated iron, mud and used bricks. Once they have gathered materials, they make themselves small shacks which are usually just one single room in size with poorly-attached roofs. The walls are often lined with sheets of newspaper and the floors are mostly just bare earth or sometimes cheap scraps of lino. It would be unusual for a shack to have a window or for there to be more than one door.

Each shack might be shared by as many as six people. The beds or mattresses are shared by everyone who lives there and the only other furniture might be a chair or two. These shanty towns do not have a power supply and so lamps and candles are the main source of light. Occasionally some people illegally 'tap in' to a power line and siphon off 'free' electricity, but the vast majority of shack-dwellers do not attempt this dangerous practice.

Health issues are a serious concern in these settlements and there have been outbreaks of diseases such as cholera because of the poor hygiene levels. The rivers which are used for drinking water are also used for bathing facilities and for emptying out buckets (toilets) and this shortage of clean water causes infections to spread rapidly. Littering is also very common and the piles of waste attract rats which make conditions ever more unhygienic. However, improvements are being made. Households with access to basic sanitation increased from 50 per cent in 1994 to 71 per cent in 2006. Progress is still being made to eliminate the bucket system in established settlements.

Figure 5.11 A South African shanty town

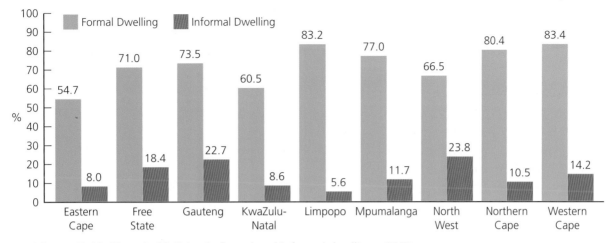

Figure 5.12 Households living in formal and informal dwellings, 2007

Source: Statistics South Africa, Statistical Release, Community Survey 2007

These settlements are also commonly the home of violence. Frustrations caused by unemployment and poor living standards are ignited by the availability of cheap beer and tempers flare when the two are frequently combined. As well as the brawls, the culture of violence and alcohol also leads to sexual assaults and rapes, which are an everyday occurrence.

In contrast, the new rich black middle class live in mansions or high rise luxury apartments with individual swimming pools and barbecue areas, surrounded by trees and tennis courts. They have controlled entrances and security guards as well as emergency security buttons connected to the police, these have become common after a number of kidnappings have taken place throughout South Africa.

Very rich businessmen, politicians, lawyers or entertainers can afford this luxurious lifestyle and quality of housing. They can expect computerised banking and fine meals at top restaurants, nights out at clubs and multiplex cinemas. Top South African executives can easily afford to hire low paid maids, cooks, nannies, chauffeurs, and gardeners.

Figure 5.12 illustrates this inequality between provinces by comparing those living in **formal** housing (e.g. a flat, semi-detached house, unit in a complex) and **informal** dwellings (shack/ squatter settlements).

This Figure indicates that the issue of informal dwellings (shanty towns) is by definition an urban problem, which explains the high figure in Gauteng, the industrial heartland of South Africa. In contrast, one of the poorest provinces, Limpopo, has the lowest number of informal dwellings because of its rural nature.

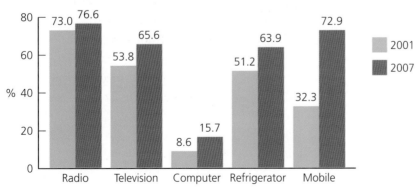

Figure 5.13 Percentage of households with goods in working order, 2007

Source: Statistics South Africa, Statistical Release, Community Survey 2007

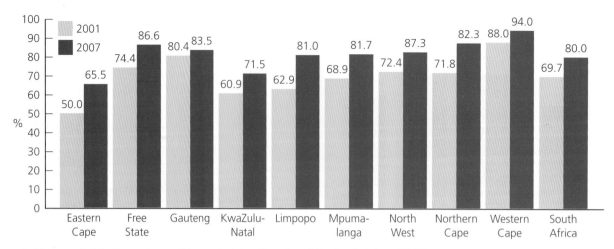

Figure 5.14 Percentage of households using electricity for lighting, 2007

Source: Statistics South Africa, Statistical Release, Community Survey 2007

As well as the progress being made in the types of household people are living in, the basic living standards of South Africans have also improved. Ownership of a radio, television, computer, refrigerator and mobile phone increased considerably between 2001 and 2007, see Figure 5.13.

The availability of electricity for lighting has increased in all nine provinces, with an average of 80 per cent of households in South Africa using electricity for lighting by 2007. The number of households with electricity in Eastern Cape and KwaZulu-Natal is below the national average, whilst in Western Cape almost all households have electricity (94 per cent), see Figure 5.14.

The Zuma Government has promised that all schools and health facilities will have access to basic infrastructure such as water and electricity by 2014. They plan to increase access to secure and decent housing for all South Africans between 2009–2014 through a new housing programme. This will involve the conversion of hostels into family housing units (known as the Community Residential Units Programme), strengthening partnerships with the private sector and the banks to increase access to decent housing. The plan is to create 240,000 more homes.

The Community Residential Units Programme targets households who cannot afford to rent formal accommodation on their low incomes. They are offered the converted hostel accommodation as secure properties to rent.

Other plans include increasing the amount of available rental and social housing by ensuring that provincial governments support the work of community self-building efforts and housing

Figure 5.15 New-build housing in Durban, KwaZulu-Natal

co-operatives. The Zuma Government also aim to ensure that land close to urban centres is made available for low cost, public housing.

Crime

Modern South Africa has a legacy of struggle and violence, resulting from the days of apartheid. Many citizens grew up in an era where brutality and violence were commonplace. White police officers, who gathered the largest share of policing skills, took advantage of the government's generous severance package after the end of apartheid and left the force. This loss of experienced personnel coincided with an explosion of crime across the country which the government has struggled to regain control over.

It should be emphasised that the crime numbers in Table 5.6 are official government figures, which many experts question. While it is true that serious crime has fallen, the perception among citizens is that individual safety is not guaranteed in the streets of South Africa.

High levels of serious crime i.e. murder, rape and serious assault have resulted from the social and economic inequalities that exist. There seems to be a connection between the crime experienced by each province and the average income of the households living in that province. In Limpopo, the province with the lowest average annual household incomes, crime rates were at their lowest. In comparison the province with the highest average annual household income, the Western Cape, had the worst rates for serious crimes. Between 1994 and 2008, the Western Cape's murder, aggravated robbery, and residential burglary rates increased the most out of all provinces (see Table 5.7).

By March 2009 the Western Cape had the second highest number of police officers per general population, one for every 300 people, while Limpopo had the lowest number of police officers per population, one for every 528 people.

Table 5.6 Broad categories of crime committed in South Africa, 2001–2006

Type of Crime	2001–2	2003–4	2005–6
Property (e.g. house burglary, car theft)	727,547	665,318	570,698
Interpersonal (e.g. murder, rape, assault)	640,572	652,959	558,325
Robbery	206,941	229,209	194,449
Theft/commercial	703,542	734,217	551,334
Damage to property/ arson	154,190	167,053	151,887
Drugs/alcohol/firearms	92,947	104,414	142,259
Total	2,525,739	2,553,170	2,168,952

Source: Development indicators, mid term review, 2007

Table 5.7 Crime statistics for wealthy and poor provinces in 2008

Crimes per 10,000 people	Limpopo	Western Cape
murder	13	59
aggravated robbery	45	220
residential burglary	220	876

Overcrowding in prisons is a further difficulty when it comes to battling crime. According to research by the University of West Cape (published in *South Africa Crime Quarterly*) the South African prison population grew from around 117,000 people to approximately 187,000 between 1995 and 2004. However, the availability of prison accommodation (approximately 113,000 places) results in overcrowding.

Figure 5.16 Communities campaign against the violent gangs which continue to undermine personal safety in South Africa

In 2005 the Department of Correctional Services (DCS) began a remission programme with the intention of significantly reducing the prisoner population. Approximately 30,000 prisoners were released at this time. However, the prisons still remained inhumanely overcrowded and in late 2006 the numbers of inmates started to increase again. One of the main causes of overcrowding in prisons is that they are used for the detention of those not yet convicted, people who are still awaiting trial. Another reason why the prison population will continue to be a challenge is that a large number of inmates (who have been convicted) are serving increasingly long-term sentences. This is because the government introduced legislation to increase the minimum prison sentences available for serious crimes such as murder and rape.

Fighting crime, as well as the causes of crime, is a government priority. The Zuma Government has tried to achieve this by recruiting more police officers and providing them with better training, working conditions and pay. They also aim to include communities in their efforts to reduce crime, for example, by establishing street committees and community

courts. The effectiveness of these is likely to be limited because of the fear that ordinary members of the public may have of criminals.

ACTIVITIES

1 What are the benefits of private health care in South Africa?
2 Why is HIV/AIDS a major problem in South Africa?
3 How is the government addressing the problem of AIDS?
4 What recent progress has been made in health care provision?
5 Why do some ethnic groups perform better in school than others?
6 'Little progress has been made in education from 1996–2007'. Give reasons to oppose this view.
7 What impact has the Schools Nutrition Program had on learners?
8 What are the main housing problems in South Africa?
9 Describe the main features of shanty towns.
10 What policies has the Zuma Government introduced to improve housing conditions?
11 Draw a memory map outlining why crime in South Africa is high compared to other developed nations.
12 Describe the main ways in which the government is trying to improve the standard of living of the poorest people in South Africa.

Economic Inequalities

Apartheid excluded the majority of South Africans from the ownership of land and the control of the natural assets and resources the land provided. It severely restricted education and access to the labour market for black people, as well as other minority groups. Although they were able to find employment in low-paid jobs, taking part in the economy in any meaningful way was heavily restricted.

Many ordinary South Africans are disappointed with the lack of progress being made and set up their own pressure group to demand fairer land distribution more quickly. The Landless People's Movement represents these rural people and has just over 100,000 members. In 2009, they participated in peaceful protests and marches outside the Supreme Court.

Land Redistribution

Apartheid meant that the majority of land was allocated to white people. This meant the forced removal of black and mixed raced people from their land, relocating them in other areas. Maintaining control of the land helped the white population to protect and extend their own wealth. This concentration of land in the hands of whites, particularly Afrikaners, contributed to the increasing economic inequality in South Africa.

This inequality in the ownership of land signalled an urgent need for land reform and this was a priority for the ANC when they were first elected in 1994. The government attempted to tackle the issue by buying back land from the predominantly white landowners who had taken over land belonging to others during apartheid. Under this system, the current landowners needed to be willing to sell their land, at a fair price. Only then can the land be redistributed to the black people who had lodged claims for it based on their prior ownership.

The land reform proved to be very slow-moving and complex. In 1994 the government set a

target of transferring a third of white-owned agricultural land to black farmers by 2014, which amounts to 24.9 million hectares. The total transferred by 2009 amounted to just over five million hectares and in November 2009 land reform officials announced the deadline was being pushed back to 2025 due to lack of funds. The government has admitted that many land claims are difficult to process because of the high illiteracy rate among rural communities and also because many claimants lack identity documents.

⬆ **Figure 5.17** The Landless People's Movement

Wealth and Employment

Since 1994, Black Economic Empowerment (BEE) has been adopted as an initiative of the South African government, aimed at improving the economic status of black people in the economy.

The South African government passed the Employment and Equity Act in 1998, which legalised **affirmative action** or positive discrimination. Affirmative action is the use of bias in favour of a group which has been discriminated in the past. This was necessary in South Africa to make up for the hundreds of years of discrimination against black, mixed race and Asian people under apartheid. This law allows non-whites to get jobs working for the government, in the civil service and in the police forces, not only at the bottom, but also in senior positions. Private companies who have a high percentage of non-whites in management positions are offered preferential treatment and secure federal contracts.

The Black Economic Empowerment Act of 2003 outlined the required targeted areas of development, i.e. improved employment and involvement within the South African economy. BEE was intended to create a fairer, more equal society. Supporters claimed that it was the best means of smoothing out racial inequalities. Initially, mining and financial sectors were the main areas of change, but this has expanded into other sectors such as tourism and education. Thousands of black people were hired as civil servants and appointed to the boards of private and state owned firms.

As a result of BEE and other efforts, South Africa's black middle class has grown by thirty per cent in just over a year (2007), with their numbers increasing from two million to 2.6 million. Their spending power, known as disposable income, also increased from 130 billion Rand to 180 billion Rand. Despite this appearance of a black 'elite', limited change in economic power has occurred and ninety per cent of the economy is still controlled by white people.

The combined annual spending power of South Africa's 'black diamonds' (middle class black people) had grown tremendously, as Table 5.8 shows.

With this growing wealth, the number of black middle class families living in the suburbs of South Africa's metropolitan areas has accelerated from 23 per cent in 2005 to 47 per cent in 2007.

Opponents of BEE point out that the best person should always be chosen for the job to be done, regardless of the colour of someone's skin. Affirmative action leads to corruption and jobs for the friends and families of the government. Zuma himself stated in 2009 that South Africa needs to review the way in which black economic empowerment (BEE) is put into effect. He said that while affirmative action and BEE had substantially increased the country's black middle class, 'we are not convinced that it has succeeded in addressing the economic and social inequalities in our society'. However, he reiterated the ANC's commitment to affirmative action as a policy, saying it was 'unthinkable' for the ANC to abandon it.

Table 5.8 Annual claimed spending power

	2005 (in billion Rand)	2007 (in billion Rand)
White population	230	235
Black population (total)	300	335
Black 'diamonds'	130	180

Source: University of Cape Town's Unilever Institute of Strategic Marketing, Black Diamond 2007: On the Move

Figure 5.18 'Black diamonds'

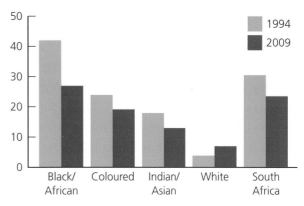

Figure 5.19 Unemployment rate by ethnic group, 2009

Source: Statistics South Africa, Statistical Release, Community Survey 2009

Table 5.9 Black senior and top managers, 2001–2005

%	2001	2005
Senior managers	25.1	27.2
Top managers	19.1	27.5

Others argue that huge differences still remain between ethnic groups and therefore BEE has had limited success. Differences in rates of unemployment still continue to exist between races.

Figure 5.20 South Africa will host the World Cup in 2010

CASE STUDY

The World Cup which is being hosted in South Africa in 2010 has created many jobs in the construction industry. The building work involved in creating stadiums and improving the country's infrastructure has offset the credit crunch in many respects. The 2010 World Cup will create a multiplier effect (boost) in South Africa, increasing the nation's income and wealth because of additional visitors etc.

Poverty

The government report *Towards a Fifteen Year Review* (published in 2008) concluded that 'income poverty' actually declined in South Africa over the last fifteen years. In 1995 about 53 per cent of households were living below that line but by 2009 that figure has decreased to 41 per cent.

South Africa's benefit system currently supports 13 million people. The social grants system is the largest form of government support for the poor. The most widespread social grant is for child support, given to 7.8 million people in 2007 compared to 34,000 in 1999. Various studies have confirmed that social grants were well targeted and contributed considerably to poverty reduction. Of social grants, the report indicated that 62 per cent of the total went to the poorest 40 per cent of households.

South Africa is proportionally one of the world's biggest spenders on social grants. It will spend an extra 13.2 billion Rand on benefits in 2009–10 to help protect poor South Africans during the global credit crisis. The amount payable for the old age, disability and care dependency grants all increased in April 2009. Zuma's Government are also considering raising the age of eligibility for the child support grant to 18, subject to affordability.

Despite the decrease in the amount of poor people in the country, the report found a widening gap between rich and poor in the country. This is because whilst many poor South Africans were lifting themselves from abject poverty, the rich in South Africa, especially the new black middle classes, were getting even richer. Economic and social inequalities among black people have widened since 1994.

ACTIVITIES

1 Why is there a higher rate of unemployment amongst the black population?
2 Why is the South African government redistributing land?
3 Describe in detail the ways in which South African governments have tried to reduce economic inequalities in South Africa.
4 Copy and complete the table below by placing the following statements under the appropriate column.

Reasons for and against Black Economic Empowerment

For	Against

- employment for non whites
- makes up for previous discrimination against non whites
- will reduce social and economic inequality
- the economy will suffer if skilled white workers lose jobs
- it opens up employment opportunities
- the best person should always be chosen for the job
- there will be growing discontent unless action is taken
- many consider it a reintroduction of apartheid
- unemployment levels for blacks and other non-whites are much higher than for whites
- social and economic policies introduced by Zuma will rectify inequalities without BEE

South African Politics

South Africa has been a democracy since the demise of apartheid in 1994. The South African constitution, which details the rights of South African people, is widely regarded as the most progressive constitution in the world, with a Bill of Rights second to none. This guarantees all citizens the right to vote and equal political rights. All South Africans are now able to participate fully in the political system through voting, joining political parties, campaigning and standing for election.

Human rights are explicitly emphasised in the constitution. They feature in the preamble, where the intention of establishing 'a society based on democratic values, social justice and fundamental human rights' is stated.

National Government

South Africa has a federal system of government which is split into three parts: legislature, executive and judiciary.

Legislature – this is national parliament and is based in Cape Town. It is made up of two houses: the National Assembly and the National Council of Provinces (NCOP). This is often referred to as a **bicameral** system because there are two distinct chambers with responsibility for passing laws in South Africa.

The National Assembly consists of 400 Members of Parliament, elected every five years. They are elected using a system of proportional representation (PR) and so the percentage of the vote that is achieved nationally is reflected in the number of seats gained by a political party.

The National Council of Provinces consists of 90 representatives, ten for each of the nine provinces. These representatives are put forward by the provincial parliaments to oversee the activities of the national government.

Table 5.10

President	Terms of Office
Nelson Mandela	1994 – 1999
Thabo Mbeki	2000 – 2008
Kgaleme Motlanthe	2008 – 2009
Jacob Zuma	2009 –

Executive – this is made up of the President, Deputy President and Cabinet. The President is elected every five years (and serves a maximum of two terms). The President is chosen by the National Assembly and then chooses their Cabinet and passes laws. The dominance of the ANC ensures that the leader of the ANC becomes President.

Judiciary – South Africa has an independent judiciary, subject only to the constitution. The judiciary is comprised of the Constitutional Court, the highest federal court in South Africa, who interpret and enforce the law. Constitutional Court justices are appointed by the President and confirmed by Parliament. They are appointed for life. There are 11 justices on the Court: one chief justice and ten

Figure 5.21 National Assembly of South Africa

associate justices. The Constitutional Court has the power to declare Acts of Parliament or actions of the executive branch or provincial governments **unconstitutional**, and they are stopped from becoming law. They are like the independent guardians of the constitution.

Provincial Government

Each province has its own system of government that closely mirrors that of the federal system. There is an executive branch in the form of a Premier, a legislative branch in the form of a Parliament and a judicial branch in the form of Courts.

The Premier acts as the head of the province along with their provincial Cabinet, known as the Executive Council. This provincial government makes decides on certain things for the area e.g. health and education.

Local Government

South Africa is also divided into local municipalities, or councils, headed by the Mayor. The Mayor works with other elected representatives to improve local conditions that have an impact on the lives of ordinary people.

Increasingly, municipal councils have come under pressure to deliver efficient and cost-effective local services. For example, the delivery of electricity is the responsibility of councils.

Elections

National elections take place every five years using a Proportional Representation system known as the National List, where the percentage of votes cast for a political party closely match the percentage of seats won by that political party. Currently in South Africa,

Table 5.11 The main political parties in South Africa's parliament

Political Party	Description
African National Congress (ANC)	The ANC remains the most popular party for historical reasons. It is the party which opposed apartheid and therefore continues to draw support from the majority of the population i.e. black Africans.
New National Party (NNP)	Formerly the Nationalist Party, the NNP ruled South Africa for the over 40 years of the apartheid era, from 1948 to 1994. The second-largest party after the first democratic elections in 1994, its voter base has since abandoned it in large numbers. In August 2004 the NNP's national executive took a unanimous decision to disband the party. Most of its former representatives now belong to the ANC.
Democratic Alliance (DA)	This party has replaced the NNP as the official opposition to the ruling ANC. It is the governing party in the Western Cape province, led by Helen Lille. Its main supporters are whites, people of mixed race and Asians
Inkatha Freedom Party (IFP)	The IFP, led by Mangosuthu Buthelezi, draws its support largely from Zulu-speaking South Africans. Its stronghold is the rural areas of KwaZulu-Natal. It lost heavily to the ANC in the 2009 elections in KwaZulu-Natal.
United Democratic Movement (UDM)	The UDM was formed in 1997 by Bantu Holomisa, who was expelled from the ANC after accusing a top party official of corruption. His party campaigns around issues which it believes the government is handling badly.
Congress of the People (COPE)	This is a relatively new political party formed in 2008 by former Xhosa members of the ANC who has supported Thabo Mbeki. It came third in the 2009 elections.

Table 5.12 National Assembly election results 2009

Political Party	Percentage of the Vote	Number of Assembly Seats
ANC	66 %	264
DA	17 %	67
COPE	7 %	30
IFP	5 %	18
Other	5 %	21

Source: IEC, 2009

thirteen political parties are represented in parliament.

Political Parties

The electoral system adopted in South Africa encourages the participation of a larger number of political parties in the electoral system.

Election Results and Analysis

South Africa held national and provincial elections to elect a new National Assembly as well as the provincial legislature in each province on 22nd April 2009.

The ANC received around 66 per cent of the 17.9 million valid votes cast, securing 264 of the 400 seats in South Africa's National Assembly. They were followed by the DA with 16.6 per cent of the vote (67 seats in parliament) and the recently established COPE with 7.4 per cent (30 seats).

The IFP secured 18 seats in parliament, while the UDM, Freedom Front Plus and Independent Democrats secured four seats each. The African Christian Democratic Party got three seats in parliament, the United Christian Democratic Party got two, and the Azanian People's Organisation, Azanian People's Convention, Minority Front and Pan Africanist Congress of Azania got one seat each.

In the provincial elections, the ANC won with an outright majority in eight of South Africa's nine provinces, including KwaZulu-Natal, Here

the IFP, who were the largest party in the 1994 and 1999 elections, suffered a humiliating defeat with its share of the vote falling to 22 per cent compared to the ANC's 64 per cent. Jacob Zuma, leader of the ANC and a Zulu himself, played the Zulu card. The province which proved to be the exception was the Western Cape, where Helen Zille's DA received 52 per cent of the vote, followed by the ANC with 33 per cent and COPE with seven per cent. This was the first time that the ANC had lost control of a province and Helen Zille declared that it was a triumph for democracy and provided hope that South Africa would not become a one party state.

Table 5.13 National Council of Provinces election results 2009

Political Party	Seats
ANC	62
DA	13
COPE	8
IFP	2
Other	5

Source: IEC, 2009

The ANC was the ruling party prior to the 2009 elections, having won nearly 70 per cent of the vote at the 2004 elections. During its term in office, Jacob Zuma was elected to the party presidency taking over from Thabo Mbeki. One of the main reasons for Zuma's victory lies in the wide degree of support he receives from the broad alliances that make up the ANC, notably the Congress of South Africans Trade Unions

(COSATU) and the South African Communist Party (SACP).

Table 5.14 Provincial results (selected parties) Western Cape, 2004

Party	Votes	Seats
ANC	709052	19
DA	424832	12
NNP	170469	5
IDM	122867	3
ACDP	53934	2
UDM	27489	1

Table 5.14 Provincial results (selected parties) Western Cape, 2009

Party	Votes	Seats
DA	1012568	22
ANC	620918	14
COPE	152356	3
IDM	92116	2
ACDP	28995	1

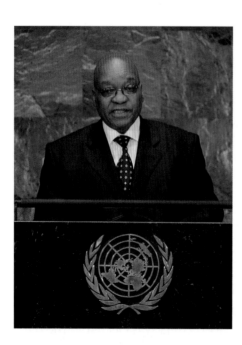

Figure 5.22 Jacob Zuma

The resignation of Mbeki and allegations of corruption made against Zuma created severe tensions and splits within the ANC. (Though the corruption scandal involving an arms deal was dismissed by the courts.) This tension eventually led to members of the ANC creating their own political party: Congress of the People (COPE). The DA capitalised on the controversy that plagued Jacob Zuma and the ANC by offering alternative politics that would be 'ethical' and open. Their share of the vote has actually increased since the 2004 elections. The mixed race and Asian voters did not trust the ANC and gave their support to the DA.

Zuma made costly campaign promises to eradicate (wipe out) poverty, raising the expectations and hopes of ordinary South Africans. Unfortunately, the world economic recession has meant that the increase in government spending has been halted. Many more South Africans are joining the 40 per cent who already live below the poverty line and high inflation has led to an increase in food and fuel prices. This has led to tension between the ANC Government and its supporters in COSATU and SACP. In July 2009, public sector strikes for higher salaries (including doctors and teachers) have taken place all across South Africa.

Opposition to the ANC

Some groups in South Africa, such as the Afrikaners and the IFP, have demanded greater self-government. They continue to oppose the ANC. Afrikaners wish to protect their language and culture which they feel has been eroded. Since the new constitution they have seen their political power slip. Indeed Orania remains the only Afrikaans community. This has led some extremist groups within the Afrikaners community to demand an independent homeland.

The Zulus, who make up the IFP, see themselves as a separate group in South Africa. They want more control over their own affairs. Their political power is confined only to KwaZulu-Natal. Tension between the IFP and the ANC spilled out into violent clashes during the 2009 elections. However the election of a Zulu as President of South Africa has weakened the IFP demand for greater autonomy.

Despite opposition, the ANC continue to dominate politics in South Africa. Tables 5.15, 5.16 and 5.17 illustrate the level of support the ANC continue to demand at all levels of government.

Table 5.15 Votes and seats won by the ANC in the National Assembly

Year	Percentage of votes	Seats won
1999	66.3	266
2004	69.6	279
2009	66.0	264

Source: ICE

Table 5.16 Votes cast for the ANC by selected province for Provincial Elections

Province	2009
Free State	71%
Limpopo	85%
Mpumalanga	86%
North West	73%

Source: ICE

Table 5.17 Votes cast for the ANC in 2006 local government elections

Province	2006
Eastern Cape	82%
Limpopo	84%
Mpumalanga	81%
North West	77%

Source: ICE

More people vote for the ANC than any other political party. The lack of an effective and united opposition partly helps to account for the ANC's success in elections. Millions of black South Africans still regard the ANC as the party that challenged the apartheid system. They played a key and active role in the struggle to topple apartheid. People feel they have a duty to vote for the party that did so much for them. There is a genuine obligation rooted in South Africans who feel that they have to vote for the ANC. There is a moral and ethical duty. Moreover, they support ANC policies that are designed to reduce social and economic inequalities.

South Africa has come a long way from the apartheid era. The first multi-racial elections were held in 1994 allowing non-whites the opportunity to exercise their right to vote. Some people argue that South Africa has remained a stable democracy since the end of apartheid, others disagree.

ACTIVITIES

1 Give two ways in which all racial groups in South Africa can now take part in politics.
2 Outline the main features of the South African political system.
3 Why do the ANC continue to do well in elections?
4 Explain in detail why the ANC Government in South Africa continues to face opposition from within South Africa.

6 The People's Republic of China

The Land and the People

The People's Republic of China is the world's fourth largest country, with Beijing as its capital. This vast country has a very diverse climate and faces natural hazards such as earthquakes, droughts, floods and tsunamis. Chinese authorities have warned that climate change may make the risk of flooding worse.

As news coverage during the Beijing Olympics in 2008 has shown, pollution from reliance on coal for power is a huge problem.

With a population of over 1.3 billion, China is the most populous country in the world. Its majority ethnic group is Han Chinese. The main language spoken is Mandarin. Other ethnic groups include Zhuang, Manchu, Uyghur and Hui.

Figure 6.1 China's location and provinces

Political and Economic Ideology

Capitalism

Capitalism is a set of ideas which form the basis of the way some countries and their governments run the economy. It is an **economic ideology**. The USA, UK, France, Japan and Germany are examples of countries that have capitalist economic systems. In a capitalist system, individuals are free to own their own land, property and businesses. Businesses are either owned by individuals, groups of people or shareholders. Decisions about what should be produced are left to individuals.

Socialism

Socialism is a political and economic theory or system in which factories, businesses and industries are owned by the community **collectively**, usually through the state. Socialists believe that equality is essential if a society is to be free and fair. Socialists believe that the state is central to creating social justice. Therefore socialists are in favour of state run, health care and education. At the very least, the most important industries should be owned and run by the state in the interests of the people and the workers. In western nations, for example, in the UK and the USA, states like China are referred to as 'communist states'. However, China does not refer to itself as communist, instead it regards itself as socialist. A country might call itself socialist but in practice, its political and economic system may not live up to the title.

Communism

Communism is a political and economic system under which all **inequalities would be eradicated**. Wealth would be distributed equally: taken from the bourgeoisie (middle classes) and redistributed amongst the proletariat (the workers). Unlike socialism, a communist country would be a stateless society. But as with socialism, there would be common ownership of factories, businesses and industries. There are different ideas of what communism actually is. In *The Communist Manifesto*, Karl Marx and Friedrich Engels argued that communism was as an inevitable end to a process where economies would move from capitalism to socialism and then to communism. Lenin believed that communism would only take place through revolution. The type of communism associated with China and Mao Zedong was influenced by Marxist-Leninism and is often termed Maoism and referred to as 'Mao Zedong Thought'. It is defined as 'Marxist-Leninism in a Chinese context'. The idea was that a strong political party would seize power on behalf of the workers and peasants and control the state.

A Brief History of Politics in China

From Emperors to Revolution: Timeline

221 BC– 1912 China was ruled by emperors.

1912 The collapse of the Qing Dynasty. Ruled by warlords. Although Sun Yat-Sen, a Chinese revolutionary with a democratic vision for China, became the first provisional President of the Republic of China. He found democracy impossible to achieve due to his struggles with the warlords who divided China.

1920s– 1930s The Kuomintang (KMT) remained the main opposition to the rule of the warlords. In 1923, the KMT allied with the Communist Party of

China (CCP) against the warlords. The CCP had been founded in 1921 and Mao Zedong was at the founding meeting. While maintaining his CCP membership, Mao served on the KMT central committee. However, the KMT broke away from the CCP in 1927. In the Autumn Harvest Uprising, Mao suffered defeat after leading a small peasant army against local landlords and the KMT in Hunan.

1945 Civil war broke out between the KMT and the CCP.

1949 Mao and his Red Army defeated the KMT in 1949. On 1st October, Mao declared the founding of the People's Republic of China (PRC). Since then the CCP has dominated politics at every level.

The Chinese Communist Party (CCP)

Mao Zedong dominated the leadership of the CCP from the 1940s until his death in 1976. Mao was a very controversial leader. A personality cult developed which spread across China. Although Mao is still revered in China, he was a ruthless leader.

↑ **Figure 6.2** Mao Zedong

In 1958 Mao launched a five year economic plan – the 'Great Leap Forward'. The private production of food was banned and peasants were instead made to work together in large communes. Together with inefficient farming techniques, these changes in farming led to famine and poverty and millions of deaths across China through starvation. This was due to the fact that there was little incentive for the peasants to produce large volumes of food as production was not for profit any more.

From 1966 to 1976, Mao maintained his grip on China's social, economic and political life during the 'Cultural Revolution'. School children spent their lessons learning Mao's sayings such as 'Chairman Mao is the red sun in our hearts'. These sayings were gathered together in 'The Little Red Book'. Everyone was given a copy and told to study it.

After Mao's death in 1976, Deng Xiaoping became *de facto* (in practice) leader of China. However, he was never officially either Chairman of the Party or President. Deng had not totally agreed with Mao's policies and acknowledged Mao had made some mistakes. While Deng was a leader during the 1949 Revolution, he was negatively labelled during the Cultural Revolution as a 'capitalist-roader'. During this period of Deng Xiaoping's leadership great changes were made to the economy. However, politically, China remains a one party state. Deng may have brought about some successful changes to the economy but he used a heavy-handed approach during the pro-democracy demonstrations in Tiananmen Square in 1989.

In the 1990s under the leadership of Jiang Zemin, China experienced substantial economic growth. China's relations with the rest of the world improved. Hu Jintao became President in 2002.

Table 6.1 Chinese Communist Party (CCP) Leaders (1945–2008)

Date	General Secretaries	Date	Chairmen
1956-1966	Deng Xiaoping	1945-1976	Mao Zedong
1966-1980	Position abolished	1976-1981	Hua Guofeng
1980-1987	Hu Yaobang	1981-1982	Hu Yaobang
1987-1989	Zhao Ziyang	1982 Position abolished	
1989 – 2002	Jiang Zemin		
2002 – present	Hu Jintao		

Table 6.2 Presidents of the People's Republic of China (PRC)

Date	President	
1954–1959	Mao Zedong	
1959–1968	Liu Shaoqi (Arrested and imprisoned in 1968)	In 1966 Chairman Mao introduced the Cultural Revolution to re-establish his authority and overthrow Liu Shaoqi government.
1968–1981	After Liu's expulsion, Mao decided there would be no presidency.	
1981	Song Qingling	Song Qingling was named Honorary President.
1982–1988	Li Xiannian	Presidency re-introduced but without much power.
1988–1993	Yang Shangkun	From 1988 the presidency became more powerful again.
1993–2002	Jiang Zemin	
2003–present	Hu Jintao	

The Composition of the Chinese Communist Party

Composition

In 2008 the Chinese Communist Party (CCP) had 70 million members. This was equivalent to around five per cent of the total population. In 2004, 13 million (18.6 per cent) of the party's members were women, and 4.4 million (6.3 per cent) were from ethnic minorities. Some 56.6 per cent of the party's membership had received a high school education and only 27.3 per cent had received a college education. Joining the party traditionally offered the promise of a better quality of life and membership is still important for ambitious government officials. However, for ordinary Chinese people the CCP is becoming less important.

The Structure of the Chinese Communist Party

The CCP continues to dominate government and society. Nevertheless, China's size (both in terms of population and geography) and its diversity means that leaders must increasingly build agreement for new policies among party members, local and regional leaders, influential non-party members, and the population at large.

Party control is tightest in government offices and in urban, economic, industrial, and cultural settings. The party has less control in the rural areas, where the majority of the people live. Theoretically, the party's highest body is the National Party Congress, which is supposed to meet at least once every five years. The primary organs of power in the Communist Party include:

- the nine-member Politburo Standing Committee
- the Politburo, consisting of 24 full members (including the members of the Politburo Standing Committee)
- the Secretariat, the principal administrative mechanism of the CCP, headed by the General Secretary
- the Military Commission
- the Discipline Inspection Commission, which is charged with rooting out corruption within the party

The Structure of Government in China

The government's role is to put CCP policies into practice. The government has always been controlled by the party. The primary organs of state power are:

- the National People's Congress (NPC)
- the President

- the State Council which includes the Premier (Prime Minister) and a Cabinet to accommodate alternate views
- 28 Ministries

Political Participation in China

In China, people have the opportunity to participate in the political process in a number of ways:

- campaigning during elections
- standing as a candidate for election
- voting in elections
- becoming a member of the Chinese Communist Party (CCP)
- holding political office
- taking part in protests and demonstrations

However, as the Chinese Communist Party (CCP) controls the political system at all levels, political positions are usually filled by

ACTIVITIES

1 Find out more about the different ethnic groups in China and draw up profiles of each group.
2 What are the main features of the following political ideologies:
   - Capitalism   - Communism
   - Socialism   - Maoism
3 In groups discuss what you perceive to be the best and the worst aspects of:
   - Capitalism   - Communism
4 Name China's leading political party since 1949. Using the information in this chapter and other sources, draw up a brief profile of each leader.
5 Summarise the composition and membership of the Chinese Communist Party (CCP).
6 Why is it increasingly important for China's leaders to find more agreement on its policies?
7 Geographically, where does the CCP have most control and where does it have least control?
8 Theoretically, what is the highest body of the CCP?
9 What is the Chinese government's main role?

members of the CCP. Moreover, Chinese citizens do not get the chance to choose their national leaders. While Chinese citizens can take part in protests, they are restricted in the issues they are allowed to protest about. For example, they are not allowed to take part in demonstrations which criticise the CCP or the political system.

Voting in Elections

Direct elections, where people can vote for their representatives only take place at the local level. This includes:

- elections to Local Congresses
- village elections where village councils and chiefs are elected
- experiments in township elections
- experiments in county level elections

Local Congresses

In each province, all people over 18 are able vote to elect deputies for the Local People's Congress which sits for five years. This is the only level of government where the CCP allows the Chinese public to participate in the choice of their representatives.

Independent candidates have had some success in elections for seats in Local People's Congresses. In 2003, two independent candidates won seats in the city of Shenzhen. However, almost all independent candidates for these district congresses do not succeed. Nevertheless the number of successes is increasing rapidly from 100 nationwide in 2003 to more than 40,000 in 2007.

Village Elections

The introduction of village elections in 1988 was welcomed by those in China who believed China's political system to be unfair and undemocratic. The introduction of these elections has been praised by those who see it

Figure 6.3 Village elections

as the road to real choice for the people of China. Almost three quarters of a million villages (involving around 700 million voters) across the country now hold such elections to elect village committees, which make decisions on important issues such as land and property rights. These elections are held every three years. The intention of introducing these competitive elections was to develop leaders who were able to lead the rural economies efficiently and also to implement national policies. With the dismantling of collective farming (the commune system), there was a need to find competent people to govern.

While there are many problems with these village elections, they have had some success.

Some of this success concerned the Chinese authorities. It became apparent to them in the early 1990s that only 40 per cent of elected village chiefs were CCP members. The national leaders of China gave instructions to local officials to ensure that the CCP kept its leading role. Now, once again, the village chiefs are mainly CCP members. However, the percentage of village chiefs that are CCP members varies from region to region. In the provinces of Guangdong, Hubei and Shandong over 90 per cent of the village leaders are from the CCP compared to an average of 65 per cent in Fujian and Zhejiang. Now, when village chiefs who are not members of the CCP are elected, they are nearly always asked to join the CCP. This is in a way a compromise, as the villagers get the leaders they want but the CCP retains its control.

Other problems such as nepotism (favouring family members), vote-buying and the selection of incompetent or corrupt leaders damage the success of these exercises in democracy. Those who are in favour of village elections think that despite the problems, village elections are a good way of introducing Chinese citizens to democratic practices.

Experiments in Township Elections

In the mid-1990s in Buyun (a remote part of Sichuan province) some experiments in township elections began. This process was conducted by political reformer Zhang Jingming who had noticed that the provincial party bosses were unpopular and wanted to improve the relationship between the people and their representatives. In this election, a mayor is elected. When it was first introduced, the media reported it unfavourably across China. It was reported that they went against the section of the Chinese Constitution which states that the Local People's Congress has the authority to choose township leaders. Nevertheless, the Buyun mayor managed to stay in his position. In subsequent elections, the election process in Buyun was adjusted slightly to bring it more in line with the Chinese Constitution. Citizens are now still able to choose their own leader. The citizens elect a candidate, this candidate is then recommended by the local CCP committee and then elected without contest by the local People's Congress.

The Open Recommendation and Selection System

In other experiments with township elections the 'open recommendation and selection'

Success of Independent Candidates

Xu Zhiyong, an independent candidate for the Haidian District People's Congress in Beijing, finally won the election with the highest number of votes in his electoral ward.

Xu, together with 22 other Beijing residents, actively promoted themselves to voters in this year's district level congress elections.

Xu, well known for his active role in guaranteeing rights of migrant workers and private entrepreneurs this year, said as a **new legislator** he will continue to be involved in social work.

'We should support Xu Zhiyong as he is a young man with a strong sense of justice,' said the voter Jiao Aiping, 'We residents long for real congress delegates that speak for us.'

Is this the development of grassroots democracy?

The fact that these village elections, township and county experiments take place might lead some to the conclusion that this is the beginnings of democracy in China. This is what is called introducing democracy 'from the bottom up'. Some researchers say that village elections are becoming more competitive and that some villagers have been successful in voting corrupt leaders out of office. Others say the elections are usually rigged and that Communist party officials remain in power at all levels.

Source: Adapted from an article in the China Daily by Liu Li 17th December 2008

system has been used. This system attempts to bring about a compromise between giving local people a say and local party officials keeping control. In this system, any adult can run for township head. A council of community leaders chooses two finalists from the list of candidates. The Local People's Congress then makes the final decision. Competitive ballots like these were taking place in about five per cent of townships by 2001. Some Chinese academics believe that this is healthy for the confidence of such leaders as they enjoy support from their voters and can challenge the local party secretaries.

Experiments at the County Level

Eleven counties in Hubei and Jiangsu conduct polls using the open recommendation and selection system to elect the county deputy chief. Although this represents less than one per cent of counties across China, they do involve quite a large number of people.

Membership of the Chinese Communist Party

In China citizens cannot join the CCP of their own accord. They have to be recommended by at least two party members. It is considered a great honour and membership carries great privileges. People have to work very hard to prove themselves worthy of membership and have to complete a probationary period, going through training and examinations. While membership of the CCP is about 70 million, this represents only five per cent of the population. Membership is attractive as it can bring opportunities for career advancement and therefore membership continues to grow.

Advancement within the CCP

The CCP has a pyramid structure. At its base are millions of local (primary) party organisations. From this base, members of Local Party Congresses are elected. The Local

Party Congresses 'elect' the next level within the party structure, the National Party Congress. The NPC is in theory, the top of the pyramid and meets once every five years, bringing together 2000 delegates from party organisations across the country. The NPC's main job is to 'elect' the Central Committee. The Central Committee 'elects' the Politburo and its Standing Committee. In practice, the power lies in the Politburo, which consists of a Cabinet of 24 members, but the greatest power lies with the nine-member Standing Committee which is an inner-Cabinet of the country's top leaders. Formally the membership of the Standing Committee is approved by the Central Committee. In practice, membership is the result of negotiations among the top leadership of the Communist Party.

At the very apex (top) of the pyramid is the position of General Secretary. In 2002, Hu Jintao was elected to this position by the Central Committee from a Party-approved list of candidates. He was then appointed President in 2003, replacing the previous CCP General Secretary in this role.

The top two rungs of the CCP pyramid are made up of the same people who form the top two rungs of the Chinese government – CCP and government are so interconnected that they could be said to be inseparable. The CCP's Central Committee in effect chooses the top level of Chinese government, but even then its power is restricted as the Politburo approves the list of candidates. If this happened in the UK, people would say it was not democratic.

In summary, those at the top of the party have control over who rises up to the top positions. Thus, those who occupy the top positions are very secure and the likelihood of major change within the party is unlikely.

Democratisation of the CCP

However, some changes are taking place. President Hu Jintao and Premier of the State Council Wen Jiaobao stated that they want more openness and discussion within the CCP. The practice of putting forward multiple candidates for positions has been introduced. In around 300 townships, local party leaders have been directly elected by party members.

In Britain, parties like the Labour Party and the Conservative Party have different groups of members who hold different positions on some issues. This has in the past led to the break-up of political parties and new parties forming. Groups or factions like this are not allowed in the CCP. However, if party members have to compete for positions within the party, then they are going to have to state what their interests are in order to attract the vote. This could lead to divisions within the CCP and perhaps eventually different policy positions. Perhaps even the break-up of the Chinese Communist Party – although this seems nowhere on the horizon.

Holding Government Office

On page 175 the CCP pyramid was outlined. It should also now be clear that there is a crossover from the CCP to the Chinese government at the top levels. To summarise the connections and overlap between the CCP and the government:

The top level position of President, this position is filled by the General Secretary of the CCP, who is also a member of the Politburo's Standing Committee.

The second top level is the Politburo's Standing Committee itself. The Premier of the State Council, who is effectively the chief administrative authority, is also a member of the Politburo's Standing Committee. All of the Vice Premiers of the State Council are either members of the Politburo or members of the CCP Central Committee.

Moreover, the heads of the State Council Ministries are also top party members. Therefore the membership of the State Council and the CCP is tightly interlocked.

Taking part in protests and demonstrations

Mass demonstrations have grown ten times in number in the last ten years. Such action includes sit-ins, strikes, demonstrations, traffic-blocking and building seizures. The average number of protestors has grown from 10 to 50. In the first six months of 2005, in fifteen demonstrations over 10,000 people took part in each. Demonstrations are not always peaceful. There seems to be a slowly growing feeling of discontent. The recent economic downturn may incite more protests. There are growing feelings of injustice, anger at poor working conditions, unpaid wages and pensions. Peasants have had their land confiscated to build airports, roads and dams. Millions have lost their homes to build new developments.

Chinese citizens can take part in protests and demonstrations but protest against the supremacy of the CCP is not tolerated nor is putting forward ideas for a new party. This can lead to heavy jail sentences in prison camps.

Environmental protests are tolerated. There is fast growing environmental lobby in China.

CASE STUDY

Authors urge Liu Xiaobo release

More than 300 major authors have signed a petition in support of the imprisoned Chinese dissident Liu Xiaobo. Wole Soyinka, Salman Rushdie, JM Coetzee and Umberto Eco are among those demanding his immediate release.

Mr Liu was arrested last month after he and hundreds of other Chinese intellectuals issued a wide-ranging call for political reform. The document, known as Charter 08, challenges the Communist Party's monopoly on power.

Tiananmen veteran Mr Liu is a government critic and veteran of the Tiananmen Square democracy protests in 1989. He was one of more than 300 prominent Chinese intellectuals to sign the online Charter 08 petition in December.

Released to coincide with the 60th anniversary of the Universal Declaration of Human Rights, the charter called for greater freedoms and democratic reforms in China, including an end to Communist one-party rule.

Mr Liu was arrested by police on 8 December, and is reportedly being held in pre-trial detention 'somewhere in the suburbs of Beijing'. Amnesty International has condemned Mr Liu's detention and called on the authorities to make public any information about his alleged crimes.

In December, more than 150 writers and activists from around the world wrote an open letter to China demanding that Mr Liu be freed from jail. In response, China's foreign ministry said the country was under the rule of law and opposed foreign interference.

Source http://news.bbc.co.uk/go/pr/fr/-/1/hi/world/asia-pacific/7842315.stm, 21st January 2009

ACTIVITIES

1 Give two ways Chinese citizens can participate in the political process.

2 Briefly identify ways in which participation in the political process is restricted.

3 For each type of election, find the following information:
- who citizens can vote for
- to what extent non-party members are successful
- how often the election is held
- evidence of democratic practice and fairness
- evidence that elections are still not democratic

4 Briefly outline the 'Open Recommendation and Selection System'.

5 Why is the 'Open Recommendation and Selection System' a compromise?

6 To what extent was Zhang Jingming successful in introducing more democracy to Buyun's mayoral elections?

7 Give examples of the success of independent candidates in elections in China.

8 What is different about joining a political party in China to joining a political party in Scotland?

9 What changes have taken place in terms of non-party members being able to hold government office?

10 What rights to Chinese citizens have to take part in demonstrations and protest?

11 What happened to Liu Xiaobo when he campaigned for political reform?

12 Read the article 'Authors urge Liu Xiaobo release'. Then read the following statement:

'The Chinese government is unhappy about foreign organisations interfering in its country's affairs but is now willing to listen to the wishes of the Chinese people regarding political change.' (View of Chinese government official)

Give one reason to support and one reason to oppose the view of the Chinese government official.

Human Rights in China

To What Extent has Progress Been Made in Recent Years?

Despite the social and economic change that has taken place in China, concern over human rights issues remains. Organisations such as Amnesty International and Human Rights Watch condemn China for its human rights record. It is very difficult to tell just how extensive these human rights abuses are as the Chinese government's controls the media on what can and cannot be reported. However, there have been signs of improvement in recent years.

Amendment to the Chinese Constitution

Changes to the Constitution (written set of rules) were made to show the rest of the world that China does have respect for human rights. The Chinese government is proud of the

Tiananmen will not be forgotten by Kate Adie

Tourists flock in their hundreds of thousands to Tiananmen Square in the heart of Beijing. They can marvel at history in the Forbidden City and gaze at modern China's fashionably dressed citizens dodging shoals of Mercedes.

What they will not see is any hint of the recent past in Tiananmen Square – there is nothing which commemorates the deaths of the hundreds, perhaps thousands of people in June 1989, the massacre which brought a brutal end to many weeks of demonstrations.

Engaging ineptitude

After months of waiting – and advice from Chinese journalists that hen's teeth might be more available – we entered the country on tourist visas.

Our first two days of filming involved uniformed policemen sticking their white-gloved hands in front of the lens, while their plainclothes counterparts attempted to tail us through heavy traffic in Chengdu – with engaging ineptitude.

At one point we were followed by five vehicles, all of which appeared to have no idea how to tail anyone – especially when we abandoned our driver and hopped on a bus.

At one point we made a detour to avoid leading them to an interviewee – who is known to the police for dissident views – and I ended up in an organic farm talking earnestly to a rather puzzled man about cabbages while the police officers bobbed up and down behind a field of flowering rapeseed.

It would all seem something of a cat and mouse game for us, except for the fact that the people we were intending to interview all suffer endless harassment and surveillance – and have done ever since 1989.

As we slipped our 'tail' and organised a rendez vous in safe and discreet locations, we became ever more aware of the mammoth security system which can be brought to bear on those whom the state designates 'trouble-makers'.

Security cameras

Tourists probably don't notice that Beijing boasts 280,000 security cameras; it is rumoured that the muscular lads who offer to be guides in Tiananmen Square, sell you postcards and ice-cream, are all members of the secret police.

The people we spoke to frequently find police outside their flat, cameras trained on their front door and their phones tapped. It is no wonder that they used their mobiles (several!) to arrange to meet us.' What is surprising – and impressive – is their determination to talk about what happened, bear witness to the massacre and explain why they continue to demand that the authorities admit what they did to their own people.

They talk of being spirited from their homes every time there is a 'sensitive time' – such as Party congresses or the Olympics, and being taken hundreds of miles away so that journalists cannot find them. Many have been imprisoned for speaking out, yet they will not give up and their determination is breath-taking.

There's Mrs Zhang, founder of the Tiananmen Mothers, a group which supports those who lost their sons and daughters, killed by an army which was firing relentlessly all the way into the city. Her son was shot – he had no idea what was happening when he went out 'just to take some photographs'. She speaks with great dignity, one of the few voices among 1.3 billion who want the truth acknowledged – and who speak of their hopes for justice and more freedom.

amendment made in 2004 that says 'the state respects and preserves human rights'. One factor that provoked this change was the reaction of the international media to the treatment of the Tiananmen Square demonstrators in spring 1989. Western governments imposed economic sanctions (refused to trade goods or services) on China and put an embargo (ban) on the sale of weapons to them.

Political Dissidents

The Chinese government, dominated at every level by the Chinese Communist Party (CCP), does not allow organised political opposition. Even where Citizens are trying to exercise their political rights in the village elections, their rights are suppressed. At first, villagers were allowed to replace unpopular village officials, but it now seems that the Chinese government is concerned because too many non-Party members were being elected.

In 2005, villagers in Taishi (Guangdong province) raised a petition to remove the head of the village committee on the grounds of corruption involving a huge land deal. The villagers had evidence (in the form of the village accounts book) which they claimed showed that the village head had been involved in embezzlement and fraud. Regional officials and police confronted the villagers and seized the accounts books. The lawyer who had helped the villagers with their claim was reported to have been arrested, and a political activist involved in the dispute was allegedly beaten up.

Hou Wenzhuo, director of the Empowerment and Rights Institute (a non-governmental activists' group in Beijing) stated: 'The Government responded in a violent and reckless way'. Mr Hou also said that the Chinese

government has changed its official policy on village elections, with provincial governments being told that non-party members should not be encouraged to stand for election.

The Chinese Prison System

In China there is a vast network of prison camps (Laogai) used to suppress political dissidents (those who oppose the Chinese political system). Laogai means '**reform through labour**'. It is the largest prison system of its kind ever to have existed. Prisoners live in squalid conditions and are subjected to inhumane and degrading treatment including torture. The majority of those imprisoned are political prisoners. Prisoners are forced to work for the state, the idea being that work will help them to become new people who will embrace the communist system. The Chinese government has stated that the Laogai system is no different from other prison systems across the world. It is there to punish and reform convicted criminals. However, the system is about more than that. One of its functions is to strengthen the control of the CCP and to suppress political dissent.

Although the name Laogai was replaced with *jianyu* (prison) in 1994, the system has not changed. After its 2004 visit to China, officials from the UN concluded that the government had made 'no significant progress in reforming the … system to ensure judicial review and to conform to international law'.

Ankang

Law enforcement authorities have the power to forcibly commit individuals to psychiatric facilities (Ankang). Political dissenters are often sent to psychiatric hospitals instead of jails because arrest warrants are not necessary. Human rights activist Wang Wanxing was held

CASE STUDY

One of China's longest serving dissident prisoners has been freed and flown to the West, allowing a rare insight into life inside its notorious psychiatric jail system. Wang Wanxing, 56, spent 13 years in the Beijing Ankang hospital for the criminally insane.

He was detained on a ward containing violent criminals and forced to watch electric shock treatment being performed on fellow inmates.

↑ **Figure 6.4** Wang Wanxing

He witnessed two deaths, one from a heart attack during treatment and one person who died while being force-fed. He was himself compelled to take anti-psychotic drugs.

His release took place quietly in August after negotiations between the German and Chinese governments and he was flown to Frankfurt where his wife and daughter were already living as refugees. News of his plight has now been made public by Human Rights Watch, a monitoring group which published a study of China's psychiatric prison system three years ago.

Mr Wang's political activism began while at school during the Cultural Revolution, when he was denounced for saying that Chairman Mao had both good and bad aspects. He was detained repeatedly in the 1970s, and became involved in the Beijing pro-democracy protests in 1989 that resulted in the Tiananmen Square massacre.

On the third anniversary he was detained when he tried to unfurl a protest banner which, according to the authorities, amounted to 'disturbing public order'. The official record said: 'He was diagnosed as suffering from 'paranoia', and his dangerous behaviour was attributed to his state of delusion'.

For seven years, Mr Wang was kept on a general psychiatric ward containing between 50 and 70 inmates. Later, after a three-month release in 1999 that ended when he announced that he intended to hold a press conference, he was

→

sent to a ward containing psychotic prisoners, many imprisoned for murder. Treatment was by drugs and 'electric acupuncture'. He witnessed one inmate die of a heart attack while undergoing the treatment.

'My guiding principle while I was there was: do not commit suicide, do not run away, do not challenge the staff,' Mr Wang said. 'As long I walked out alive, that would be enough'.

As he was being put on the aircraft, a hospital official told him: 'If you ever speak out about your experiences at our hospital, we'll come and bring you back here'.

Source: Richard Spencer, the Telegraph, 4th November 2005

in an Ankang in Beijing for 13 years for unfurling a banner in Tiananmen Square in 1992. Wang was released in August 2005. People who have been detained in asylums have reported being forced to take sedatives and to undergo electric shock therapy. A peasant woman from a Shanghai suburb, Liu Xinjuan, was committed to psychiatric hospitals five times between 2003 and 2006. All she wanted was to gain possession of her house after her divorce.

The Laogai Economy

Laogai camps are also a vital part of China's national economy. The government does not fully fund the prisons and they are encouraged to pursue enterprise (business) models to help cover their costs. In practice, prisons make a healthy profit and the most productive ones are rewarded for their success. However, prisoners are not paid for their work. Inmates have no way of expressing their grievances as trade unions are not allowed. Local and national governments receive huge amounts of revenue from prison enterprises.

Laogai products are sold all over China and even exported to different parts of the world,

earning large amounts of foreign currency. A thriving example is Jinzhou Prison (Liaoning Province), also known as Jinzhou Switch Factory and Jinzhou Jinkai Electrical Group. This camp has assets worth 302 million yuan (approximately £30 million), annual sales of approximately £30 million and an annual profit of approximately £3.7 million.

One Child Policy

In 1979, the One Child Policy was introduced by the Chinese government to control population growth. Families are restricted to having just one child each and this is enforced nationally. It is the responsibility of the local family planning officials to ensure that targets are met. While the policy has had some success in reducing the birth rate, improved social conditions have had a greater impact. The tragic negative impact of this policy is that it led to abortion and a large gender imbalance in the population. There is evidence that the preference for boys has led to widespread **infanticide** (murder of newborns). The fundamental human right of these children – the right to life itself – has been denied as a result of this policy.

The Chinese authorities are now concerned about the future imbalance between those of working age and the number of elderly. A debate is taking place amongst the Chinese leaders over allowing some regions/cities to relax the one child policy.

Religious Freedom

Article 36 of the Chinese constitution states:

'Citizens of the People's Republic of China enjoy freedom of religious belief. No state organ, public organisation or individual may compel citizens to believe… nor may they discriminate against citizens who believe in… any religion.'

The Chinese government admitted in the 1990s that, during the Cultural Revolution, believers had been persecuted and they also reopened sites of religious worship. Five religions are recognised by the Chinese state: Buddhism, Taoism, Islam, Catholicism and Protestantism.

In recent years the numbers of religious believers has grown rapidly to around 200 million. The Chinese government recognises that religion can be used to create social harmony and the Chinese Communist Party

CASE STUDY

Ethnic Han Chinese make up more than 90 per cent of China's population and, over the last 60 years, the Chinese Government has sent millions of Han Chinese to the remote regions of China such as Tibet and Xinjiang. The Chinese leadership argues that they are modernising these backward regions and bringing prosperity.

The idealised image of harmony throughout China was further shattered in July 2009 when savage fighting between the native Uighurs and the Han Chinese led to the death of more than 160 citizens in Xinjiang region. The Chinese army quickly restored order and placed the blame on outside forces. In November 2009 the Chinese Government announced the execution of nine Uighurs involved in the disturbance.

The conflict is widely believed to have escalated into violence because Uighurs believe that the massive influx of Han Chinese is undermining their traditions and Muslim religion. In 1949, Uighurs made up 75 per cent of the Xinjiang population, today it stands at about 45 per cent (Han Chinese make up 40 per cent). In the capital city, Urumqi, 70 per cent of the population is now Han.

Xinjiang is rich in reserves of oil, minerals and natural gas and this vast region is of strategic importance to China. The eight million Uighurs feel that they are second class citizens in their own region. They are concerned that the CCP is promoting the use of speaking Mandarin in Xinjiang's schools at the expense of their traditional Uighur language. Meanwhile, the Han Chinese are resentful that the Uighurs are exempt from the One Child Policy.

has addressed this issue by acknowledging the importance of religion. However, the CCP still sees religion as something that needs to be controlled. The image they strive to convey is one of harmony between all the nationalities that make up China but there are doubts surrounding this ideal.

Tibetan Buddhism

Religious Tibetans are not allowed to worship their spiritual leader, the Dalai Lama. China is trying to control Buddhist leaders in Tibet. They have stated that Tibetans cannot be reincarnated without government permission. This is an extreme example of the Chinese state extending its authority into religious affairs.

ACTIVITIES

1 Give the names of two organisations that are concerned about human rights issues in China. Explain why it is so difficult to get accurate and reliable information on the human rights situation in China.

2 Quote the section from the 2004 amendment to the Chinese Constitution on human rights. Why is the Chinese government keen to promote this amendment?

3 Prepare a brief report on what happened in Tiananmen Square in 1989.

4 Consider the amendment to the Chinese Constitution and also read the article 'Tiananmen will not be forgotten' by Kate Adie. What conclusions can be drawn about improvements in human rights in China since the Tiananmen Square massacre in 1989? You should reach conclusions on the following:
   ● The evidence that the amendment to the Constitution is being upheld by officials in China.
   ● The willingness of people to speak out about what happened in Tiananmen Square.

5 What happened to the villagers in Taishi in 2005, when they tried to exercise their political rights?

6 Describe the following:
   ● The Laogai
   ● The Ankang

7 The Chinese government has stated that 'the Laogai system is no different from other prison systems across the world.' Explain in detail why the Chinese prison system could be said to violate human rights.

8 Explain why the Chinese prison system is important to the economy.

9 Find out about when, why and how the One Child Policy was introduced and implemented.

10 Construct an information booklet that the Chinese government might give to citizens to inform them of their rights in relation to having children. What information would not be contained in this booklet?

11 Giving detailed information about religious freedom in China, explain why the Chinese government would want to control religion. Mention at least three religious/ belief systems in China.

12 Explain why there is unrest in Xinjiang region.

In 2008, protests by Buddhist monks, in Lhasa, ended in violence. Tibetans said that over 100 Tibetans were killed. Chinese sources said that Han Chinese shopkeepers were burned to death when their premises were set on fire. The issue in Tibet is not only religious, it also concerns the status of ethnic minorities. The 2009 unrest in Xinjiang region highlights the nationality problem faced by the Chinese government (see page 183).

Islam

Most of the Muslims in China live in the north-east. Amongst the Uighurs in Xinjiang, there is a separatist movement. These separatist groups have been labelled terrorists by the Chinese government.

Christianity

In the 1950s, under Mao's leadership Catholics were told to end their relationship with the Pope. The Chinese government continues to fear that the Catholic Church might undermine the authority of the CCP. Interestingly, there are far more Christians in China now than there were in 1950. Many Chinese citizens have turned to religion as they have lost faith in the CCP.

Falun Gong

'Truthfulness, compassion and forbearance' are the ideals sought by the Falun Gong, yet they were labelled an 'evil cult' by the Chinese authorities. Probably because this was a large group over whom they had little control. Sources say there is evidence of violent crackdowns on the Falun Gong and that thousands of their members have been sent to prison camps without trial, or to mental health institutions or for re-education.

Economic Change and Progress in China

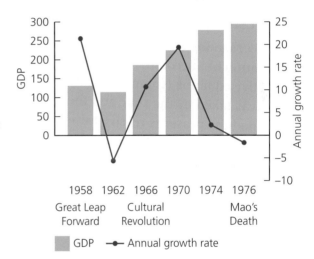

Figure 6.5 China's Gross Domestic Product and annual growth rate (in billion yuan) 1958–1975

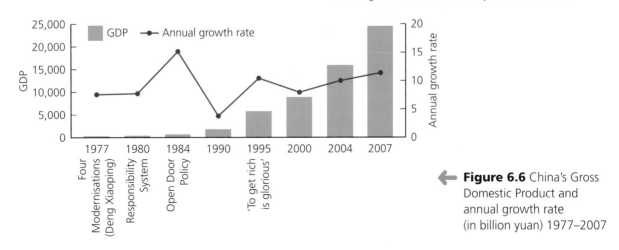

Figure 6.6 China's Gross Domestic Product and annual growth rate (in billion yuan) 1977–2007

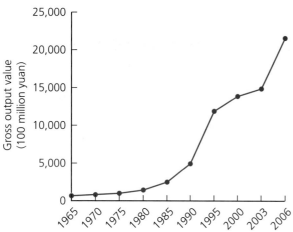

Figure 6.7 Gross output value of crops 1965–2006

Mao's China

In Mao's China, all industries and businesses were owned by the state. The period from the early 1950s until the mid 1970s was dominated by Mao's influence. Figure 6.5 shows the effect Mao's policies had on GDP (the value of goods and services produced in an economy) and economic growth. The devastating effect that the Great Leap Forward had on agriculture is reflected in the fall in GDP in the early 1960s. Falling GDP in the late 1960s followed the Cultural Revolution.

Collectivisation

In 1955 Mao forced the entire population of the countryside into collectivised farms (communes). All food was taken by the state and the only food the peasants received was what was handed out to them. The first stage of collectivisation involved taking the land from the landlords and redistributing it amongst the peasants. Communes were introduced in 1958.

In the commune system households were organised into teams, then teams formed brigades, and brigades formed the commune. Each level of organisation was responsible for certain activities: the team for organising farm labour, the brigade for establishing small workshops and elementary schools; the commune for large-scale land reclamation projects, a hospital, a high school, small factories, and other sideline industries, as well as a welfare fund to aid the poor communities within the commune.

The Great Leap Forward

Mao's economic policy (the 'Great Leap Forward') was launched in May 1958. Mao's intention was to industrialise China as fast as possible and for China to become a superpower. Some historians argue that Mao wanted even more than that – he wanted to dominate the world.

During the four-year period of the Great Leap Forward, 38 million people died of starvation due to famine or exhaustion from being over-worked. Mao's regime took food from the peasants, often by force. Government sources claimed there was an excess of food in China, while people starved. This was known to Mao but his ambition to industrialise was more important to him than people's lives. While people starved, grain was exported to pay Russia for knowledge of how to build nuclear submarines. Grain was also used in the nuclear programme – turned into alcohol to be used as fuel.

Cultural Revolution

In the 1960s, Mao wanted a return to communist ideals. Anyone who opposed these ideals was called a 'capitalist roader' and punished. It was during this period that the Mao cult developed. Billions of badges with an image of Mao's head on them were made, billions of portraits hung around the streets and buildings across China and everyone received Mao's Little Red Book. Mao ordered students in schools to condemn their teachers for filling their heads with middle class ideas. Exams were abolished.

Children were encouraged to join the Red Guards. They embarked on a campaign of terror, first targeting teachers and children and society as a whole. Writers, opera singers and other people from the arts were beaten and tortured. Books and paintings were burned. Musical instruments trashed. Any sign of culture was destroyed.

Mao then turned against Party officials, those bosses he saw as taking a capitalist road. New groups called the 'Rebels' were formed from the grassroots of the Communist Party. As they hated their bosses they were willing to follow Mao's orders. In 1967, Deng Xiaoping was put under house arrest, denounced as 'the second biggest capitalist roader.' Deng called this period the most painful of his life. After Mao's death in 1976, he became *de facto* leader in 1977 and set China on a new journey.

The Great Leap Forward and Cultural Revolution failed. China did not become a great industrial nation during Mao's leadership.

Changes to the Chinese Economy under Deng Xiaoping

Figure 6.6 shows GDP and economic growth rates under Deng Xiaoping's leadership (see page 185).

Overall, the economy grew steadily during this period with sustained growth.

The Four Modernisations

Under Deng Xiaoping the government introduced the four modernisations which involved agriculture, industry, science and technology and defence.

Modernisation in agriculture meant that the emphasis on human labour in the communes was replaced by machinery under Deng's modernisation. Modern fertilisers, pesticides and technology increased agricultural output and ensured more reliable food supplies.

Modernisation in industry led to rapid developments in the chemical, textile, metal and engineering industries which created greater efficiency and productivity.

Modernisation in science and technology was spurred when the scientists who had been imprisoned or sent to work as peasants in the communes were released and their skills employed. Schools and universities were encouraged to help more people gain qualifications to feed the research projects into modern technology.

The fourth modernisation involved defence and the modernisation of the armed forces.

The Household Responsibility System

Zhao Ziyang, who was general secretary of the CCP in Sichuan Province, launched the Household Responsibility System in 1975. He became Prime Minister of China in 1980 and it was his influence that led to almost all households across China adopting this system by the end of 1983.

With the Household Responsibility System, each family is independently responsible for managing plots of land. The family units, which could consist of either an individual family's plot or the combined plots of a group of families, enter into a contract with the government. The land is leased to the unit for a certain number of years and the farmers receive contracts from the government to produce certain crops. The decisions about what to produce and how to produce it are made by the farmers. Once the amount required by the government has been reached, any surplus crops produced on the plots can be sold for profit on the open market.

The fact that surplus crops can be sold on the open market gives the farmers an incentive to work hard and make a return on their efforts. This contrasts with the commune system which rewarded effort and cooperation rather than the end result of that effort i.e. the crops themselves and their market value. This system encourages farmers to take responsibility for efficient production and increasing the range of crops grown and the yield. Farmers can choose to grow non-food crops such as tobacco and cotton. The farmers can spend their profits on reinvesting in their land and machinery or spend it on consumer goods. As a result of the Household Responsibility System, crop yields rose and the national grain harvest shot up from 304.8 million tonnes in 1978 to 407.3 million tonnes in 1984. The introduction of fertilisers and other technological innovations further raised grain output well above the 500 million tonne mark by the late 1990s.

The changes have brought improved living standards for many farmers and there is now a wider choice of quality food available. However, falling rural incomes in comparison to those achievable in the cities, and the fact that many less successful farmers have sold their land, have resulted in millions of peasants migrating to cities such as Beijing and Shanghai to seek employment.

In the late 1990s and early 21st Century, this migration from rural areas and the rapid industrialisation of cities led to a decrease in grain production. This made it necessary for China to increase its grain imports. In 2004, agricultural tax reductions and other incentive measures contributed to a recovery to 469.5 million tonnes.

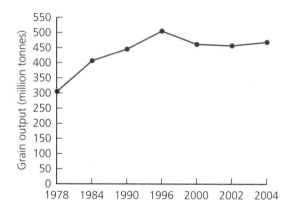

Figure 6.8 Grain output (million tonnes) 1978–2004

Sources: China Statistical Yearbook 2003: National Bureau of Statistics

A Shift Away from Communism

The Household Responsibility System is seen as the key to economic change. Deng Xiaoping called economic reform associated with the household responsibility system 'Socialism with Chinese Characteristics.'

Farmers can sell their surplus produce at open markets for profit. However, the Chinese government aims to encourage a socialist market economy system. For example, urban and rural people on low incomes will be able to purchase grain at subsidised prices.

Township enterprises: Secondary and Tertiary Industry in the Countryside

China's large population and limited arable land make it necessary for the government to be able to develop policies which will maintain grain production and keep rural incomes rising.

The government therefore encourages rural areas and small towns to develop secondary and tertiary industries. Reasons for this are to reduce rural-urban migration and to improve rural incomes. This encourages entrepreneurs and allows people with new ideas to set up secondary and tertiary businesses. One area of growth has been developing food processing factories, allowing rural people to get involved in the next stage of food production.

Chinese farmers have been very successful in developing Township and Village Enterprises (TVE). Farmers are making business decisions for themselves, rather than the CCP. While there have been ups and downs for these TVEs, some farmers who have learned business skills have taken this initiative to another stage and led the development of further innovation in local industry.

Small towns and cities have developed around these industries. This has reduced distribution problems for these scattered farm units and also ensured the provision of necessary services to farmers. It has also helped to absorb the rural population and reduce migration to the big cities.

The Great Leap Outward

By the beginning of the 21st Century, China had become very important to the international economy. This opening up was necessary if Deng's modernisations were to be successful. In the 1990s Deng Xiaoping sought help from countries such as the UK, the USA and France to help China modernise industrially. The realisation was that economic development depended on being part of the international economy.

The Open Door Policy

The Open Door Policy of the early 1990s aimed to attract foreign businesses to invest in China. Foreign investment was necessary for economic growth. There was to be continuity in the political system but more daring reform in the economic system.

The Open Door Policy led to a massive increase in foreign trade and investment.

In the early 1980s, Special Economic Zones were set up. The first was set up in Shenzen City, because of its proximity to Hong Kong. Foreign investment grew steadily in the 1980s but suffered after the Beijing massacre in 1989. Investment from western countries was halted for a time but investment from Taiwan offset the damage. Foreign investment in the 1980s mainly took the form of joint ventures involving cooperation between foreign and Chinese companies.

In the 1990s greater foreign investment was encouraged by allowing subsidiaries of foreign companies to invest in Guangdong and Shanghai. In 1997–98 foreign investment peaked at $45 billion a year.

China was admitted to the World Trade Organisation in 2001 and this fuelled a further surge in foreign investment.

CASE STUDY

SEZs

A Special Economic Zone (SEZ) is a geographical region that is allowed to run its economy differently from the rest of the country. The most successful SEZ in China, Shenzhen.

Figure 6.9 Shenzhen, a Special Economic Zone

Shenzhen is a city of over 12 million people. Just over 30 years ago it was a small fishing village. In 1979, under the leadership of Deng Xiaoping, it became the first SEZ. It is now the largest manufacturing base in the world and southern China's major financial centre.

It is close to Hong Kong and this also been a reason for its huge growth. There are plans for the two cities to integrate over the next decade to create a metropolis large enough to rival New York and Tokyo. The cost of living in Shenzhen is considerably lower than living in Hong Kong.

The SEZ was created to be an experimental ground of capitalism in 'socialism with Chinese characteristics'.

Economic policies of SEZs

1 Special tax incentives for foreign investments in the SEZs.

2 Greater independence on international trade activities.

3 Economic characteristics, represented as 'four principles':
- construction primarily relies on attracting and utilising foreign capital
- primary economic forms are joint ventures between Chinese and foreign firms as well as wholly foreign-owned enterprises
- products are mainly for export
- economic activities are primarily driven by supply and demand

Government Response to Economic Downturn

China's Household Income Reform Plans

- China will fast track its payment system reforms to boost household income and spur consumption, especially those of the medium and low-income group.

- Executives of state-owned enterprises may see their salaries trimmed to narrow the gap between the rich and the poor.

- An improved social security safety net will be introduced, to encourage spending, and the income for rural and low-income households will be increased through taxation reform.

- Analysts believe these measures would help boost consumption, which accounted for just 40 percent of China's GDP growth in 2008.

20th November, BEIJING – A top Chinese official on Thursday described the country's employment outlook as 'grim'.

Speaking at a news conference, Minister of Human Resources and Social Security Yin Wenmin warned of a rise in the number of newly jobless workers as the latest in a series of indications that China's economy is not escaping from the broader global downturn. Already, growth in the country's gross domestic product has slowed to single digits, and Yin warned that China's urban unemployment rate could rise to 4.5 per cent by the end of the year, up from four per cent.

'Stabilising employment is the top priority for us now', Yin said.

Source: Adapted from an article in the Washington Post by Lauren Keane, 21st November 2008

ACTIVITIES

1 'Change in GDP in China has had very little to do with the economic policies of its leaders but everything to do with factors not within its control.' (View of Chinese Communist Party Official) Explain, using Figures 6.4 and 6.5, why the Chinese Communist Party Official is being selective in the use of facts.

2 Explain why the economic policies during Mao's rule damaged the economy and prevented economic growth and development.

3 Explain the changes Deng Xiaoping made to the economy under the following headings:
   - Four Modernisations
   - Household Responsibility System
   - Great Leap Outward
   - Open Door Policy
   - Township Enterprises

4 To what extent were these policies successful?

5 Draw up a brief profile of Shenzen.

6 Research information about Pudong – a Special Economic Zone.

7 Why was the Chinese government concerned about the economy in 2008–9? What did it plan to do to minimise the impact of the international economic recession.

'The government's policies to create jobs and raise household income will definitely boost consumption,' said Sun Mingchun, economist, Nomura Securities. 'The real potential for consumption growth is in China's rural areas. While on an average almost every Chinese urban family owns a washing machine, refrigerator, and air conditioner, less than half of their rural counterparts enjoy such luxuries. But as rural household incomes rise, the demand for consumer durable goods will also go up,' Sun said. (*Source: China Daily*)

Inequality in Wealth and Income

Wealth in China is unevenly distributed. Half the population earn 2000 yuan (£140) a year whilst the top four per cent earn ten times the amount. There is also a big difference between rural and urban areas. The average urban income is three times the average rural income and migrant workers from the countryside earn even less. In 2007, the average annual income of an unskilled migrant worker was 1200 yuan (£84) compared with the national average of 9600 yuan (£660).

Ownership of electrical items is far higher in the urban areas. Only 15 in 100 households in rural areas have fridges compared to 87 in 100 households in urban areas. Far fewer people in urban areas own colour televisions and computers.

Chinese children are supposed to have nine years of free compulsory education but the system is unequal. Children in rural areas often drop out to begin work and boost the family income. Only 1.5 per cent of children in Tibet receive secondary education compared with 60 per cent in Beijing.

Under the old system, the danwei (work unit) provided health coverage, but now half the urban population, and 90 per cent of the rural population, have no medical coverage from employers.

There are also differences in living standards within cities. While the wealthy people in the cities live in luxury apartments, migrant workers are not so fortunate. For example, at a mobile phone factory in Shenzen they live in dormitories close to the factories where they work. Conditions in these factories are often very dangerous and workers can suffer severe injuries. Many migrant workers live in shelters made from scaffolding on the building sites where they are building luxury apartments.

Due to the Hukou System (the Household Registration System) set up in 1958, the city populations in China are divided onto two major groups: Hukou urban population and the rural (the outside) population. It is a kind of passport system and means that the urban, local population can get access to health and education services that the 'outside' population cannot. The non-Hukou population is also known as the 'floating population'.

⬆ **Figure 6.10** A cramped dormitory for migrant workers in Beijing

The massive increase in urban population has led to an increase in urban poverty and an urban underclass.

Employment and Unemployment

The end of the state system, and the 'Iron Rice Bowl' of a guaranteed job for life, means that those without the skills necessary for the private sector have fallen behind. 43 million jobs have been lost from State Owned Enterprises (SOEs) but only 16.5 million new ones have been created by the private sector. Economic recession has made matters worse and the Chinese government is trying to prevent a rise in social unrest and demonstrations.

'This is not just an economic issue, but a social issue,' said Hu Xingdou, an economics professor at the Beijing Institute of Technology. 'China's social security system is imperfect – no job means no food. Rising unemployment could lead to serious social unrest.'

One policy tried by the government was to shelve a plan to raise the minimum wage. A lower minimum wage would not help struggling companies, nor reduce the number of job losses. 'We have to first worry about whether workers have a job – then worry about how much they're getting paid later,' Hu said.

It was not only the national government that took steps to prevent job losses, but also local governments. In 2008–9, businesses in Shandong province began to have to apply for government permission to lay off more than 40 workers. Business bosses are concerned that they won't be able to pay the wages.

China's reform commission also recommended subsidising dairy farmers and dairy companies to keep them in business until consumer confidence returned after the melanine scandal. Milk powder contaminated with melanine caused the deaths of four infants and more than 50,000 became sick.

Education

Figure 6.11 Education in China

The improvements in literacy in Mao's years, have almost stopped. China will not meet UNESCO's goals for literacy levels by 2015. Children in China's cities can receive a very high standard of education. It can be very stressful as they are expected to achieve highly for the government and China's economy as well as for their ambitious parents. There is a lot of pressure on school students to do well in the Gaokao university and college entrance exams. This problem is made worse by the one child policy because parents have only one child to focus their ambitions upon. Chinese children are supposed to have nine years of free compulsory education but the system is unequal. Children in rural areas often drop out to boost the family income.

The national government contributes only one-fifth of the education bill for Chinese citizens. This is only two per cent of China's GDP, whilst in comparison to low income countries the average spend is 3.4 per cent of GDP. Townships pay for the other four-fifths of the education bill, collecting this from fees and taxes. In the rural areas the schools have to charge fees; the poorer the area, the poorer the education.

Only 1.5 per cent of children in Tibet receive secondary education compared with 60 per cent in Beijing. Local authorities charge fees for books and other expenses, which poorer families cannot afford. If migrant workers do not have an urban hukou (a residency permit) they have to pay more. The 2003 Law on Promotion of Private Education allows many better off Chinese families to send their children to private schools, or abroad, to be educated.

Health

While there have been significant improvements in the standard of living of many people in China due to the economic reforms of the past two decades, this progress has not been matched in terms of healthcare. Under the old system, state-owned enterprises provided healthcare – this is no longer the case. In rural areas the 'barefoot doctor' system, whereby farmers were trained in very basic medical skills to tend to local people, has also ended.

Rural areas are particularly hard hit, with 39 per cent of the rural population unable to afford professional medical treatment. Only 12 per cent of people in rural areas have health insurance, compared to 54 per cent in urban areas. In 1997, the overall performance of China's healthcare system ranked 144th in the world.

This situation is largely due to the end of farming communes and their rural health clinics that were replaced with private medical practices in the 1980s. Over one-third of the urban population also find they cannot afford the medical treatment they need.

The state-owned enterprises provide health care under the **danwei** system, which was a work unit providing people with a place to live. However, many SOEs have gone out of business. Workers who lose their jobs also lose any insurance coverage. The better-off can afford private medical insurance. There is also considerable corruption in the system. Half the money for doctors' salaries comes from drug sales, leading to over-prescribing and unnecessary procedures.

Table 6.3 Distribution of healthcare beds and medical staff in urban and rural settings (per 1000 population)

Number of beds		
Year	Urban	Rural
1980	4.47	1.48
1990	4.18	1.55
2000	3.49	1.50
2003	3.67	1.50
Number of health professionals		
1980	8.03	1.81
1990	6.59	2.15
2000	5.17	2.41
2003	4.84	2.19

Source: China Statistical Yearbook, 2003: China Health Statistics Summary 2005

Commitment to Improving Health Services

The Chinese government has set out the following objectives for healthcare improvement:

- to improve public health and rural health services with more investment
- to improve hospital management to raise quality of patient care and to develop plans to establish and build a national health infrastructure

- central government has allocated £0.27 billion RMB to help every province, city and county set up its own disease control and prevention centre

- some initiatives include allocating special funds to central and western China, and funding graduates of medical colleges to serve in rural hospitals for one or two years

- the government has set clear, although ambitious, goals of improving the national healthcare infrastructure by 2010

However, health care in China is so poor that, even with these admirable intentions, progress will be slow and fraught with problems.

Housing

The end of the danwei system means less subsidised state housing is available. The Property Law of 2007 allows the buying and selling of property and has given a legal basis to a housing boom.

However, the less well-off cannot afford house prices, which are rising by 25 per cent a year in some areas. The construction boom has also lead to urban sprawl and pollution, as well as protests against some developments.

Crime

In the last 20 years, crime in China has grown even faster than the economy. Crimes like theft, drug use, internet fraud, prostitution and gambling show the change from the former strictly run Chinese society. School drop-out rate and large numbers of migrant workers leaving children in the care of relatives are blamed for the fact that two-thirds of the criminal cases involve juveniles. 'Mafia capitalism' involving organised gangs (triads) in crimes like counterfeiting, people trafficking, smuggling and money laundering has created a huge hidden economy. Twenty per cent of China's consumer goods are counterfeit and China's business reputation and standing in the world is threatened by corruption among officials.

ACTIVITIES

1 Describe in detail the social and economic inequality between urban and rural areas in China.

2 Describe in detail the social and economic inequality within cities such as Beijing and Shenzen.

3 'Since China has opened up its doors to the international economy, health care and education have improved for all citizens. Crime rates have also reduced.' (View of Sue Wenmin) Read the sections of education, health and crime. Explain why Sue Wenmin is being selective in the use of facts.

7 The United States of America

The United States of America (USA) is the third largest country in the world after Russia and Canada. It is roughly two and a half times the size of the European Union. The entire UK would fit into the State of Oregon alone! The sheer size of the country helps explain why there are so many levels of government. It is also one of the most populated countries in the world with a population of just over 305 million. As a result, there are great variations in how people live, their wealth and overall quality of life.

The United States Census Bureau divides the nation into four main regions: west, mid-west, south and north-east. These are important in explaining the distribution and settlement patterns of minorities.

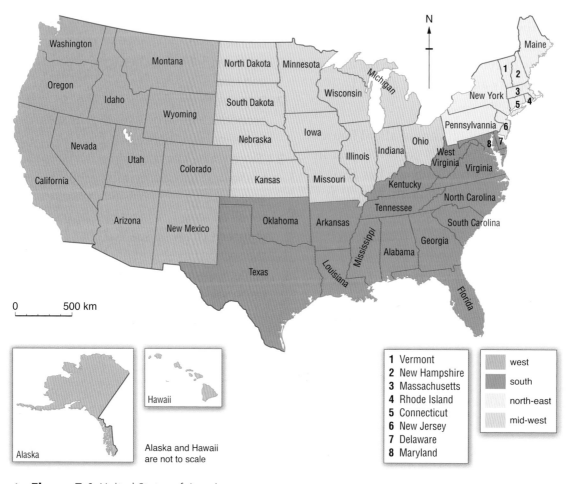

1 Vermont
2 New Hampshire
3 Massachusetts
4 Rhode Island
5 Connecticut
6 New Jersey
7 Delaware
8 Maryland

west
south
north-east
mid-west

Figure 7.1 United States of America

Figure 7.2 The population of the USA has a diverse ethnic mix

Ethnic Groups

The population of the USA is mixed. The five main ethnic groups in the USA include white, black (or African Americans), Hispanics (or Latinos), Asian and Pacific Islanders, and Native Americans. These are broad general sweeping terms used to describe various cultures and groups of people. There are important differences within each ethnic group.

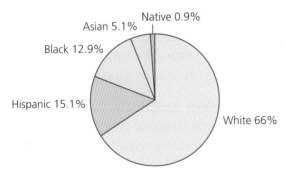

Figure 7.3 US ethnic groups, 2008
Source: US Census Bureau, 2008

Minority groups currently make up roughly one third of the USA population and are expected to become the majority by 2042. By 2050, the minority population is projected to be 235 million out of a total population of 440 million. Hispanics will make up 30 per cent of the population by 2050, followed by black people at 15 per cent and Asian and Pacific Islanders (APIs) at 9.2 per cent.

Settlement Patterns

White Americans

There are approximately 200 million Americans who are white. The majority of white people in the USA originate from Europe. At 66 per cent of the nation's population, white people are more evenly distributed across the four regions and less concentrated in large metropolitan areas. The cities with the highest proportions of white people are located largely in the north-east and mid-west – regions that have not received as many immigrant minorities over the past several decades as the west and south.

Hispanics

Hispanics are the largest minority group in the USA and originate from former Spanish colonies in Latin America. They are made up of Mexicans, Puerto Ricans, Cubans and immigrants from Central and Latin America.

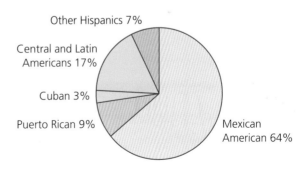

Figure 7.4 Hispanic subgroups, 2008
Source: US Census Bureau, 2008

Hispanics are also the fastest growing minority group in the USA because of rising immigration (just over 40 per cent of Hispanics residing in the USA were foreign born in 2008) and the high birth rate amongst this ethnic group.

The south and west account for more than 80 per cent of the Hispanic population growth in this decade, while the north-east and mid-west account for just under 20 per cent. As Hispanics can be divided into subgroups, we will look at each subgroups settlement pattern.

Table 7.1 Hispanic distribution pattern, 2008

Region	Hispanics as % of total population
West	44
South	34
North-east	13
Mid-west	9

Source: US Census Bureau, 2008

Over 90 per cent of **Mexican Hispanics**, increasingly known as Chicanos, are concentrated in the western and southern Border States of Texas, Arizona, New Mexico and California (known as Gateway States) because they are the nearest point of entry

from Mexico. Many Mexicans settled in these Border States have crossed over illegally.

The Mexico–USA border spans four States and runs for nearly 2,000 miles. The border is unfenced in many places making entry relatively simple, though this is changing. A common means of border crossing is through the hiring of 'coyotes', people-smugglers who transport illegal immigrants in return for money.

Besides the proximity of Mexico to the Border States, colonial legacy also explains why Mexican Americans are concentrated in the South. Many of these states belonged to Mexico prior to the Mexican American War in 1848. Mexicans living in these States were offered US citizenship and began working in manual type jobs.

The majority of **Puerto Ricans**, who do not need a visa for entry to the USA, live in the north-east in States like New York and New Jersey, which are nearest to Puerto Rico. People born in Puerto Rico are born as citizens and, as such, they are entitled to enter the USA freely. Today, more Puerto Rican descendants live in continental USA than in Puerto Rico itself. Unfortunately, many Puerto Ricans face poverty and hardship as a result of racial discrimination. They chose to retain their identity and culture instead of integrating fully to become American.

Cuban Americans form the third-largest Hispanic group in the USA. Cubans have settled in Florida because it is their closest point of entry and because there is an established community who speak Spanish and have done well economically. Other Cubans are attracted to Florida, because it is here that they will be most likely to be accepted given that there is an established Cuban community there. This means that they are more likely

Figure 7.5 Mexico–USA border

to be accepted and find suitable employment. Many other Cubans also enter the USA via Mexico. Before the 1980s, all refugees from Cuba were welcomed into the USA as political refugees. The USA welcomed Cuban immigrants for many years as part of their anti-communist stance. This changed in the 1990s and, more recently, in 2008 Mexico and Cuba created an agreement to prevent immigration of Cubans through Mexico.

Although the Hispanic population has been heavily concentrated in long established settlement areas, they are now spreading out from their traditional metropolitan areas. Many minorities have begun to disperse or spread out from traditional port of entry States. This is especially the case for longer term and USA-born Hispanics. Many lower skilled Hispanic migrants are moving to fast growing areas of the country in response to retail, service and construction job growth. Although this group has dispersed to different parts of the nation, about half of all Hispanics live in ten metropolitan areas (see Table 7.2). The top ten Hispanic housing areas are largely the same as in 1990, with the exception of Phoenix. Among the ten fastest growing metropolitan areas for Hispanics over 2000–2008, those in the south-east dominate. Florida has witnessed huge rates of Hispanic growth.

Table 7.2 Hispanic population by State, 2008

State	Region	Number of Hispanics	Number as percentage
California	west	13,087,981	35.9
Texas	south	8,379,992	35.6
Florida	south	3,642,610	20.1
New York	north-east	3,139,787	16.3
Illinois	mid-west	1,889,528	14.7
Arizona	west	1,796,643	29.1
New Jersey	north-east	1,360,784	15.6
Colorado	west	927,453	19.5
New Mexico	west	874,125	44.7

Source: Pew Hispanic Centre, 2008

African Americans

African Americans commonly referred to as black, have their origins in Africa. The majority of black Americans live in the south. They were brought to the USA as slaves to work on cotton and tobacco plantations in the former slave-owning States of Louisiana, Mississippi, Alabama, Georgia, and South Carolina.

Table 7.3 Distribution pattern of black Americans, 2008

Region	Percentage of black population settled
West	7
South	56
North-east	18
Mid-west	19

Source: US Census Bureau, 2008

When slavery was abolished, many black people remained in the south and became seasonal labourers. However, some decided to migrate to the north in search of employment and escape discrimination. New industries grew up in the north and this attracted many black people who were seeking to improve their living standards. However, they found that the states in the north (like New York, North Carolina and Maryland) did not better their living standards. Many were trapped in inner city ghettos in a life of poverty. However, some managed to improve their economic status by gaining promotion and moving out to suburbs. Middle class black people tended to move to their own segregated suburbs.

As more black people entered the middle classes, and as images of the segregated south drew back with time, black migration started to flow back to the south. This 'reverse migration' saw many black people move to the south in increasing numbers – though less to historic 'Old South' States such as Louisiana, Mississippi and Alabama, and more to 'New South' growth States such as Georgia, North Carolina, Texas and Florida. 72 per cent of the USA's black population growth between 2000 and 2008 occurred in the south. The bulk of this growth took place in large southern metropolitan areas like Atlanta, which is likely to overtake Chicago as the second largest black metropolis in the USA by the end of the current decade. The significant draw that areas like Atlanta hold for black people can be linked to the area's continued strong economy, coupled with a cultural comfort zone. Many young, educated black people feel that these areas offer a community where they can network with other professional black people. In addition, the costs of living are lower in the south than in the north, adding extra appeal.

High rates of population growth are also evident in Las Vegas, Phoenix and Orlando. These are among the fastest growing metropolitan areas in the nation overall, and the jobs created there – both low and high skilled – appear to be attracting black migrants. Still, the south plays a significant part in black population increase, as the region contains five of the ten metropolitan areas experiencing the fastest black population growth in recent years.

Asian and Pacific Islanders

Asian and Pacific Islanders (APIs) are a diverse ethnic group who have come from countries in Asia, such as China or the Pacific Islands.

The API population continues to cluster in traditional immigration magnet areas to a somewhat greater degree than the Hispanic population. Indeed, the ten metropolitan areas with the largest API populations are the same in 2008 as in 1990. Led by Los Angeles, New York and San Francisco, these ten metropolitan areas were home to 57 per cent of the nation's API population in 2008, down from 61 per cent in 1990.

Over half of APIs are concentrated in the west – mostly California. Historical reasons for this include immigrants being brought to work on the Union Pacific Railway on the West Coast. It also remains the closest point of entry from the Pacific. Around a third of APIs, including Vietnamese immigrants in Florida, have settled in the south because of similarities in climate and the availability of service sector jobs. For API immigrant minorities, family networks and friendship have drawn them to traditional ports of entry, even during times when employment opportunities are more favourable elsewhere.

Just over half of all APIs live in wealthier suburbs because they are in high earning white-collar jobs. Some have referred to them as 'model minorities' because the API culture promotes a hard work ethic, respect for elders, academic success and value on ethical and moral behaviour.

Table 7.4 API Distribution Pattern, 2008

Region	Percentage of API population settled
West	61
South	16
North-east	1
Mid-west	9

Source: US Census Bureau, 2008

Native Americans

Native Americans were the first settlers and therefore original inhabitants on the land which is now the USA. Tribes within the Native American camp include the Cherokee and Navajo. Native Americans also include Alaska native tribes such as the Eskimo and the Aleut who inhabit Alaska.

Over a third of Native Americans are concentrated on reservations in States such as Arizona, California and Oklahoma. A reservation is an area of land managed by a Native American tribe, recognised in law as foreign territories, and therefore not subject to USA laws. Native Americans have managed to retain their culture and tradition in these reservations.

A slight majority of Native Americans live somewhere other than on the reservations, often in big western cities such as Phoenix and Los Angeles. Phoenix has maintained a massive growth streak in recent years, growing by 24.2 per cent since 2000. This makes it the second fastest-growing metropolitan area in the USA behind Las Vegas.

Table 7.5 Native American Distribution Pattern, 2008

Region	Percentage of Native American population settled
West	61
South	16
North-east	14
Mid-west	9

Source: US Census Bureau, 2008

ACTIVITIES

1 Outline the five main ethnic groups in the USA.
2 What conclusions can be drawn about the ethnic composition of the USA?
3 Why are Hispanics more likely to live in States such as California and Texas?
4 What role does slavery play in accounting for the high percentage of black settlers in the south?
5 Draw a spider diagram to show the distribution patters of APIs and Native Americans.

Immigration

The USA's immigrant population (legal and illegal) reached a record of nearly 38 million in 2007 (see Figure 7.6). Illegal immigrants account for an estimated 11.3 million of the total national population. An estimated 1.5 million legal and illegal immigrants settle in the USA each year. If immigration continues at current levels, the nation's population will increase from 305 million in 2008 to 440 million in 2050 – an increase of just over 130 million. This will have a huge impact on the American economy and society.

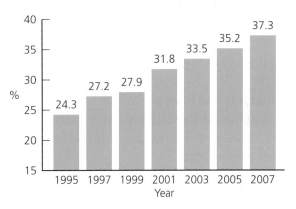

 Figure 7.6 Number of immigrants living in the USA

Source: Immigrants in the United States: A Profile of America's Foreign Born Population, Centre for Immigration Studies, 2008

Figure 7.7 shows the ethnic origin of illegal immigrants in 2008. Well over half of the illegal immigrant population originate from Mexico, followed by other Latin American countries. This makes Hispanics the largest ethnic group settling in the USA illegally.

According to estimates for 1990, about 88 per cent of the illegal immigrant population lived in only six States that had been traditional settlement areas for the foreign-born: California. New York, Texas, Illinois, Florida and New Jersey. But, by 2008, only 62 per cent of the illegal immigrants lived in those six States.

201

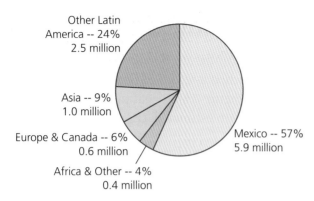

Other Latin
America -- 24%
2.5 million

Asia -- 9%
1.0 million

Europe & Canada -- 6%
0.6 million

Africa & Other -- 4%
0.4 million

Mexico -- 57%
5.9 million

Figure 7.7 Ethnic origin of illegal immigrants, 2008

Source: Pew Hispanic Centre, 2008

In the past, immigrants, both legal and illegal, were highly concentrated in certain States. But, since the mid-1990s, the most rapid growth in the immigrant population in general and the illegal population in particular has taken place in new settlement areas where previously the immigrants had been a relatively small presence. For example, in 1990, 45 per cent of immigrants were settled in California but this had fallen to 24 per cent by 2008.

Arguments for Immigration

Immigration is a deeply divisive issue in the USA and one that dominated the November 2008 elections for Congress and President.

The main argument about immigration centres on the economic contribution that immigrants make. Immigrants contribute to the economy because they fill the kind of jobs that most Americans will not take. In Texas and California especially, immigrants are vital for the economy – businesses rely on their cheap labour. If industry cannot employ cheap immigrant labour, businesses may suffer. In the south, many agricultural businesses depend on cheap labour to harvest crops. Farmers cannot afford to employ American citizens as they would have to pay them the minimum wage. Paying higher wages would increase business costs and consequently the price of goods and many consumers would end up paying more for their agricultural products. Therefore, it follows that the low wages given to immigrants help keep prices in the USA low. In addition, immigrants who are working legally pay taxes. This money is used to pay for welfare services.

Arguments against Immigration

Immigration places huge strain on welfare services in states like California, Texas and Florida where many immigrants settle. In California, immigrants and their young children comprise nearly 60 per cent of the total number of people without medical insurance with illegal immigrants alone making up 27 per cent. The latest data for 2008 also shows that almost half of those in the States public schools are either immigrants or the child of an immigrant. The Centre for Immigration Studies also found that 39 per cent of immigrant-headed households in California used at least one major welfare program, twice the rate for American born households. This places a huge strain on welfare services in California. Taxes might need to be increased in California to fund healthcare, education and welfare. This might prove difficult because voters don't like paying extra taxes, especially towards immigrants. In addition, the Governor of California is a Republican and they favour low taxes and minimal state support.

Reform

The terrorist attack on September 11, 2001 led many to argue that immigration was a security issue. Large sections of the general public demanded that immigration laws be tightened up and tougher measures on illegal immigrants be introduced.

After 9/11, new legislation in the form of the Border Security Act (2001) and the USA Patriot Act (2001) restricted and controlled the entry of immigrants into the USA. The USA–Mexico border has the highest number of both illegal and legal crossings of any land border in the world. As a result, the federal government passed the Secure Fence Act in 2006 in an attempt to prevent people crossing illegally, and doubled border patrol agents to over 16,500 to apprehend illegal immigrants.

Crossing the border illegally is just one of the ways people enter the USA illegally. The main way people become illegal immigrants is staying beyond the authorised period after legal entry. They normally stay beyond the time their visa expires. While many are caught and returned home, most simply repeat the process over and over until they are successful.

As a result, worksite enforcement, such as the E-Verify Program implemented in States like Arizona, is increasingly deployed. They impose stricter rules by forcing companies to screen workers to see if they are authorised to work in the country. E-Verify is a voluntary web based program to help USA firms hire legal workers. Within three days of hire, the employer submits the new employee's social security number, name, date of birth and other details over a secure web connection. That information is then verified for accuracy. In 2009, federal contractors will be required to use E-Verify, it will remain voluntary for other employers. Congress re-authorised funding for the E-Verify program in 2009 because they believe that the program has been highly successful.

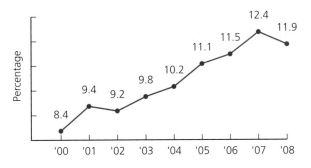

Figure 7.8 Illegal immigration, 2000–2008
Source: Homeward Bound, Centre for Immigration Studies, 2008

Many argue that stronger immigration enforcement has reduced illegal immigration from 12.5 million in 2007 to 11.2 million in 2008 – a decline of 11 per cent.

However, illegal immigration may increase if a legal path is offered to illegal immigrants. Barack Obama pledged to offer legal status or amnesty to an estimated 11.2 million illegal immigrants in 2009, with certain conditions attached. The Democrats now control both Houses of Congress therefore increasing the likelihood of this proposal passing as legislation. Remember you need a majority of votes in the Senate and the House of Representatives to pass a bill.

ACTIVITIES

1 How many immigrants were there in the USA in 2008?
2 What country do most illegal immigrants come from?
3 What States do most illegal immigrants settle in?
4 Briefly describe one argument for and one argument against immigration.
5 Explain, in detail, the measures that the government have passed to reduce immigration.
6 Do you agree or disagree with offering amnesty to illegal immigrants? Justify your answer.

Social Inequalities and Responses

It is important to bear in mind that although minorities continue to suffer social and economic inequality, progress has been made.

This improvement has not been equally shared between and within ethnic groups.

Housing

Table 7.6 Percentage home ownership by ethnic group, 2000 and 2007

Ethnic Group	2000	2007
White	71.1 %	72.9 %
Black	47.2 %	47.3 %
Hispanic	52.8 %	46.3 %
API	46.3 %	53.7 %

Source: Pew Hispanic Centre, Statistical Portrait of Hispanics, 2007

Black people are more likely than white people to live in poorer housing. While some black and Hispanic people have moved into better quality housing, many urban black and Hispanic residents remain trapped in inner city ghettos. A ghetto is a poverty stricken and deprived urban area. They have social problems like violence, poverty and derelict housing. Increasingly, the term 'barrios' is used as a Latino equivalent of a ghetto – barrios are neighbourhoods with largely Spanish speaking residents.

Black and Hispanic people find it harder to get a mortgage than white and API people because they are more likely to be unemployed and living in poverty (largely as the result of low qualifications). Banks are reluctant to give out home loans to minorities because they find it difficult to keep up with mortgage payments. This means that many black and Hispanic people live in poor quality housing because it tends to be cheaper. Minorities, therefore, remain trapped in ghettos by a combination of an economic barrier of poverty, poor education and unemployment. The credit crunch (which led to the collapse of financial giants like Fanny Mae and Freddy Mac) meant that banks were even more reluctant to lend money to poorer households.

Barriers of prejudice and discrimination also helps to explain why minorities were concentrated in ghettos. Segregation, where black and Hispanic people congregate in housing schemes (like the former Robert Taylor Homes in Chicago), was largely the result of 'white flight'. The expansion of highways and cars paved the way for affluent white people to move to the outskirts of major town and cities known as the suburbs. They left the inner cities to buy nice houses with gardens on tree-lined streets. The escape to 'vanilla suburbs' as they came to be known left inner cities increasingly made up of black people.

Figure 7.9 Contrast of lifestyles in suburbs and ghettos

There were, of course, some wealthy minority families who were able to afford to escape the ghettos. However, they were not all welcomed by white residents in vanilla suburbs. White people feared that the value of their property would decline with the influx of black families. Many white people used intimidation to keep black households out of the area. API families find it easier to move into vanilla suburbs. The perception of APIs is different to that of black people.

The number of minorities (blacks, Hispanics and particularly APIs) who have been able to move into residential suburban areas has increased in recent years. Over half of black and Hispanic Americans are considered to be middle class and are able to afford the more expensive housing in the suburbs. Do not stereotype ethnic minorities – they do not all live in ghettos or barrios.

Health

The healthcare costs of most Americans are met by private health insurance, which they or their employer pays for in employer sponsored insurance. There is no free, universal health service in the USA.

The number of people covered by private health insurance sits at around 202 million – roughly 67 per cent of the population in 2007. Nearly a third of Americans have no health cover at all. This varies between ethnic minorities (see Table 7.7).

Minorities are less likely to have health insurance than white people because they cannot afford it and because many minorities who work are in jobs where insurance is not provided. The work they tend to do may be low paid, unskilled and part time. Therefore, firms are not able to finance health insurance for their workers.

Table 7.7 Americans without medical insurance by ethnic group

Ethnic Group	2000	2007
White	9.1%	10.4%
Black	18.3%	19.5%
Hispanic	32.6%	32.1%
API	17.5%	16.8%

Source: Income, Poverty and Health Insurance Coverage in the US 2007 Report, US Census Bureau, 2008

Consequently, health indicators such as life expectancy (see Figure 7.10), infant mortality, coronary heart disease and cancer remain higher for minorities. Lifestyle factors (smoking, drinking, taking drugs, eating junk food) and poverty have a significant impact on the health of minorities. People living in inner city ghettos are more likely to make unhealthy lifestyle choices.

Poor quality housing that is damp and overcrowded leads to health problems. Mental health problems like depression and stress are related to the physical environment. Children going home to a run down sink estate with vandalism and a lack of amenities will be psychologically affected. Their outlook on life might become bleak.

Tackling poverty lies at the heart of improving the health status of minorities.

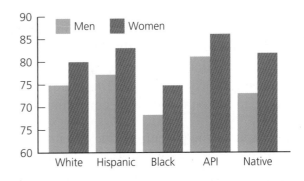

↑ **Figure 7.10** Life expectancy by ethnic origin and gender, 2007
Source: US Census Bureau, 2007

Education

White Americans usually live in areas with good schools, with some being able to afford private education and many going on to higher education. Whilst black Americans are making progress in education, some are disadvantaged by social and economic inequalities. Ghetto schools tend to have a 'blackboard jungle' image with high drop out and low academic success rates.

Academic success is not valued highly in ghetto schools, particularly for black boys – being good at sports such as football or basketball is valued more highly. The 'no brains – gold chains' culture is rife in inner city ghetto schools. While not all minority students in inner city ghetto schools lack the drive to succeed or do well, it is more often the case that their determination to succeed is inhibited by social factors. This is reinforced by attitudes towards learning. It is not cool to study and very few want to have a reputation as the school nerd especially in rough end neighbourhoods. Even the white media portrays nerds and geeks in a negative light showcasing them as losers. As a result, many minorities end up dropping out of school in the hope of helping out their family financially by getting a job, albeit poorly paid and part time.

Inner city schools are also likely to be in a state of disrepair. Problems with the roof, heating, ventilation, equipment and resources are common in inner city schools. This has an adverse impact on the learning environment.

The reason for the widening achievement gap between black and white students is likely related to differences in teacher quality and educational spending. According to the National Urban League Report *The State of Black America 2008*, 21 per cent of teachers in

Table 7.8 Educational attainment by ethnic group, 2008

	School Graduates	College Graduates
White	89%	30%
Hispanic	60%	12%
Black	80%	17%
APIs	85%	49%

Source: US Census Bureau, 2008

majority black districts had less than three years experience, compared to 10 per cent in majority white districts. On top of that, dollars spent per black student was only 82 per cent of what was spent per white student.

Those minorities that do succeed, despite mounting obstacles, face financial constraints when attempting to extend their education to college and university. In the USA, students have to pay to attend further education. It can cost hundreds of thousands of dollars to attend a prestigious university to study a highly regarded course such as law or medicine. Therefore, minorities (particularly black and Hispanics people) remain under-represented in these types of subjects and courses.

The vast majority of Hispanic public school students (84 per cent) were born in the USA. Therefore, many Hispanics speak English well. However, in those States with high Hispanic settlement patterns, many choose to speak Spanish with their friends and are often less likely to integrate with other ethnic groups. Indeed, 70 per cent of Hispanic students speak a language other than English at home. It is important to bear in mind that speaking fluent English at home varies according to how long Hispanics have lived in America. Recently arrived immigrants are less likely to speak fluent English than those who were born in the country. This may have an impact on their qualifications.

APIs do particularly well in education (see Table 7.8). This is because they are pushed harder by their parents to do well at school and to attend university. Parents value education highly and see it as a means of achieving success for their children. In their minds, having a good degree and a strong work ethic helps them to overcome discrimination.

The Obama government plans to reform the No Child Left Behind Act to improve attainment for all Americans. The No Child Left Behind Act set strict targets for schools and moved students from poorly performing schools to 'good' schools. This has had limited success in improving attainment for minorities. Obama plans to reform the Act by raising the quality of early learning programmes, encouraging better standards and recruiting and rewarding outstanding teachers. In addition, the College and Affordability Act (2008) which doubled the grants available to students and increased funding for colleges serving low income and minority students will continue. Other provisions designed to lower the cost of college education were passed under the Higher Education Opportunity Act (2008).

Crime and Law

Black and Hispanic crime statistics are likely to be worse than white crime statistics because crime is concentrated in inner cities. Economic segregation breeds resentment and young Blacks grow up 'street wise' and are drawn into the destructive gang culture of crime, drugs and 'territorial' battles against other neighbourhoods.

Some Republicans argue that the decline in the nuclear family leads to crime and disorder. They point out to the increase in lone parent families in the black community in ghettos as a reason for the corresponding increase in crime.

Table 7.9 Household types by ethnic group, 2006

	Married Couples	Lone Parent	Other
White	66.5	15.6	17.9
Black	37.8	46.4	15.8
Hispanic	59.5	31.1	19.4
API	72.3	16.0	11.7

Source: Pew Hispanic Centre, American Community Survey 2006

For many years, people have asserted that young black boys need positive male role models. They need fathers to instil a sense of discipline within them. The absence of fathers and with it an authority figure has meant that boys get their sense of identity by joining gangs. Their sense of worth is measured by the actions they take in the gang. Those activities that will earn respect are ones associated with assault and violence.

Territorial gang battles generally tend to be over drug sales. Inner city ghettos are rife with drugs like cocaine and z that residents take to escape their poverty stricken life. Drug dealers use gangs for protection and to control territories.

↑ **Figure 7.11** Gangs in the USA

Black and Hispanics people feel that they face discrimination and prejudice from the police and courts – despite making up only 12 per cent of the population, nearly 40 per cent of prison inmates are black. Although high profile politicians deny racial bias, a report by Amnesty International *Death by Discrimination* concluded otherwise.

CASE STUDY

⬆ **Figure 7.12** Winners and Losers of the American Dream

Name: Venus Williams

Date of Birth: 17 June 1980

Profession: Tennis player

Achieved the American Dream by working hard and becoming highly successful in tennis. She has won 17 Grand Slam titles.

Williams is the chief executive officer of her interior design firm 'V Starr Interiors' located in Florida.

Name: Yetunde Price (sister of Venus and Serena Williams)

Date of Birth: 9 August 1972 (died 14 September 2003)

Profession: Personal Assistant to her sisters Venus and Serena Williams.

She was the victim of murder by shooting on 14 September 2003 in a poor section of Compton, an area of Los Angeles, California, known for its history of gang violence. Robert Maxfield, 25, a Southside Crips gang member was sentenced to prison for the crime.

Table 7.10 Percentage of prison inmates by ethnic origin

	1995	2004	2008
White	33.5 %	34.3 %	34 %
Black	45.7 %	40.7 %	38 %
Hispanic	17.6 %	19 %	20 %

Source: Bureau of Justice Statistics, 2008

Half of all black inmates are sentenced to prison under State jurisdiction as the result of violent offences – murder and assault ranking high within this category. Following this just under a quarter of all black prisoners are in prison as a result of drug related offences. Hispanics follow a similar pattern to Blacks.

State and local responses to crime vary across the nation with some opting for more punitive

ACTIVITIES

1 Outline the differences between housing in ghettos and vanilla suburbs.
2 Why do some minorities have lower rates of health insurance compared to others?
3 Describe in detail inequalities in health between ethnic groups.
4 What measures have the government put in place to address health inequalities?
5 Why do APIs do particularly well in education?
6 Explain in detail why ghettos suffer greater crime problems than vanilla suburbs.
7 Explain in detail why many Blacks are concerned with their treatment within the USA justice system.

measures. The Gang Abatement and Prevention Act (2009) with the Gang Intervention and Suppression Act (2009) have made state law crimes into federal offences, carrying harsher penalties. It also resulted in the federal government extending their commitment to help fight criminal gang violence nationwide by devoting more than one billion dollars over the next five years.

Economic Inequalities and Responses

The USA is the wealthiest nation in the world with an estimated Gross Domestic Product (GDP) in 2009 of $14.3 trillion. This accounts for just under a quarter of world GDP making it perhaps the most powerful and influential country in the world. Despite its wealth, the United States remains one of the world's most unequal societies. Huge disparities in income and wealth, not only continue to exist, but continue to grow.

Unemployment

Table 7.11 Percentage unemployment by ethnic group, 2008–9

Ethnic Group	2008	2009
White	6.1 %	8.7 %
Black	11.2 %	14.7 %
Hispanic	8.6 %	12.2 %
API	4.8 %	8.2 %

Source: US Labour Department, December 2009

Table 7.11 clearly shows that black and Hispanic people have higher rates of unemployment than white and API people. The rate of unemployment has increased for all ethnic groups as the result of the credit crunch. An economic recession hits minorities harder than white people because they tend to be concentrated in lower skilled jobs which tend to be made redundant first. In addition, their contracts tend to be flexible and therefore employers find it easier to lay off these workers. The credit crunch also destroyed many white collar jobs in industries like finance and IT. This accounts for the increase in unemployment amongst APIs.

On the whole, taking both 2008 and 2009 into account, black and Hispanic people continue to have higher rates of unemployment. Education is one of the most important factors in determining employment. Those who do well at school are more likely to get better paid jobs and are less likely to be unemployed. Employers and businesses are going to hire well educated individuals over those who have dropped out early or with fewer qualifications. In addition, many newly arrived Hispanics might not speak fluent English and therefore may find it difficult to fill out application forms and perform successfully at interviews.

Discrimination also continues to exist because even black and Hispanic people with similar qualifications have higher rates of unemployment than white people. Many minorities face racial prejudice by employers.

However, economic progress is being made. America is a less racist place than it was 50 years ago and many minorities are in middle class jobs. As a result, middle class black people have experienced great improvements to their living standards. They live in nice residential suburbs, are in good well paid jobs, with their children attending good magnet schools. The snowy peak, used to describe a situation where white people are more likely to be found in promoted posts, is beginning to collapse.

Better education, especially for APIs, has led to improved job prospects and greater earning potential. Many APIs work in white collar jobs in 'sunrise' industries, such as electronics. Nearly one third of APIs earn over $100,000 a year. The recent reforms to education by the

Obama government may also improve the economic status of minorities.

The increase in positive role models for minorities to emulate (try to be like) has also contributed towards improvements in their living conditions. Hard working black people like Oprah Winfrey and Barack Obama have demonstrated the value of success. They have used education to do well in life. Many minorities who lack confidence and self esteem can look up to these role models for inspiration.

Income and Poverty

Income refers to earned money such as wages and salaries and unearned money such as social security benefits known as welfare. The average household income was $50,233 in 2007.

The average income for white people is higher than for black and Hispanic people because minorities tend to be found in low paid work. The highest earners are those who have graduated from university and hold degrees. Table 7.12 shows the industries that minorities work in.

Table 7.12 Percentage (%) of types of occupation by ethnic group, 2008

Occupation	White	Hispanic	Black	API
Management	9.9	4.4	4.9	8.9
Finance	2.3	1.1	1.6	3.7
Computing	2.1	0.8	1.2	7.2
Health Care	4.8	1.9	3.9	7.8
Construction	7.7	12.7	4.1	1.6
Farming and Fishing	0.6	2.5	0.4	0.2
Transportation	5.7	8.3	9.3	3.2

Source: US Bureau of Labour Statistics, 2008

The types of occupation minorities work in account for the differences in income between ethnic groups.

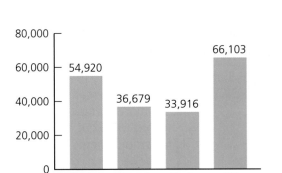

Figure 7.12 Average weekly earnings of full time workers in 2007 by ethnic group
Source: US Bureau of Labour Statistics, 2008

Figure 7.13 Vicious Circle of Poverty

Consequently, poverty rates are higher. Poverty is linked to income. The Federal Poverty level in 2007 for a family of four was $21,386. The official poverty rate in 2007 was 12.5 percent, that's around 37.3 million people who were in poverty, up from 11.3 per cent in 2000. The poverty rate increased for children under 18 years old (18 per cent in 2007, up from 17.4 per cent in 2006).

Table 7.13 Percentage (%) of poverty levels in the USA in 2007 by ethnic group

Ethnic Group	1990	2000	2007
White	9.4	7.4	8.2
Black	31.9	22.5	24.5
Hispanic	28.1	21.4	21.5
API	12.2	9.9	10.2

Source: Income, Poverty and Health Insurance Coverage in the US 2007 Report, US Census Bureau, 2008

Black and Hispanic people are more likely to live in poverty than other ethnic groups because of their employment status or lack of it. Black families are the victims of the poverty cycle. Many people from minority groups are stuck in the 'vicious circle' of poverty from which they cannot break free. Being born poor generally leads to poor education, a low paid job or unemployment, reliance on welfare, lone parent families and poverty which in turn results in the children of these people being poor. This repeats itself down the generations.

Black families in the ghetto suffer from low incomes due to unemployment and welfare dependency. Black people face higher unemployment caused by lower educational attainment and discrimination in employment.

Middle class black families took advantage of the education system and affirmative action programs to leave the ghetto and move to residential suburbs. This left a gap in terms of positive role models. Financially, those that do well in the ghetto are those that sell drugs or are involved in criminal activity. Children growing up in ghettos want to grow up like them. The sense of belonging and respect associated with gang culture is more appealing than working a menial 'nine to five' job.

Hispanics suffer from poverty as the result of immigration. As we already saw, the majority of immigrants to the USA are Hispanic. More specifically, they are Mexican and Puerto Rican immigrants escaping poverty in their own country. They tend to be found in the lowest paid jobs because they are willing to accept low pay and because they lack the qualifications to do professional jobs. However, over time their children become fully integrated into society and may either get a good job or decide to open up their own business with their relatives. This has been the case for Cuban Americans who immigrated decades ago. Miami city in Florida is home to millions of Cuban Americans. It is the financial hub for many entrepreneurs from Latin America. They save money in American banks not only because they are they safer, but also because financial advisers can communicate in their own language and provide many related services like consultancy and accountancy. As a result, poverty rates for Cuban Americans remain lower than for other Hispanic immigrants. Their children are fully integrated into American society and indeed many Cuban Hispanics have married white Americans. As a result, children are of mixed origin making it difficult to discriminate on racial grounds as their skin colour is lighter. Consequently, rates of poverty differ between and within ethnic groups.

Temporary Assistance for Needy Families

While Temporary Assistance for Needy Families (TANF) and State support may have helped lift some out of poverty, inequality continues to exist. TANF is a block grant of money for States to provide financial assistance to low income families. It provides benefits on a temporary basis to needy families until they find employment. It was re-authorised by Congress in 2005 with a focus on work and strengthening families through responsible fatherhood and healthy marriage. Some Republican Senators argued TANF was encouraging an increase in lone parent households. If the nuclear family was encouraged then there would be a decline in lone parent families and consequently welfare. This was because lone parent families are more likely to be in poverty and therefore rely on welfare. Under the current TANF program, fathers are being encouraged to support their family instead of forcing them to rely on the State.

Table 7.14 TANF

Aspects of TANF	How it helps
Five year lifetime limit on claiming welfare	Forces people to rely on TANF in emergency situations. People are forced to accept and search for employment. There is no dependency culture.
Workfare	This welfare to work scheme equips the unemployed and poor with skills and training to help secure a job.

Affirmative Action

Earlier solutions to tackle economic inequalities included affirmative action programs. Affirmative action is a term used to describe those measures taken by the government to eliminate discrimination against minorities in social and economic areas like employment and education. It is designed to give ethnic minorities a helping hand by giving them special consideration. In employment, firms were given targets for minority recruitment. This allowed opportunities, especially for black Americans, to further their social and economic status by undoing the wrongs of previous discriminatory practices. However, this preferential treatment of minorities over suitably qualified white people has been challenged by the Supreme Court and deemed unconstitutional. It has been opposed on the basis of discrimination because it promotes less qualified individuals. In 2003, there was a legal challenge directed at the University of Michigan for their admissions policy. They gave preference to minorities over white students applying for courses. This was deemed unconstitutional. Many minorities themselves felt patronised by affirmative action because they were left questioning their place in the workplace. Were they hired because they were the best or because of the colour of their skin?

For Affirmative Action	Against Affirmative Action
Minorities have made social and economic progress as the result of affirmative action.	Leads to resentment. White people can legitimately express anger and hostility towards minorities who have denied them a place at university or a job. This form of reverse discrimination fuels resentment.
Inequalities continue to exist and therefore direct action is needed. Previous social and economic policies have not been successful in bridging the gap between minorities and white people.	The majority of Americans oppose affirmative action. Minorities themselves feel that they have made progress in their own right.

ACTIVITIES

1 Why are APIs and white Americans more successful in employment than black and Hispanic Americans?
2 What economic progress has been made by minorities in recent years?
3 What impact has the credit crunch had on unemployment?
4 Describe fully the vicious cycle of poverty.
5 Explain in detail the ways in which TANF helps to meet the needs of those living in poverty.
6 Explain in detail recent policies introduced by the Obama government to reduce economic inequalities.
7 What are the arguments for and against affirmative action?

Political Structure

With American Independence in 1776, the 'Founding Fathers' laid down how the country would be run in a written document called the Constitution. This outlined the rules for the political system and also listed the rights that each American citizen would have.

Figure 7.14 The Constitution document

The Constitution divided the Federal Government into three branches based on the separation of powers.

The Constitution clearly lays down what each of the branches of the government can do. These branches were deliberately kept distinct to ensure that no one branch of the government could dominate the others.

It also gives the 50 States the power to look after their own affairs. The job of government is split between national and State government – this is called a federal system of government. Federal laws made by the national government in Washington DC are the same for the whole nation, but State laws can differ.

The separation of powers was reinforced by a series of checks and balances designed to avoid any one branch being too powerful. Each State has its own elected government making laws on

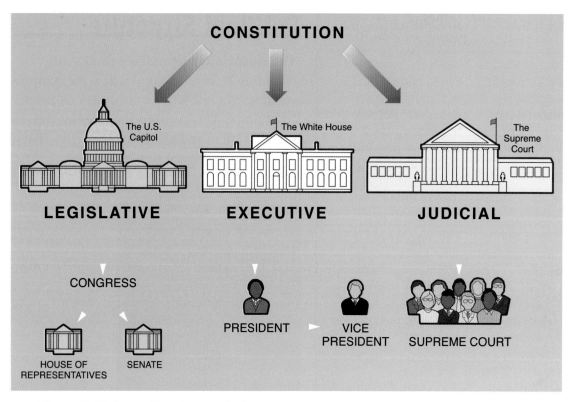

↑ **Figure 7.15** Separation of powers in federal government

education, health etc. The State governments have the greatest influence over most Americans daily lives. The State government is a replica of national government and it is also split into three parts.

It is important to remember that the USA is a huge country and individual States, like Texas, are often the size of small countries themselves. The States are divided into smaller regions known as counties.

Electoral College

America has fixed term elections that occur every four years for the presidency. The President is elected using the Electoral College system. In this system, each State is awarded a certain number of Electoral College votes. The number is equal to that State's representation in Congress – the number of Senators (two per State) plus the number of Representatives. Thus in 2008, California had 55 votes (2 + 53) while

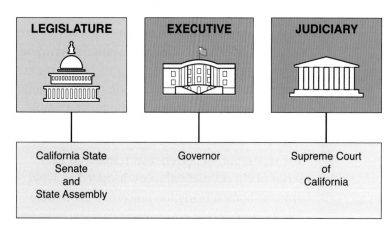

← **Figure 7.16** State government

Wyoming had just three votes (2 + 1). There are 538 Electoral College votes in total. To win the presidency, a candidate must win an absolute majority, which is 270.

The popular votes for each candidate are counted in each State. In all but two States, whichever candidate wins the most popular vote receives all the Electoral College votes of that State – the so called 'winner takes all' rule.

Barack Obama gained 365 Electoral College votes, way beyond the 270 you require to win. As a result, he became President.

Representation

Remember Congress is the legislative branch of the federal government. It is made up of two houses: the House of Representatives and the Senate. A term of Congress lasts for two years. The 111th Congress began its business at the

Table 7.15 USA presidential election results, 2008

Candidate	Party	Electoral College votes	Popular votes	Percentage of vote
John McCain	Republicans	173	58,421,377	45.9 %
Barack Obama	Democrats	365	67,066,915	52.7 %

Source: Adapted from BBC News

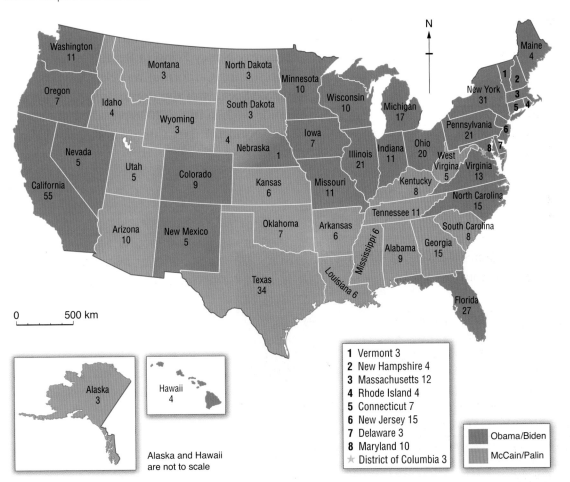

Figure 7.17 Electoral College map 2008

beginning of January 2009. For the first time in 12 years, both Houses were controlled by the Democrats.

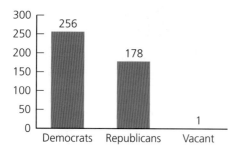

Figure 7.18 Composition of Congress, 2009
Source: Adapted from Congressional Demographics, 2009

Women

Congress in general, and the Senate in particular, has for most of its history been seen as a men's club. It was not until the passing of the 19th Amendment in 1920 that American women were guaranteed the right to vote in elections for Congress. Altogether, 37 women have served in the Senate. Only one new women was elected in 2008: Jeanne Shaheen of New Hampshire. That brings the number of women in the Senate to a record high of 17.

Three States – California, Maine and Washington – are currently represented in the Senate by two women.

Table 7.16 Gender composition of Congress, 2008

	Senate seats	House of Representatives seats
Men	83	361
Women	17	74

Source: Congressional Demographics, 2008

A record number of 91 women serve in the 111th Congress; 74 serve in the House of Representatives and 17 in the Senate. Of the 74 women in the House of Representatives, 61 are Democrats and 13 are Republicans. Of the 17 women serving in the Senate, 13 are Democrats and four are Republicans.

With most female Senators being Democrats, the fact that Democrats have regained control of the Senate means that women Senators have a higher profile in the 111th Congress, as well as greater numbers. At the start of the 110th Congress, Nancy Pelosi (a Democrat representing California) was elected as the first female Speaker of the House. In addition, high profile women in the 2008 presidential election race included Hilary Clinton and Sarah Palin.

Figure 7.19 Female State Senators

FACTFILE

Name: Hillary Clinton

Date of Birth: 26 October 1947

Profession: Secretary of State

Hilary Clinton is the wife of the former President Bill Clinton. She was the first female Senator to represent New York.

She was a leading candidate for the Democratic presidential nomination in the 2008 election.

In the 2008 presidential nomination race, Clinton won more delegates than any other female candidate in American history, but she narrowly lost to Senator Barack Obama.

↑ Figure 7.20 Hillary Clinton

FACTFILE

Name: Sarah Palin

Date of Birth: 11 February 1964

Profession: Governor of Alaska (until July 2009)

Palin was the first female governor of Alaska and the youngest person elected governor of that State.

Palin was the Republican Party's vice-presidential nominee for the 2008 election.

Since the McCain-Palin defeat in the 2008 election, there has been speculation that she will run for president in the 2012 presidential election.

↑ Figure 7.21 Sarah Palin

However, women make up 54 per cent of the American population. If women were represented in proportion to their population size there would be 54 Senators and 235 members of the House of Representatives.

There are 92 male Governors and only seven female Governors – two Republicans and five Democrats.

Ethnic Groups

Minorities are not proportionately represented in Congress. They make up a third of the total population and if minorities were represented in proportion to their population size there would be 33 Senators and 143 members of the House of Representatives.

Black membership of Congress over the past 15 years has always been low in comparison to their population size. Representation at Senate level is particularly poor. It fell back to just one black representative in 2009 because Barack Obama had to resign as Senator when he became President.

Table 7.17 Ethnic composition of Congress

Ethnic Group	Senate seats	House of Representatives seats
White	94	365
Hispanic	3	28
Black	1	41
API	2	4
Native	0	1

Source: Congressional Demographics, 2008

There are 41 black Members of the 111th Congress, all serving in the House of Representatives. All of these are Democrats, including two Delegates. Fourteen African American women, including two Delegates, serve in the House.

There are a record number of 31 Hispanic Members of the 111th Congress, one more than the record number who served in the 109th and 110th Congresses. 28 Hispanics serve in the House of Representatives and three in the Senate. Of the Members of the House of Representatives, 22 are Democrats (including one Delegate), three are Republicans, and seven are women. The Hispanic Senators include two Democrats and one Republican. All are male. In May 2009 President Obama appointed Sonia Sotomajor to the Supreme Court. The 54 year old Puerto Rican became the first Hispanic appointed to the Supreme Court.

Age

The average age of Members of the 111th Congress is among the highest of any Congress in recent history. The average age of both combined Houses is 58.2 years.

The average age of Senators at the beginning of the 111th Congress is 63.1 years, approximately 1.5 years greater than those of the 110th Congress. The youngest Senator is Senator Mark Pryor (a Democrat representing Arizona), who is 45. The oldest Senator, as well as the oldest current Member of Congress, is Robert Byrd (a Democrat representing West Virginia) aged 91. The average length of service of Members of the Senate is 12.9 years (2.2 terms).

The average age of Members of the House of Representatives is 56. The average length of service of Members of the House of Representatives is 11.0 years (5.5 terms).

Table 7.18 Age composition of Congress, 2008

Age	Senate	House
30s	–	16
40s	9	79
50s	28	155
60s	37	143
70s +	26	42

Source: Congressional Demographics, 2008

In the current Congress, law is the dominant declared profession of Senators, followed by public service/politics. For members of the

House of Representatives, politics is first, followed by business and law.

As has been true in recent Congresses, the vast majority of Members (95 per cent of the 111th Congress) hold university degrees. Research indicates that 27 Members of the House and one Senator have no educational degree beyond a high school diploma. Forty years ago in the 91st Congress (1969–1971), at least 45 Representatives and nine Senators had no degree beyond a high school diploma.

Responses

In many cities, where minorities have tended to concentrate, the Mayor is either black or Hispanic. This is particularly the case in parts of the south and inner city areas of the north where the black population is heavily concentrated. For example, cities such as Detroit and Philadelphia both have a black Mayor.

Obstacles to becoming a Politician

Constitution

The Constitution states the the President must be a natural born citizen of the USA, be at least 35 years old, and have been a resident for 14 years. The natural born citizenship requirement has been the subject of controversary.

In addition certain requirements to hold public office discriminate against newly arrived immigrants who may wish to stand as candidates. For example, to stand as a Senator, you not only need to be at least 25 years old but you also must have lived in the State you wish to represent for the last seven years. Equally, to stand as a member of the House of Representatives, you have to be at least 30 years old and have resided in the USA for at least nine years. This makes it difficult for minorities such as Hispanics to become elected.

Finance

In addition to the constitutional requirements, there are a number of other elements which reduces the likelihood of women, minorities and younger candidates being elected. Probably the most important of these is the ability to raise money. This is crucial to a successful bid for Congress and presidency. Campaigns are so expensive that very few candidates can afford to finance their own campaigns. At State and national level, most candidates spend millions of dollars on leafleting, posters, billboards and media coverage in the form of television infomercials to secure their victory. For most minorities, poverty and low income act as a barrier. Black and Hispanic people are more likely to be found in lower paid burger flipping jobs and their level of education is likely to be restricted at high school level. The level of education people have is linked with political participation and the likelihood of being elected.

Discrimination

Discrimination and prejudice may also play a part in explaining the low level of representation. Some white voters in the 'conservative South' or 'bible belt' States like Texas may be less inclined to vote for a minority candidate. They may view minorities as being inferior and certainly not to be elected for public office. Women are also under-represented as the result of sexist stereotypes. This discourages women from standing as candidates. This is especially true for southern States that are conservative in their views. For example, in the state of Alabama there have never been any female Senators elected. In addition, politics is dominated by men and therefore standing for election may intimidate certain women.

The redrawing of electoral boundaries to create districts with predominantly ethnic minority electorates has increased opportunities for black and Hispanic candidates in American politics. As most voters in these districts are black or Hispanic, political parties are more willing to select a black or Hispanic candidate to run for office, as they believe they will have a greater chance of being successful. Some think that the reason for this is because minorities are more likely to elect another minority who knows what they are going through. The minority candidate, if elected, would do more to support their cause and might push through policies to reduce inequalities. This is one of the main reasons why minorities in particular should go out and vote. They are able to elect candidates at local and federal level who will represent their interests on issues from healthcare and education to welfare and immigration.

All black Representatives in the House are Democrats are collectively known as the Black Caucus (group). They have a degree of influence in Congress because they have over 20 per cent of the votes needed for a Bill to pass as legislation. Combined with Hispanic members, they could push forward greater equality legislation which would help to improve the economic position of minorities. Many Democrat representatives depend on the minority vote in Congress to pass Bills. Therefore many white Democrats are sensitive to minority issues.

Regarding gender inequality, EMILY's List is an organisation which supports female Democrat candidates running for office at local, State and federal level. This group is committed to increasing the election chances of pro-choice Democratic women. To achieve this, it recruits and funds possible women candidates and helps them to run effective campaigns. The group also works to mobilise women voters to turn out and show their support in elections.

Since they formed the group in 1985, they have helped to elect 79 Democratic members of Congress, 15 Senators, nine Governors and hundreds of women to State and local office. In 2008, EMILY's List helped elect 12 new women to the House of Representatives, two new women to the Senate, and 175 women at the State and local level. In 2009, they supported Nina Totenbergs nomination to become a Supreme Court judge. They also raised finance for Judy Chu who won her seat in July 2009 for the State of California as a member of the House of Representatives.

◀ **Figure 7.22** Black Caucus

ACTIVITIES

1 What is the Constitution?
2 'Barack Obama won the 2008 Election comfortably.' Using Table 7.15, what evidence is there to support and oppose this view?
3 What impact would high profile female politicians such as Hillary Clinton and Sarah Palin have on female representation?
4 'Minority representation has always been over half in Congress.' (Karen Salvage) Give two reasons to show how Karen Salvage is exaggerating.
5 'Most representatives are young'. (Margaret Webster) What evidence is there to oppose this view?
6 Explain in detail why either women or minorities are under-represented in the USA political system.
7 How influential is the Black Caucus movement?
8 How do members of EMILY's List support female candidates?

Participation in Politics

Voter Registration

In the USA, Americans must register themselves in order to vote for representatives at local, State and federal level. The responsibility for registering lies with individuals, unlike in the UK where the government attempts to ensure that everyone eligible to vote is registered by sending a voter registration form to every household containing a pre-paid return envelope. In the USA, individuals need to take that initiative. They must complete lengthy and often complicated voter registration forms accurately in order to vote.

While the process is now more convenient with the passing of the National Voter Registration Act, different States have different rules and procedures, particularly with respect to closing dates, times and places for registration, residency requirements, documentation to be presented, and the availability of postal and absentee ballots. Many minorities are intimidated by the process, especially where offices are far from their homes, or where they are required to produce their identity card, social security

Table 7.19 Voter turnout by ethnicity, 2004–2008*

2004			2008			Change in Total Ballots from 2004 to 2008		
Total Ballots Cast 122,295, 345			Total Ballots Cast 126,276,331			Total Ballots Cast 3,980,986		
Demographic	Exit Poll	Estimated Total Ballots**	Demographic	Exit Poll	Estimated Total Ballots**	Demographic	Change in Total Ballots**	Percent change
Race			Race			Race		
White	77%	94,167,000	White	74%	93,444,000	White	−723,000	−1%
African-American	11%	13,452,000	African-American	13%	16,416,000	African-American	2,964,000	22%
Latino	8%	9,784,000	Latino	9%	11,365,000	Latino	1,581,000	26%
Asian	2%	2,446,000	Asian	2%	2,526,000	Asian	80,000	3%
Other	2%	2,446,000	Other	3%	3,788,000	Other	1,342,000	55%

Note: These are preliminary tables – 2008 vote counts have not yet been certified.

Source: Federal Election Commission, 2008

number or driving licence. To most people, the need to register to vote is a simple form filling exercise, but for many minorities it is a daunting ordeal. Fear of criminal record checks, language barriers and racial intimidation at polling stations continue to put off many minorities from registering to vote.

The NCBCP Unity 08 Campaign did a great deal to increase voter registration among African Americans. Alongside celebrities, the campaign organised voter registration at churches, salons and college campuses. Internet banking and direct mail information supplied by sympathetic black business people allowed Unity 08 to target black households. Equally, Hip Hop Vote 2008, featuring notable celebrities, stressed the importance of participating in elections to voters (mainly young black people inclined to listen to hiphop) through internet sites such as YouTube and concert appearances with stars wearing t-shirts with the slogan 'Respect My Vote'. They followed the success of the 'Rock the Vote' campaign in 2004 (which was repeated in 2008) using celebrities to encourage young people to go out and register to vote.

Figure 7.23 Celebrity campaigners encouraging black voting

Measures such as 10–4 Campaign and Campaign for Communities increased the Hispanic vote. All these measures contributed to increased voter turnout in the 2008 presidential election with 62.8 per cent of the electorate turning out to vote.

Voting

There are many opportunities for Americans to exercise their right to vote. Elections are important because they allow American citizens to participate in choosing their local and national political representatives. Americans can vote at different levels:

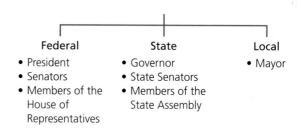

Federal	State	Local
• President	• Governor	• Mayor
• Senators	• State Senators	
• Members of the House of Representatives	• Members of the State Assembly	

Figure 7.24 Voting representatives

The USA has fixed term elections: every two years for the House of Representatives, every six years for the Senate (with one third re-elected every two years) and every four years for the presidency.

Voter turnout for minorities tends to be lower than that of white voters. Many black people remain trapped in inner city ghettos, despite promises made by political parties to help their plight. Their social and economic position remains poor because inequalities continue to exist. They therefore see no point in voting because nothing much will change for them. They may have voted in the past in the hope of positive change but this change has not happened. As a result, they may now feel let down by the government. This apathy and sense of alienation helps to account for low black turnout rates.

In addition, there is a strong correlation (link) between voting and education. The higher the level of education, the more likely a person is to turn out and vote. This is because they understand the political process and issues being debated and therefore have a vested interest in voting. They are aware of the importance of carrying out their civic duty. Many minorities, Hispanic and black people, drop out of school early and leave with few qualifications. They are less likely to vote.

Minority participation certainly increased in the 2008 presidential election. Celebrity campaigns were successful in spreading the message that politics has a major impact on people's lives. Issues such as the economy, immigration and the 'war on terror' hit a nerve with minorities. They were aware of their need to go out and vote to oust the Republicans and bring in 'change' in the form of Obama.

Both political parties were also increasingly aware of the importance of the minority vote. Their settlement and distribution patterns meant that States with a large concentration of minorities like Texas, California and Florida were crucial for candidates to win the race to the White House. This is because these States have a lot of Electoral College votes.

Many States use methods that allow for a degree of direct democracy so that people are able to vote on a single measure. This is known as a referendum. Voters also have the opportunity to propose or initiate laws themselves. Referendums operate in some form or another in 24 States.

Standing as a Candidate

Ordinary Americans have the opportunity to put themselves forward for election by standing as a candidate at local, State or federal level. There are hundreds of elected posts in the USA that provide individuals with the opportunity to stand as a candidate and make a difference to the lives of people. The majority of candidates tend to align with the two main political parties (Democrats and Republicans) who are able to fund election campaigns and finance air time for advertising.

In addition, there are certain requirements for wanting to hold public office. The Constitution sets out criteria for standing as a candidate, for example, each Senator must be at least 25 years old, and ought to have resided in the State they wish to represent for the last seven years.

Joining a Political Party

For almost 150 years, the USA has had two major political parties: the Democrats and the Republicans. Political parties in the USA do not have a set of standard values upon which policies are based. They are not like Scottish political parties, who tend to have a 'party line' or stance on each issue. Democrats have differing attitudes to others within their own party on certain issues. For example, Democrats from the 'conservative' south – the 'bible belt' – e.g. Texas are very different from Democrats from the 'liberal' north-east such as Maine.

Figure 7.25 Democratic Party convention

Primaries give the ordinary voters a say in the process of nominating a Presidential candidate for election. There are two types of primary election: open and closed. Participation in a closed primary is limited to voters who have declared their attachment to a party, whereas in an open primary voters can declare their attachment on the day on the primary election. In the primaries, candidates from the same party have to run against each other and therefore fund election campaigns. Once the State by State nomination process is over, each State party sends delegates to a National Convention.

The Democrats and Republicans hold a National Party Convention during an election year which usually lasts for four days. The 2008 Democratic Convention was held in Denver (Colorado) in August 2008. It is here that they officially nominated Barack Obama for President and Joe Biden for Vice President. Nearly 90,000 people were in attendance – the highest turnout ever seen! Equally, the 2008 Republican Convention took place in Saint Paul (Minnesota) in September 2008. The attending delegates at the convention nominated John McCain as the Republican Presidential candidate and Sarah Palin as the Vice-Presidential candidate.

Interest Groups

An interest group is made up of people who strongly believe in the same cause. They want to influence decision makers at all levels and get them to take action in their favour. An increasingly popular way of participating in politics is for Americans to join and campaign for an interest group. Influential interest groups include the National Rifle Association, Coalition to Stop Gun Violence, EMILY's List, US Chamber of Commerce and the National Association for the Advancement of Coloured People.

US interest groups share many of their methods and tactics with the UK. The Constitution, through the separation of powers and checks and balances, serves to divide up power. This gives interest groups many potential points to influence the government.

Interest groups are massively involved in the work of Congress. Most will lobby Congressmen directly, highlighting the impact of certain measures on the voters in the Congressmen's states. They also provide up to date, accurate and detailed information to those who need it. Interest groups maintain offices in Washington DC and State capitals. This allows them to be on hand to lobby members of federal, State and local government.

At election time, interest groups back candidates who support their cause by fundraising and media advertising. Some people felt that interest groups were 'buying' power. As a result, Congress passed legislation in 2007, the Honest Leadership and Open Government Act, to make procedures more open and honest.

ACTIVITIES

1 What are the main differences between voter registration in the UK and USA?
2 What conclusions can be drawn about voter turnout in the 2008 presidential election?
3 Give the measures used to encourage turnout in the 2008 election.
4 Describe two ways American people can take part in choosing who becomes the Governor.
5 Draw a spider diagram outlining the posts Americans can stand election for.
6 Describe in detail how people support their political party during election campaigns.
7 Why do people join interest groups?
8 Describe the methods that interest groups use to influence the government.